DEVON & CORNWALL RECORD SOCIETY
New Series, Vol. 23

DEVON & CORNWALL RECORD SOCIETY

New Series, Vol. 23

THE DEVON CLOTH INDUSTRY IN THE EIGHTEENTH CENTURY

SUN FIRE OFFICE INVENTORIES OF MERCHANTS' AND MANUFACTURERS' PROPERTY, 1726–1770

Edited with an Introduction by

STANLEY D. CHAPMAN

Pasold Reader in Textile History, University of Nottingham

Printed for the Society by
THE DEVONSHIRE PRESS LTD.
TORQUAY

1978

CONTENTS

INTRODUCTION

Insurance policy registers are one of the exciting new sources located within the last decade by the ever-widening interests of economic and social historians. This class of records presents opportunities for research on a variety of national, regional, and local problems that have remained obscure for want of adequate evidence. The insurance inventories, collected for particular industries, localities, or periods, can provide a wealth of detailed evidence on such vital topics as the growth (or contraction) of particular industries, the size of workshops, factories, and firms, and their ownership, the distribution of handicrafts and trades, the size and value of farms, inns, shops, mansions and town houses, the pace of local building and property ownership, capital formation, and vernacular architecture. It can safely be predicted that the registers will in course of time take their place as one of the ' standard ' sources for all historians of trade, industry, and the local economy and society. However, the source is as yet little known and appreciated outside a small group of university researchers. This volume is intended to introduce the material to a wider circle of interested historians and laymen, both in Devon and other counties.

Readers of Professor W. G. Hoskins' pioneer work *Industry, Trade and People in Exeter, 1688–1800* (Manchester 1935, reprinted Exeter 1968) will be familiar with the salient features of the Devon serge industry in the eighteenth century. The essence of the organisation lay in the division of function between merchant and manufacturer. The merchants, very largely resident at the centre of the industry in Exeter and Tiverton, made themselves responsible for supplying the wool which, whether grown at home or abroad, was generally transported by sea to Exeter and Barnstaple. It was sold at the Exeter Wool Market or by private treaty to the serge makers, who lived in the county town and a circle of towns and villages in the Exe valley and (to a much smaller extent) in the Dart valley. The serge manufacturers worked up the raw material on their own premises, carding, spinning, and weaving, employing their own families and possibly other workers as well. It required something like eight spinners working on the old hand wheels to serve one weaver, so that a proportion of the yarn fed into the looms had to be spun outside the domestic unit, and the weaving area was encircled by a penumbra of villages where middlemen known as ' yarn jobbers ' employed scores of females and juveniles. The cloths were taken out of the looms ' in the white ' and sent to Exeter for sale to the cloth merchants, who either forwarded them to London for sale, or sent them to local specialists for fulling, dyeing, finishing, and packing. The finished cloths were shipped to London for sale by the Blackwell Hall factors, or they were exported to Holland, Germany, Spain, Portugal, and other destinations abroad. The development of this overseas commerce owed something to the enterprise of foreigners as well as the local merchants, and several families of German and Dutch extraction (notably the Barings, Duntzes, and Passavants) rose to eminence in local society during the course of the century.

The thousand or so Sun Fire Office insurance policy inventories assembled in this volume add extensive detail to this basic framework, identifying hundreds of families that were engaged in the trade and manufacture, demonstrating the size and structure of the manufacturing units, and modifying the broad generalisations of Hoskins's outline. A sequence of disastrous fires in Devon clothing towns through the eighteenth century served to impress the public mind with the wisdom of insuring their property. In 1731, 298 of the best houses in Tiverton were destroyed by fire; they were said to be worth over £56,000, but the total insurance in London and Bristol offices was only £1,135.[1] At Honiton there were major fires in 1747 and 1765; the earlier one destroyed three-quarters of the town including the working tools and furniture of ' many hundreds of the poor laborious inhabitants, such as weavers, combers, etc.'[2] Consequently the habit of insuring property became common among the ' middling ' class of society to which merchants and manufacturers belonged, and the Sun Fire Office, which was the first company to establish agencies in the provinces and was far and away the largest fire insurance business until the end of the eighteenth century, took the lion's share of the business.[3] Over fifty Devon towns and villages involved in the woollen industry are represented in the Sun's long series of policy registers, though some five of these contain only yarn jobbers. There is also a considerable number of policies for the clothing districts of the adjacent parts of Somerset (Taunton, Wellington, and villages in the locality) which formed a part of the Devon textile region but which, for want of space, cannot be included in this publication. However, three Cornish yarn jobbers' policies have been located, and the distribution of the industry for the three counties, so far as this can be determined from insurance sources, is shown on the adjacent map. Unfortunately, there is no means of calculating the precise proportion of Devon tradesmen of any occupation who were insured at any point in the century, but the large number of manufacturers' policies collected here can leave little doubt that we have a secure basis for generalisations about the industry.

There are of course numerous Sun Fire Office policies available for other counties, both for the textile industry and for a great variety of other property, especially farming, corn milling, brewing, tanning, paper making, sugar refining, ship building, the small metal trades, and the numerous small craft industries of London.[4] The Devon policies all in

[1] Martin Dunsford, *Historical Memoirs of Tiverton* (1790), pp. 216–221.
[2] *Universal British Directory*, III (1794), p. 389.
[3] P. G. M. Dickson, *History of the Sun Fire Office, 1710–1960* (1960), pp. 67–72. Public Record Office, Chatham Papers, 30/8/187, shows that in 1797 the Sun insured property for £1.17 m. out of a total of £1.95 m. for the county, or about 60 per cent. The percentage must have been much higher in the period 1720–1770.
[4] Policies for some industries have already been exploited, e.g. S. D. Chapman, ' Fixed Capital Formation in the British Cotton Industry, 1770–1815 ', *Economic History Review*, XXIII (1970), and the same author's ' Textile Factory before Arkwright ', *Business History Review*, XLVIII (1974). D. T. Jenkins, *The West Riding Wool Textile Industry 1770–1835: A Study of Fixed Capital Formation* (1975).

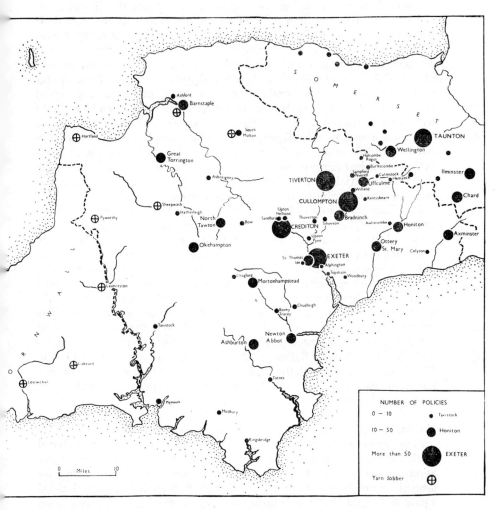

MAP OF DEVON AND ADJACENT AREAS SHOWING THE DISTRIBUTION
OF POLICIES FOR TEXTILE MANUFACTURERS, 1726-1770.

Exeter includes Heavitree and Culmstock includes Hillmore.

all will be found to be particularly valuable up to about 1775, both
because the number of policies appears to be greater than those for any
other county outside London, and also because they possess a peculiar
flavour of their own, a quality compounded of more detail and more
vernacular expression than those of any other county at the period. It
is not easy to account for this rare quality. The habit of insuring spread
from London into the home, southern, and western counties before it
reached the midlands and north of England, and in Devon arrived
ahead of the stereotyping that became a feature of later policies. So far
as the unusually large numbers are concerned, one can only repeat
Defoe's claim, made just before the policies commence (and no doubt
with some journalistic licence), that Devon was ' so full of great towns,
and those towns so full of people, and those people so universally employed in trade and manufactures, that not only it cannot be equalled
in England, but perhaps not in Europe.' [1] Extensive rebuilding in the
fireproof materials (brick, stone, slate, etc.), noticeable in numerous
policies, also contributed to the desire to insure.

It is important to know the basis on which the insurance valuations
were made, whether historic cost, market value, replacement cost, or
some other criterion. Unfortunately the ample records of the early
insurance companies contain no precise definition of property valuation,
but a general inference may be drawn from records of fire claims, which
show that insured property was valued at its cost of replacement. [2]
Comparisons between the policies and surviving business records might
offer some confirmation of this, but in fact Devon possesses very few
business accounts relating to the period, and only one set can be used
for the purpose suggested. The Kennaway Mss. contain the ' Debts
and Credits ' (Annual Balances) of William Kennaway II from 1746 to
1794, and so coincide with the Kennaway policies published in this volume,
but comparison of the two sources is not easy. The most that can be done
is to put relevant entries from the two sources alongside each other and
note the basic similarities (Table 1). A similar exercise for mills in
Nottinghamshire and in the West Riding is also reassuring. [3]

Some evidence for a slightly later period than the policies reproduced
in this volume suggests the ideal criterion for insurance property valuations in the eighteenth century. In 1798 the Phoenix Fire Office informed one of its agents that '. . . in Fire Policies it has been decided
again and again that the Insurer is to pay so much (& no more) than
the sum which will *reinvest* the sufferer . . . & in this the Managers of the
Royal Exchange and Sun Fire Office authorise us to say they coincide.' [3]
This policy statement leaves no doubt that it was the long-established
practice for the insurance offices to indemnify policy holders to enable
them to replace their property and goods, and it seems no less than
reasonable to infer from this that the property value stated on the policy
was the cost of replacement, stated to the nearest £10 or so. For the
period covered in this book replacement cost might well be higher than

---

[1] D. Defoe, *Tours* (Everyman Edn.), I, p. 221.
[2] H. A. L. Cockerell and Edwin Green, *The British Insurance Business 1547–1970* (1976),
pp. 30–1.
[3] D. T. Jenkins, *op. cit.*, Appendix III. S. D. Chapman, ' Fixed Capital ', Appendix A.

Table 1

Comparisons of Insurance Policy Valuations with those in Business Accounts.

WILLIAM KENNAWAY, EXETER MERCHANT, WOOLSTAPLER, AND SERGEMAKER

Sun Fire Office policies for 1761, 1764, and 1765
(Volumes 136/183250, 157/212605, 158/215763)

		£	£
1761	Dwelling house, brick, timber and slated	195	
	Office	5	200
1764	Household goods and stock in his dwelling house	100	
	Household goods and stock in adjacent house used as warehouse, combshop, and offices	100	200
	all stone, brick, lath, plaster & slated		
1765	Intended dwelling house & offices adjoining	500	500

KENNAWAY MSS., 'DEBTS AND CREDITS' (ANNUAL BALANCES), 1746–1794
(Devon Record Office, 58/9)
The early accounts are crude, and separate valuation of particular items
emerges only slowly:

		£
1757	House and household goods together valued at	300
1756	Household goods valued separately at	100
	Value of house	200
1766	'Old House' depreciated to	170
1767	'Old House and Garden'	220
1769	'Old House'	200
do.	'House, late Peirie'	608
1773	'Dwelling House' (newly built)	700

historic cost or market value, so it is wrong to assume (as some historians tend to do) that insurance policies typically undervalue assets.

A handful of policies in the Sun series detail the number of rooms in particular properties, and this valuable information provides a key for the researcher to assess the size of properties insured for particular sums. For Devon, the earliest policy to disclose such details is that of Ralph Fowler, a Cullompton woolcomber, in 1726 (22/39491). The policy reads:

	£
One hall [i.e. living room] and parlour and chambers over ...	100
One [work-]shop and one buttery and chambers over ...	20
One porch and chamber only	10
One cellar only (all the above tyled)	5
One room formerly called the yarn [work-]shop and chamber over it	20
One room called the warping shop and chambers over it ...	20
Two kitchens and chambers over	60
Two butteries or pantry and chambers over	15
Two [work-]shops and chambers over...	15
One barn and stable converted into other rooms	30
One linney only (these thatched)	5
	£300

Fowler's property, like that of many of his contemporaries in the Devon serge industry, seems to have been extended in an *ad hoc* manner in response to the need to provide more accommodation for machines and employees; it could have started as a farmhouse and later have been turned over to textiles. The four-roomed house has been described as the product of a process of evolution spread over several centuries, in which the original one room (or hall) was divided up so as to create a private room (parlour) at one end for the master of the house and his wife, and two bedrooms over, both, according to Prof. M. W. Barley (*The English Farmhouse and Cottage*, 1961), originally built in the rafters. This basic type of house must lie behind hundreds of other policies transcribed in this volume. Though its precise value is frequently concealed by the common practice of bracketing the house and adjacent workshops in one valuation, making a total figure of £150 to £300 for all the buildings, the central 'hall', parlour, and chambers must have been worth something like the £100 suggested in this unusually illuminating policy.

This early policy makes only slight reference to building materials, but those that follow generally list all the materials of which the insured building was composed. A wide variety of materials seems to have been employed, commonly stone, cob, timber, plaster, thatch, brick, and tiles, more occasionally weather boarding and nogging (i.e. brick infilling in a timber frame). The policies show that the traditional local materials were still the most popular, with some shift towards brick, slate and tile to reduce fire risk; evidently the woollen industry and trade did not provoke any change in traditional materials. The policy descriptions may help local historians to identify the actual buildings referred to in the policies.

The fixed capital component of insurance policies (buildings and plant) cannot of course be used as an index to the total assets of the persons insured. The policies commonly cover stocks, but the valuations of this item are at best only a rough guide,[1] while the main component of working capital (trade credits) was not insured simply because it was not vulnerable to fire risk. As a broad generalisation, merchants held only a small proportion of their capital in fixed assets; Kennaways, to take the only well-documented example for Devon, conducted all their business from a modest house (value £200) in Exeter until 1769, when profits were already in excess of £10,000 a year. The accounts are not sufficiently clear to make precise calculations of fixed and working capital until about 1790, but the contrast between the two remains:—

					£
Fixed capital: Dwelling house (1770–3)	...	...	...	1,170
Warehouse (1771–2)	...	...	...	550
Drying house (1788)	...	...	...	800
Racks...	...	...	...	...	670
					£3,190

---

[1] Chatham Papers, *loc. cit.* Hugh Watts, Secretary of the Sun Fire Office, conceded in 1797 that insurance on merchants' stock was commonly a quarter or fifth of the value. This was because goods held in trust or on commission were not always insured, but if loss was sustained the policy holder pretended they were his own insured goods.

Working capital: Italian debts 43,520
               Spanish debts 6,411
               Home debts 3,012

                                               52,943

Stock: of wool and worsted 5,237
      of goods 5,148

                                              £63,328

These proportions are broadly consistent with financial data from a
handful of surviving textile merchant accounts for other regions.[1] It
seems very probable that the cloth manufacturers invested a much
larger proportion of their capital in buildings and machinery, relying on
the merchants to find markets for their output, but unfortunately there
are no surviving business records to demonstrate this point. The most
that can be said, if Kennaways' records can be generalised, is that
merchant credits to serge makers were extensive in the 1790s, and that
this practice was by no means novel at the period.[2] Indeed, it may well
have been the experience of providing credit for manufacturers that
encouraged several leading Exeter merchants, notably the Kennaways,
Barings, Duntzes, and Milfords, to graduate to banking.[3]

The insurance policies offer some useful information on another
problem of industrial organisation in the period, that of the ownership
of the Devon industry's domestic capital, i.e. looms, spinning wheels,
combing pots, and other utensils employed by the operatives in their
cottages and workshops. In some textile regions, notably the West
Riding and West of England (Gloucestershire, Wiltshire, and its Somerset
borders) all the weavers appear to have owned their own looms,[4] while
in another (the East Midlands framework knitting region) the merchant
organisers were steadily acquiring the frames operated in the knitters'
homes.[5] In the West Riding the valuation of looms in the early and
middle decades of the eighteenth century varied from 5s to £2 (£0.25
to £2.00), a price range that does not appear beyond the reach of weavers,
especially since many looms were built by village joiners.[6] The insurance registers contain policies for numbers of Devon weavers and
combers who owned property valued at £100 to £500,[7] and the policies

[1] E.g. Wm. Hussey of Salisbury in S. D. Chapman, 'Industrial Capital', Harte and
Ponting, see n. 18, p. 121, and Arthur and Francis Beardsley of Nottingham in S. D.
Chapman, 'The Genesis of the British Hosiery 1600–1750 ', *Textile History*, III (1972).
pp. 27–8.
[2] D[evon] R[ecord] O[ffice], Kennaway Mss., ms. entitled ' 1794, Sept. 8th. List
of Creditors '. The inventory of John Andrews, Tiverton merchant, dated 1722, lists
credits to serge makers and others: P.R.O., PCC 21/76.
[3] List of Exeter banks in W. G. Hoskins, *op. cit.*, p. 49.
[4] M. Dickenson, ' The West Riding Woollen and Worsted Industries, 1689–1770 ',
Ph.D. thesis, Nottingham 1975, pp. 61–2, and J. de L. Mann, *The Cloth Industry in the
West of England, 1640–1880* (Oxford, 1971), p. 103.
[5] S. D. Chapman, ' The Genesis of the British Hosiery Industry ', *Textile History*, III
(1974), pp. 26–8.
[6] M. Dickenson, *loc. cit.*
[7] The policies of weavers and combers have been omitted from this volume, partly
for want of space, and partly because the numbers are relatively small and unrepre-

continued on page xiv

give the impression of an unbroken spectrum of wealth between the clothiers and serge makers with little property to the more substantial weavers and combers. The evidence seems clear that there was a class of master weavers and combers with ample means to own the modest fixed capital required. This interpretation does not of course preclude the existence of a large proletariat of dependent operatives. Dunsford's record of the rise of trade unionism among Tiverton combers and weavers leaves no doubt of the existence and unity of this class.[1] Most of the class were probably dependent on the sergemakers and clothiers whose attempts to secure tighter control of the manufacture are illustrated by many of the policies collected in this volume; one of them, Perring of Modbury, already owned more than a hundred looms in 1754,[2] and there is no reason to suppose that the extent of his interest was unique.

The insurance policies illustrate the range of specialists that the regional industry maintained in the middle decades of the eighteenth century. The entrepreneurial function was represented by such specialised occupations as woolstaplers, yarn jobbers, and wool merchants, with only a handful of general merchants. Manufacturers appear as serge makers, clothiers, cloth makers, weavers, combers, and various combinations of these specialisms, while the finishing trades comprise fullers, dyers, pressmen, hot pressers, and various joint occupations. Moreover, the uncertain course of the textile trades through the eighteenth century persuaded numerous entrepreneurs in the region (and indeed in other regions) to retain a residual agricultural interest, or to diversify by taking a secondary occupation such as shopkeeping, malting or cider making, innkeeping, or investment in property. The large number of surviving insurance policies allow us to make some cautious generalisations on the extent and nature of this process of diversification, and on the retention of interest in farming, in two periods: from when the policies begin in 1726 to mid-century, and from 1751 to 1770. If we define a farming interest as the inclusion of barns, linhays, hovels, milkhouses, cowhouses, dairies, granaries, etc. (but not stables) in the policies, about 30 per cent can be so described in both periods. This figure, if it can be relied on, places Devon in an intermediate position between the West Riding of Yorkshire, three-quarters of whose clothiers are said to have had some sort of agricultural interest at the period, and the Wiltshire cloth industry, ten per cent of whose clothiers retained a link with farming.[3] However, it should be added that the Yorkshire figure is derived from probate inventories, which give a more detailed picture of farm stock, and it

continued from page xiii
sentative, and they generally lack the interesting detail of the policies reproduced. They seldom contain anything more than small rented properties, and rarely exceed £100. For examples of higher valuations see e.g. Isaac Tucker, Axminster shopkeeper and fillet weaver, £1,200, 149/202317 (1763); Bartholomew Coombe, Hatherleigh comber, malter and shopkeeper, £500, 136/182547 (1761); and Michael Barrett, Plymouth woolcomber, £500, 160/219632 (1765).

[1] M. Dunsford, *op. cit.*, pp. 205, 228–32, 239–240.

[2] Journal of Reinhold Angerstein, trans. by Torsten Berg, to be published by the Royal Historical Society. There were said to be 700 serge weavers at Modbury at this time.

[3] S. D. Chapman, ' Industrial Capital before the Industrial Revolution ' in N. B. Harte and K. G. Ponting (eds.), *Textile History and Economic History* (Manchester, 1973) p. 129. cp. J. de L. Mann, *op. cit.*, p. 96.

seems likely that if the Devon probate materials had survived the proportion might appear appreciably higher. Nevertheless, the link between textiles and agriculture clearly varied between the regions.

The development of retailing during the eighteenth century offered opportunities for the more enterprising. Devon records provide very little specific evidence of this, apart from Dunsford's references to Tiverton innkeepers incurring the wrath of the local textile workers by dealing in serges.[1] In fact, it was quite common, taking the country as a whole, for innkeepers to deal in other commodities because the yards and public rooms were convenient places for business transactions.[2] Serge makers, looking for investment opportunities, would easily recognise the commercial attractions of the inn and alehouse. Another obvious second occupation was that of mercer and draper, where a man already in the textile trade could readily utilise his experience and connections. Over the period covered by the policies in this volume, one in eight of the entrepreneurs listed united retailing in one or more commodities to their activities in the textile industries. Property investment was another obvious insurance against the instability of the textile trade; in the first half of our period half the entrepreneurs for which we have evidence had some such investment, and cottages were frequently rented to weavers and combers. This fraction fell to two-fifths in the second half of the period, probably because the Devon textile industry was in gradual decline, and entrepreneurs were finding it impossible to build up their reserves of capital.

Such combinations of economic activity were however only one characteristic of Devon industry at the period. It was paralleled by the sergemakers' attempts to extend their interests *within* the industry, a process which can be measured in a rough way by studying the variety of premises (and hence of processes) listed on manufacturers' policies. Fairly consistently over the period, half of them owned their own workshops as distinct from their domestic accommodation, a quarter had their own warehouses, and fifteen per cent their own dyehouses. The policies regularly mention sorting rooms, washrooms, breaking shops, combing shops, yarn shops, warping shops, weaving shops, dyerooms (or dyehouses) and presshouses, indicating the range of processes carried on by the sergemaker, and the attempt to take over the functions said to have been conducted by Exeter merchants or other specialists at the centre of the industry. A handful of sergemakers can be seen to have retained their own warerooms or a warehouse in Exeter. From other sources we learn that sergemakers, including those from Exeter and Tiverton, were accustomed to contract with farmers for their wool supplies or to go to Barnstaple to buy their own imported wool, so by-passing the Exeter Wool Market.[3] The fulling mills seem largely to have remained in the hands of the great landowners and town corporations. The scale of investment by sergemakers was typically less than that of the largest Exeter dyers and fullers (men like Henry Wilmott and William Fryer), but there is ample evidence here of a class of small thrusting entre-

---

[1] M. Dunsford, *op. cit.*, pp. 226, 228–9.
[2] A. Everett, *Perspectives in English Urban History* (1973), Ch. 4.
[3] W. G. Hoskins, *op. cit.*, p. 36, n. 25, and *Universal British Directory*, II (1793), p. 313.

preneurs much like those that have been described as characteristic of Yorkshire at the period.[1]

Further evidence of the enterprise of the manufacturers can be seen in the growing habit of building workshops and workers' tenements alongside the employer's house in enclosed courts, so that the various processes could be more effectively supervised. The farm with buildings enclosing a yard was typical of Devon, and this traditional plan was adapted to the needs of the woollen industry. The insurance registers provide examples of this practice at Exeter, Tiverton, Crediton, Cullompton, South Molton, North Tawton, Chagford, and Uffculme, and a local historian described it at Bradninch.[2] There are also large numbers of L-shaped and U-shaped groups of buildings which may have become quadrangular in the course of time. The occasional reference to gatehouses and gateways seems to imply adherence to an ancient local tradition, for these were a feature of the larger farmhouses.[3] Linhays (open fronted cattle stalls) in the sergemakers' yards were sometimes adapted for textile processes, so that they are called ' hanging linney ', ' chain linney,' or ' spinning linney ' in the policies. The yards themselves were used for warping (i.e. preparing the warp threads for the looms), though any other large open space would have served as well. The assembly of sequential processes in a collection of adjacent buildings in this manner has been identified as the ' proto-factory ', a very significant intermediate stage between the workshop (defined as the location of the main process) and the fully evolved factory (defined as the location of a sequence of semi-automatic machine processes).[4] In Devon, as in Lancashire, Yorkshire, Wiltshire, and other industrial counties, the eighteenth century saw a process of evolution from the workshop to the fully-evolved factory, though the latter was of course much more common in the north of England by the 1780s and 1790s.

The building of employees' tenements adjacent to the master's house was a way of tying weavers, combers, and other employees to their employer, and of bringing them under more immediate work discipline. If Dunsford's graphic accounts of trade union militancy and popular riots are to be trusted, the domestic labour force was anything but docile. One would like to learn something of the quality of these tied cottages, but the insurance valuations offer no descriptions beyond their locations, and the most that can be done is to compare the valuations with those of other kinds of property. The policies do not always give the number of tenements in a row, and the valuations sometimes bracket a number of domestic and industrial buildings together. However, a valuation can be set on 483 tenements insured in the period 1750–1770, four-fifths of which were insured for less than £30 each. A stable was usually insured for £10 at the period, and a small ' linney ' of the kind that would stand

---

[1] H. Heaton, *The Yorkshire Woollen and Worsted Industries* (Oxford, 1920).

[2] M. W. Barley, *English Farmhouse and Cottage*, p. 222. C. Croslegh, *Bradninch, A Short Historical Sketch* . . . (1911), p. 300.

[3] See the policies of J. Fowler (Cullompton), J. Pulling (Tiverton), W. Salter (Tiverton), and P. Tucker (Crediton). Elkand Widgery, a South Molton woolcomber, insured a ' college of tenements and outhouses adjacent in East Street ' for £100 in 1753 (117/153411).

[4] S. D. Chapman, ' Textile Factory before Arkwright ', *loc. cit.*, elaborates these definitions.

in the yard for about the same sum. A tenement valued at less than £10 (of which only fourteen cases can be found) implies something inferior to a stable, a £10–£19 valuation (226 cases) suggests a one-roomed dwelling rather more comfortable than a stable, perhaps with a loft for sleeping, while the third category (£20–£29, 133 cases) suggests a two-roomed dwelling. The implication is that the general standard of craftsmen's cottages must have been most rudimentary.[1] Even so, it was probably better than that of the dwellings of the agricultural labouring class; as late as 1808 it was said that ' three mud walls and a hedge bank form the habitation of many of the peasantry ' in Devon moorland parishes.[2]

The insurance policies include valuations of fifteen fulling mills, a rather small number considering that there were fourteen mills in Tiverton alone at the beginning of the period.[3] Exeter Corporation, who owned the freehold of a number of mills in the suburbs, may have insured with the Bristol Fire Office, or some other company. However, the mill policies that have survived are of considerable interest. They show valuations from £50 to £200, but this figure sometimes included a house, and quite often the mill was also used for some purpose in addition to fulling. Grist mills, a dyehouse, a calendar house and a malthouse are mentioned in different Devon policies. The low figures may occasion surprise and suggest under-valuation by the owners. In fact, the valuations are fairly typical of those found for mills in other counties, and are not inconsistent with data from other sources. At the beginning of the period a competent millwright would install a water wheel and transmission system on the latest principle (the breast wheel) for £25. Breast and overshot wheels were more efficient than the traditional paddle wheels, and were becoming general, especially in the north of England, in the first quarter of the century.[4] However, there is no reason to suppose that Devon (and the south-west generally) was particularly backward in the process of rebuilding mills on the improved plan. A set of five water wheels at Exeter used for fulling and grist were working ' breastwise ' in 1720.[5] Forty years later, a millwright from Derby (the home of that eighteenth-century prodigy of delicate mechanism, the Derby silk mill) advertised the quality of his services by recording that he had ' travelled all over the south west parts of England and Wales in order to obtain a further knowledge of whatever might be useful relating to Corn Mills, Paper Mills, Cloth Mills, Leather Mills, Forges of all kinds, Slitting Mills, Logwood Mills, and Snuff Mills, and all sorts of Mill Machinery. . . .'[6] Evidently the south-west was a region where a millwright could still learn something to his advantage, though visits

[1] M. Dunsford, *op. cit.*, p. 297, refers to Tiverton dwellings on the west side of the Exe in the area where fullers' workers lived as ' low ' (i.e. one storey, probably with thick cob walls about six feet high) and thatched, a detail that adds substance to the impression drawn from the policies.

[2] C. Vancouver, *Agriculture of Devon* (1808), p. 94.

[3] M. Dunsford, *op. cit.*, p. 216.

[4] E. Laurence, *The Duty of a Steward to his Lord* (1727), pp. 161–2.

[5] P.R.O. E134 5 Geo I, Mich 25, and 6 Geo I, Mich 39, *John v. Stafford.* Witnesses agreed that Duryard Mills were worth £250–£300 p.a., and £1,500 had been spent on renovation *c.* 1714. This implies a capital value of £5,000–£6,000, much higher than anything recorded in the insurance policies.

[6] *Nottingham Journal*, 9 Apr. 1763.

were probably limited to unusually big concerns like the mill at Exeter just referred to.

Professor Hoskins partly accounts for the decline of the Devon serge industry by reference to what economic historians now call ' entrepreneurial failure ', that is, the failure of entrepreneurs to respond to changing market conditions. ' What a contrast there is between the old men of the South and the new men of the North, typified in Sam Hill of Halifax, rising from nowhere, constantly experimenting, altering and adapting, studying the markets closely for openings in new classes of goods! ', he writes.[1] Hoskins modifies this remark by quoting Dunsford's accounts of the attempts that were made in 1720 to introduce fine druggets in Tiverton, and in 1752 the lighter type of worsteds associated with Norwich.[2] As already indicated, other evidence can be collected to show that the region was not devoid of entrepreneurs with drive and foresight, and that the contrast with the north of England can be over-drawn.

Some of the individual insurance policies collected here can contribute to the more optimistic view already drawn from the general evidence of dynamic response among the body of serge makers. The Weres, the Quaker serge makers of Wellington who (as Fox Bros.) are still in business there, built up an extensive trade to Amsterdam, Bruges, Rotterdam, Hamburg, and Ostend.[3] Their insurance policies show that they retained stock worth £3,000 in 1761, an unusually large figure at the period. Another striking example of business success was the Kennaways of Exeter whose surviving accounts show a steady increase in profits from £1,382 in 1751 to nearly £30,000 in 1785. Between 1784 and 1790, when the accounts reveal their markets for the first time, some 80 per cent of their sales were being made in Italy.[4] The insurance records show William Kennaway senior both at the commencement of his business as a wool factor in one of the numerous yards of mid-eighteenth century Exeter, and also after the later purchases of his own houses and warehouses. A more familiar success story is that of the Baring brothers, the former Bremen family, who were still active as cloth manufacturers, dyers, and merchants on the eve of the French Wars, but were moving quickly towards ' pure ' finance. The policies reveal them as extensive property owners in the 1760s and 1770s. The contribution of other migrant entrepreneurs is represented by Claudius Passavant, a member of one of the two important Huguenot families that traded to Exeter in the eighteenth century.[5] Samuel Milford provides yet another example of spectacular mercantile enterprise in Exeter in the second half of the

---

[1] W. G. Hoskins, *op. cit.*, p. 53.

[2] M. Dunsford, *op. cit.*, pp. 209–235.

[3] H. Fox, *Quaker Homespun. The Life of Thomas Fox of Wellington, Serge Maker and Banker, 1747–1821* (1958), pp. 17–19. Were's earliest policy (vol. 15, 26 July 1723, £800) shows that he already owned one of the biggest firms.

[4] DRO Kennaway Mss.

[5] R. W. Hidy, *The House of Baring in American Trade* (Harvard, 1949), Ch. 1. The firm's manufacturing and financial activities are disclosed in more detail in P.R.O. C12/227/2, C12/947/18. Barings had an interest in a dyeing business up to 1795, as well as the fulling mills revealed in their insurance policies. For Passavant and the other Huguenot family (Du Fay), see A. Dietz, *Frankfurter Handelsgeschichte* (F'furt 1925), IV (1), pp. 311, 316.

eighteenth century. He appears to have come of a modest local background, but married the daughter of an Exeter fuller and found his way into the cloth export trade to Italy, making enough money to open the Exeter City Bank in 1786.[1] He established three sons in business but still had sufficient fortune remaining to leave his widow between £60,000 and £70,000. His father, Richard Milford, can probably be identified with the Crediton sergemaker of the same name whose 1751 policy is included in this volume. The £700 policy is a little above average valuation, but otherwise typical of scores of country sergemakers at the period.

The enterprise of Devon textile entrepreneurs is evident almost to the end of the century. It is not appropriate to use this Introduction to attempt a comprehensive study of the Devon mills that were built to meet the challenge of cheap machine-spun cotton and worsted in the age of Arkwright, but it is useful to mention a few leading concerns to provide illustrations of the scale of enterprise introduced in the 1790s. Serge was a relatively inexpensive cloth made for popular consumption, and suffered severely from the competition of Lancashire cotton. The earliest response was the erection of extensive cotton mills in Exeter (by J. & J. Parker, who already had cotton mills at Clitheroe), at Tiverton (by Heathfield, Denny & Co., who had a big cotton mill at Sheffield), and at Barnstaple (by William Fry & Co., who owned the Raleigh mill at Keynsham, near Bristol). In the early 1790s there was still sufficient confidence in Devon for London financiers to inject capital into these concerns; John Parker was a London money scrivener, Heathfield was in partnership with Wells, a London banker, while the Barnstaple concern enjoyed the support of partnerships of Bristol and Dublin merchants.[2] When it was realised that Arkwright's technique could be applied to worsted spinning, the Tiverton mill was turned over to the more familiar fibre, and worsted mills were built by Sir George Yonge at Ottery St. Mary, by James Chappell, an Exeter linen draper and banker, in his native town, and by Thomas Fox, ' sergemaker and banker ', at Wellington.[3] These were the giants; in addition numbers of serge manufacturers struggled to maintain a place in the industry by introducing some of the new mechanical principles to their own workshops.[4]

Unhappily for Devon, expertise was not easily transferred from north to south, and in the difficult trading conditions of the French Wars large and small firms alike capitulated to the competition of Lancashire and Yorkshire. An American visitor to Exeter in 1796 soon realised the truth. ' Baring informed me that the coarser kinds of cloths are made cheaper in Yorkshire than here—also shalloons, tammies, callimancoes,

---

[1] Milford pedigree and family papers in possession of J. R. Milford of Chedworth, Gloucs. Copies kindly lent by Prof. Joyce Youings.
[2] For J. & J. Parker (Exeter Mill Co.) see P.R.O. C12/254/15 and E112/1532/295; also O. Ashmore, ' Low Moor, Clitheroe: a 19th C. Factory Community ', *Trans. Lancs. & Chesh. Antiq. Soc.*, LXXII, LXXIV (1963-4). For Heathfield, Denny & Co., see W. Harding, *The History of Tiverton* (Tiverton, 1845-7), pp. 198-202, and P.R.O. C12/1431/40. For Raleigh Mill, P.R.O. C12/658/18, E112/1939/664, and B1/87/283-6.
[3] Sale of Yonge's Mill, *St. James's Chronicle*, 13 Aug. 1796, and handbill in Harvard Univ. Library Mss., U.S.A. For James Chappell see P.R.O. B1/86/52-6.
[5] E.g. Wm. Cole, Farringdon, £1,200 in Sun ' Country Series ' 12/648736 (1795); Mat. Barnett, Exeter, £650, in Sun C.S. 19/667848 (1797); Cresswell, Fowler & Brown, Cullompton, £1,700, in Sun C.S. 8/636173 (1794). Devon has a very meagre representation in the Sun registers by this period.

camblitts, sagathies, etc. at Norwich ', he noted in his journal. Later in his travels he recorded that ' The present manufacture of Norwich is cambletts and stuffs [i.e. worsted cloths] of like kind chiefly for the Russian, Italian and Assyrean trade; some of these have greatly declined and the manufacture of cotton goods similar to Manchester has been since decreed; they are not however made so cheap [as in the north].' Norwich was on the way out, too.[1]

The competitive position of Devon and the Norwich region was also undermined by the narrowing price differential between the price of wool and the price of cotton (see chart opposite). The extraordinarily rapid extension of cultivation of cotton in the United States practically coincided with the period of the French Wars, when it became increasingly difficult to import wool fleeces from the traditional continental sources. It has been estimated that from the 1770s consumption of wool per head of population actually declined as cotton was gradually substituted in one use after another.[2] Yorkshire was best situated to meet this challenge as buildings and plant were more readily switched to cotton and the new technology more easily borrowed from the neighbouring county and adapted to wool. Devon, the most distant English competitor, was obviously more vulnerable to competition from northern innovators. Even so, the best available figures, which are summarised in Table 2, suggest that in the 1770s and 1780s the effect was to rob Devon of the benefits of growing national prosperity, rather than produce actual decline in the county's staple manufacture.

Table 2

VALUE OF EXPORTS OF CLOTH FROM EXETER IN THE EIGHTEENTH CENTURY

1700–1715	£0.5 mn.
1763–1778	£0.5 mn.
1788–1791	£0.5–0.6 mn.

Source: W. G. Hoskins, *Industry, Trade and People in Exeter, 1688–1800*, pp. 68–70 and 79, for first two estimates. India Office Library Mss., Charter Series, A/2/11, petitions of Exeter merchants, 24 March 1793, for third estimate. *Universal British Directory*, III (1794) p. 6, estimates £600,000, probably inspired by the same source.

The estimate for the years 1788–91, which is reproduced here for the first time, is based on a calculation made in 1793 by twenty leading merchant houses of Exeter. By this time they were ready to voice their fear of cotton, and blamed their difficulties on competition from Swiss and Silesian cottons and linens, and coarse cottons from Catalonia.[3] Their sentiments fell short of frank admission, for the continental cotton producers were already a long way behind Manchester in both fine and coarse cotton production.[4]

[1] Journals of Joshua Gilpin (1765–1840), vols. 9 and 10. (Ms., Pennsylvania Historical Museum, U.S.A.). J. B. Gribble, *Memorials of Barnstaple* (1830) p. 544 confirms Gilpin's reference to the introduction of worsted and cotton mixtures in Devon.
[2] P. Deane, ' The Output of the British Woollen Industry in the 18th C.', *Journal of Economic History*, XVII (1957).
[3] India Office Library Mss., Charter Series, A/2/11, petitions of Exeter merchants to the East India Co. directors, 24 Mar. 1793.
[4] M. Lévy-Leboyer, *Les banques européennes et l'industrialisation internationale* (Paris, 1964), p. 27.

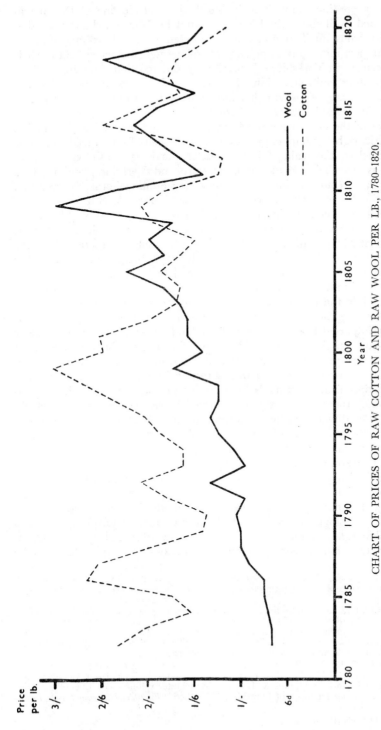

CHART OF PRICES OF RAW COTTON AND RAW WOOL PER LB., 1780–1820.

The wool prices are the average for South Down in Wiltshire for August, September and October of each year (Bischoff, J., *A Comprehensive History of the Woollen and Worsted Manufacturers* (1842), II, p. 125). The cotton prices are the mean of the annual price range for West Indian Cotton (Tooke, T., *History of Prices* (1928 edn.), I, p. 401).

The suggestion, implicit in Table 2, that the decline of Devon was suspended until the early 1790s, must not be interpreted to mean that the numerous small manufacturers represented in this volume had the same opportunity to become captains of the new factory system as their counterparts in Yorkshire. It has been estimated that the output of the West Riding multiplied eight times during the course of the eighteenth century,[1] a rate of growth that inevitably generated more capital than the static Devon industry could command.

Most of the capital for the Devon cotton and worsted mills built on the Arkwright system came, as we have seen, from outside sources. Nevertheless, the scale of investment in particular mills was quite as large as that being made in Lancashire and Yorkshire, and made a spectacular contrast with the typical serge manufacturer's premises. Both the Exeter and Tiverton mills were launched with a capital of £24,000, of which the insured capital of the latter reached £13,100 in 1797; probably the Exeter mill cost about the same.[2] Yonge's mill at Ottery St Mary realised £11,000 when it was sold by auction the same year.[3] Fox Brothers' first mill was built to a similar plan so probably cost about the same. The power unit had to increase in proportion to the size of mill; the ' millwright's work ' at Tiverton was insured for £800, while the two wheels and transmission at Foxes' Tonedale Mills (1802) cost £850.[4] The technical expertise for these innovations was largely imported from the north of England. J. & J. Parker (the Exeter Mill Co.) employed Peter Atherton, Arkwright's former partner at Warrington, to build carding, drawing, roving, and spinning machines for them.[5] Foxes bought machinery from a Manchester builder in 1791 and castings from Dearman's Foundry at Birmingham in 1802.[6] Heathfields had their Tiverton labour force trained at the firm's Sheffield mill.[7] The difficult trading conditions of the French War years exposed the south-western manufacturers to the most severe competition from the north, and they were particularly vulnerable in this position of dependence on northern technology.

The final phase in the history of the Devon textile industries began at the close of the French Wars when it became clear that the county had a large low-paid and under-employed labour force habituated to industrial employment, and a stock of redundant industrial buildings available at knock-down prices. The solution was found by James Dean, an Exeter ' Parliamentary Agent and Land Surveyor '. In 1816 he

---

[1] R. G. Wilson, ' The Supremacy of the Yorkshire Cloth Industry in the 18th C.', in N. B. Harte and K. G. Ponting (eds.), *Textile History and Economic History* (Manchester, 1973), p. 231.

[2] P.R.O. C12/254/15; Harding, *loc. cit.*; Royal Exchange registers 32a/154794 (1797) and Sun C.S. 18/663527 (1797).

[3] Ms. notes on handbill cited in note 39.

[4] H. Fox, *op. cit.*, pp. 91–5; J. H. Fox, *The Woollen Manufacture at Wellington, Somerset* (1914), pp. 54–5. Sun C.S. and Royal Exchange, *loc. cit.*

[5] P.R.O. E112/1532/295. Atherton was at one time a partner in the famous Holywell cotton mills (C12/250/35), then opened his own mills at Mold (near Chester), then became a partner in Phillips & Lee, the Manchester spinners: E. J. Foulkes, ' The Cotton Spinning Factories of Flintshire, 1777–1866 ', *Flintshire Historical Society Publications*, XXI (1964).

[6] H. Fox, *op. cit.*, p. 94.

[7] W. Harding, *loc. cit.*

explained that ' The woollen manufacture of Devonshire has ceased to be profitable, and has therefore in great measure been abandoned. The [lace] manufacture of Leicestershire and Nottinghamshire cannot find a market for their goods at prices adequate for the cost of manufacturing them by the old machinery. Messrs. Heathcote & Boden of Loughborough feeling existing restraints applied to me a year ago [i.e. December 1815] to purchase a suitable situation for them in Devonshire to erect improved machinery and I obtained for them the fine mill of Heathfield, Milford & Co. at Tiverton. . . . Application has lately been made to me by upwards of twenty of the principal manufacturers in Devonshire to sell their mills for them. . . .'[1] Heathcote was the innovating entrepreneur in the bobbin net lace manufacture, and his migration in search of cheap labour soon brought other lace manufacturers to Devon. Lace factories were opened at Barnstaple (Rawleigh Mill), Taunton, Chard and Exwick, and the Ottery mill converted to silk reeling, probably to supply the other mills; but this enterprise could not replace the losses sustained by the declining serge industry.[2] It was, moreover, accompanied by the decline of Devon's traditional hand-made lace industry, for bobbin-net, embroidered by hand, found no difficulty in undercutting Honiton lace. Within a generation (1795–1825), both of Devon's traditional textile industries had been eclipsed by their northern rivals.

[1] P.R.O. HO 42/156, James Dean to Home Sec., 6 Dec. 1816. For Heathcoat's career, see W. Gore Allen, *John Heathcoat and his Heritage* (1958) and D. E. Varley, ' John Heathcoat (1783–1861) Founder of the Machine-made Lace Industry ', *Textile History*, I (1968). Neither source attempts to link Heathcoat with the previous history of Devon textiles.
[2] W. Felkin *History of the Machine-wrought Hosiery and Lace Manufactures* (1867), p. 251; first census of the lace industry reported in *Nottingham Review*, 11 Se , . 1829. Ottery Mill deeds in Devon C.R.O.

EDITORIAL NOTES

The long series of Sun Fire Office policy registers now deposited at Guildhall Library, London, begins in 1710, but the earliest volumes are of little value to the historian of trade and industry. For the first ten years the policies did not regularly include valuations, and until 1726 or 1727 the detail is sparse. Devon policies make their first appearance in the registers in 1723, but the first forty or so of them, like those of other counties, were fairly stereotyped, recording only a dwelling house and/ or merchandise, invariably for a total of £300 or £500. These inferior policies are not worth transcribing, but to maintain a complete record they are listed in the order in which they appear in the registers in an Appendix. The more detailed policies begin with that of Ralph Fowler in 1726 (reproduced in full above, p. xi), but for some years after this some agents omitted interesting details, notably building materials and street locations in the larger towns (Exeter and Tiverton). The transcription is concluded about 1770, when the Devon policies in the registers begin to dwindle.

The policies reproduced in this volume are limited to those of principal textile manufacturers and merchants. Weavers, woolcombers, hosiers, and mercers are omitted because the numbers are much smaller (and therefore less representative) and because these policies seldom contain any detail about manufacturing. All the policies have been extracted from the so-called ' Old Series ' of Sun registers (Ms. 11,936 at Guildhall Library, London) which comprise some 500 volumes of up to 600 pages each; there are generally three or four policies to each page, depending on the clerk who wrote them up. The reference numbers shown for each policy (e.g. 114/152601) consist of the volume number (114) followed by the policy number.

The dates are the original policy dates. The English calendar was reformed during 1751 when eleven days were ' lost ' during September. New Year had begun on 25th March but this too was altered and became 1st January from 1752 (1751 was only nine months long). 1751/2 is marked N.S. for this reason.

The policies are listed under the place of residence, town or village, of the insured. They are then classified into the following occupational categories: Merchants; Woolmerchants, Woolmen and Woolstaplers; Sergemakers; Clothiers; Fullers and Tuckers; Dyers; Pressmen and Hot Pressers; and Miscellaneous (including Yarn Jobbers). Within each occupational group the arrangement is by alphabetical order of surnames. Where there is more than one policy for any individual, they are listed in date order. A man following two or more trades is listed under his textile occupation; for example, a tanner and clothier is categorised as a clothier.

Partnerships are cross referenced in the text but details are shown for the first-named partner only, e.g. Brook & Reed, Exeter, are listed under Brook, while Smale & Baring, Tiverton and Exeter, are listed under Smale. Where the first named partner was not concerned with textiles, the details are given under the textile manufacturer, e.g. Reynolds (Ironmonger) & Woodman (Fuller) is listed under Woodman. In case of doubt reference can be made to the name index at the end of the book.

The text assembled in this volume is not intended to be a complete transcription of the original policies for this would have taken up too much space. The primary objective has been to show the location, ownership, size, and structure of the so-called 'domestic' industry in the county, but as far as possible the detail and eccentricities of the original inventories have been retained.[1] A good deal of the common form and repetitive phrasing has been omitted, the usual omissions being italicised in the following typical examples:

£

On his now dwelling house *only*, timber and thatched, *not exceeding one hundred pounds* 100

His household goods *and furniture* therein *only, not exceeding eighty pounds* 80

His cellar and office *only*, adjoining, *not exceeding five pounds* ... 5

His stock in trade in his dwelling house *only, not exceeding one hundred and fifty pounds* 150

Urban policies often give the parish of the policy holder or his property but these have been omitted except for the city of Exeter. The only other details omitted are the names of tenants not occupied in cloth manufacture.

Capitalisation and punctuation have been modernised and, as far as possible, spellings of place and street names, but in all cases where there is any doubt or where identification has been impossible the original spelling has been given in italic type. Christian names have been given as far as possible in their modern form but all alternative spellings of surnames have been retained, e.g. Thomas Corsway, Cossway or Cosway and John Read, Reed, or Reid. The following abbreviations have been used throughout the text:—

adjoining/adjacent	adj.
dwelling house	dwho.
house	ho.
household	hshld
goods	gds
New Style Calendar	N.S.
stock	stk
trade	trd.

[1] A few details about location of properties, particularly in Tiverton, which came to light after the text had been set up, have been inserted at the end of the relevant inventories, where necessary with the use of asterisks: General Editor.

Acknowledgements

The splendid collection of business records at Guildhall Library was assembled by the former archivist, Dr. A. E. J. Hollaender, and my thanks are due to him and his successor, Mr. C. Cooper, for providing every assistance over a period of several years. The most difficult problem of the historian exploiting the insurance registers has been that the hundreds of heavy volumes are not indexed in any way; altogether there are estimated to be some 1,200,000 unindexed policies for the eighteenth century alone. To work systematically through the Sun Fire Office registers for fifty years is a formidable task, and has only been accomplished with the aid of a number of hard-working collaborators. I am particularly grateful to Dr. M. W. Dickenson and Mr. T. Rath, who in turn served me as research assistants and, from time to time, engaged other assistants, mostly teams of vacation students. Mr. K. G. Ponting, Director of the Pasold Research Fund, encouraged me with regular financial support and, more recently, Mrs. Valerie Glass, Statistical Assistant to the Department of Economic History at Nottingham University, has spent many hours sorting and standardising the transcripts. Professor M. W. Barley and Mr. Edwin Green read the first draft of the Introduction and suggested several considerable improvements. Mrs. Shirley Smith and Mrs. Gwen Parker translated my manuscript into an orderly typescript.

In February 1977, when this volume was passing through the printer's hands, the Social Science Research Council announced that it had awarded a grant of £35,186, spread over two years and three months, for the preparation of a machine-readable index of eighteenth century fire insurance registers. If all goes well, the index should be available to researchers towards the end of 1979. The registers will be indexed by name, place, and occupation, but will contain no information on the contents of the policies. It is hoped that the present volume will illustrate the kind of information that insurance registers can offer, and consequently be of service to all potential users of the registers and index.

It has been a great pleasure to respond to the Devon and Cornwall Record Society's invitation to contribute a volume to their New Series, and I should particularly like to express my appreciation to Professor Joyce Youings for her encouragement and advice. The Society's Council will join me in thanking the Pasold Research Fund and the Sun Alliance and London Insurance Group for making grants to assist publication. My final thanks are to the subscribers to the Record Society Series, whose annual tribute makes the publication of such specialised scholastic work possible. I hope they find the present volume opens up new areas of interest in local historical studies, to their profit and enjoyment.

STANLEY D. CHAPMAN

ALPHINGTON

67/96873
BURNETT, John, Sergemaker.   3 Nov. 1743
Dwho., stone, cob and thatched £150; Hshld gds and stk in trd. therein
£100; Comb shop, stables and linneys adj., stone, cob and thatched £50.

£300

ASHBURTON

149/201080
FOOTT, Philip, Sergemaker.   20 July 1763
Dwho., stone, lath and plaster and slated, £70; kitchen and chamber
over behind the house, thatched £30.

£100

108/143988
SOPER, John, Sergemaker.   11 Dec. 1754
Dwho., office and stable under one roof, stone and slated £100; Hshld
gds and stk in trd. therein £300.

£400

202/292522
SUNTER, William, Sergemaker and Maltster.   28 Dec. 1770
Dwho. and maltho. adj., stone and slated £300; Hshld gds £100;
Utensils and stk £150; Linney separate, weather boarded and slated
£200; Utensils and stk therein £50.

£800

173/241430
TOZER, John, Sergemaker and Shopkeeper.   8 Jan. 1767
Dwho. and adj. stables, lath, stone, plaster and slated £145; Hshld gds
therein £50; Utensils and stk therein £350; Range of offices slated,
barn and shop adj. stone, cob and thatched £54; A sty £1; Utensils,
stk. in trd. in dwho and in wareroom therein, stone, lath, plaster and
slated £100.

£700

197/282453
TOZER, John, Sergemaker and Shopkeeper.   20 Mar. 1770
Dwho. and woodho. adj. £400; Hshld gds therein £50; Utensils and
stk therein £950; Wareho. and stable adj. £20; Utensils and stk in a
dwho. and warerooms adj. £500; Stk in dwho. of B. Buckingham £80.
Stone, plaster and tiled.

£2,000

168/233091
TOZER, Richard, Sergemaker.   23 April 1766
Hshld gds in his dwho., stone, cob, lath, plaster and slated £50;

1

Utensils and stk therein, £190; Utensils and stk in his brewho., chamber and stable adj. separate from above, thatched, £60.

£300

171/236633

WINSOR, John, Sergemaker.   22 Aug. 1766
Stk in 5 warehos. 6, 7, 8, 9, 10 Hay's Wharf, Bridge Yard, Southwark.

£3,000

108/145043

CAUNTER, John, Clothier.   18 Feb. 1755
Dwho. and offices under one roof, stone, cob and slated £100; Hshld gds and stk in trd. therein £100.

£200

199/285568

CAUNTER, John, Clothier.   12 June 1770
Dwho. and offices adj., stone, cob and slated £100; Hshld gds therein £50; Utensils and stk therein £100; Ho. and linney adj. called the Dock Inn in tenure of sergemaker, stone, weather boarded and slated, £300; Ho. and offices in tenure of himself and others, stone, cob and slated £200; Utensils and stk therein, £100; Drying linney near in own tenure, stone, weather boarded and slated £200; Utensils and stk therein £50; Another ho. in own tenure, stone and slated £80; Utensils and stk therein £20.

£1,200

86/117195

FABYAN, Peter, Clothier.   26 July 1749
Dwho., Maltho., two tenements in tenures of two persons, a stable, shippen and wareho. all under one roof, stone, brick and slated £200; Hshld gds and stk in trd. in that part only he occupies £200.

£400

94/127834

SHELLABEAR, Walter, Clothier.   18 Oct 1751
Dwho. and small stable adj., stone, cob and slated £150; Hshld gds and stk in trd. therein £50.

£200

ASHFORD

153/208614

PRICKMAN, John, Sergemaker.   20 April 1764
Dwho., combshop, warehos and stable adj., stone, cob and thatched £130; Hshld gds and stk therein £170.

£300

171/239366

PRICKMAN, Peter, Sergemaker.   8 Nov. 1766

Hshld gds in his dwho. and millho. adj. £60; Utensils and stk therein and in combshop, warping rooms, wool chamber all adj. £140. All stone, cob and thatched.

£200

ASHREIGNEY

50/78204
DENIS, Roger, Sergemaker. 21 Sept. 1738
Dwho., wareho., yarn chamber, wool chamber and stable, under one roof, stone, cob and thatched £90; Hshld gds and stk in trd. therein £150; Thatched workshop and offices to it in the yard £10; Utensils and stk. therein £50.

£300

148/199619
ISAAC, John, Sergemaker. 7 June 1763
Ho. in tenements. Stable and tallet over adj. in Ashreigney. Stone, cob and thatched £150; Hshld gds and stk therein £150.

£300

AWLISCOMBE

151/205094
BING, Francis, Clothier. 13 Dec. 1763
Dwho., cellar, stable, wash-ho., poundho., pound therein and offices adj. £160; Hshld gds and stk therein £130; Wareho., workshop, stable and cellar adj. £40; Stk therein £70. All stone, cob and thatched.

£400

AXMINSTER

145/193542
HAYCROFT, Richard, Tanner, Woolstapler and 22 Oct. 1762
Leather dresser.
Dwho. and offices adj. at Westwater £100; Hshld gds and stk therein £50; Stable adj. warerooms and storerooms and tan pits under in the yard £50; Gds and stk therein £380; Dryho. £20; Ho. and outho. adj. late the Valiant Soldier now in warerooms in his own possession £50; stk therein £100; Mill ho. and mills therein, with all their running tackle and workho. adj. £150; stk therein £150; Ho., offices adj. late the Red Lion in tenure £50. All stone, cob and thatched.

£1,000

157/213191
HAYCROFT, Richard, Tanner, Woolstapler and 18 Oct. 1764
Leatherseller.
Dwho., workshops, storerooms and offices adj. £100; Hshld gds and stk therein £100; Millho. and mills therein with all running tackle and workho. adj. £100; stk therein £100; Ho. and offices adj. in his own

occupation £70; Hshld gds and stk therein £30; Backho., millho., leatherho., warerooms over in yard £100; stk therein £300; Ho. and offices adj. in tenure of his servants £70; Dryho. and stable adj. £29; stk therein £1, stone, cob and thatched.

£1,000

40/64048
BILKE, Edward, Clothier.   25 June 1734
Dwho. and dyeho. under one roof, thatched.

£200

167/230982
BRYANT, Robert, Clothier.   18 Feb. 1766
Hshld gds in his dwho. and workshop adj., stone, cob and thatched £40; Utensils and stk therein £160.

£200

159/216713
CHAMP, William, Clothier.   29 Jan. 1765
Dwho. and offices adj. £50; stone, cob and thatched. Hshld gds and stk therein £50.

£100

31/51311
COLEMAN, John, Clothier and Shopkeeper.   17 Aug. 1730
Hshld gds, stk in trde in his dwho., timber, stone and thatched.

£300

149/202339
FINNEMORE, Elizabeth and FINNEMORE, Thomas,   6 Sept. 1763
    Widow and Clothier.
Their dwho., cellar and shear shop with chambers over, above, adj. £130; Hshld gds, utensils and stk therein £100; Pressho., breaking shop with chambers over the pressho. £40; Utensils and stk therein £30; Ho., dyeho. and long linney adj. with three furnaces therein in tenure £100; All stone and brick.

£400

63/92955
FINNEMORE, Thomas, Clothier.   22 Oct. 1742
Dwho., thatched £100; Hshld gds and stk therein £80; Cellars and shearshop with chambers over adj. the dwho. on the south £30; Utensils and stk therein £20; Pressho. adj. the shearshop £40; utensils and stk therein £30. In Chard St.

£300

149/202664
HARVEY, Israel, Clothier.   24 Sept. 1763
Two dwhos under one roof and range of buildings behind and adj. in tenure £350; Hshld gds and stk therein £200; stable behind £10.

Workshops in his own possession and stable behind and adj. in tenure £20; Utensils and stk therein £10; woodho., wool wareho. under one roof £10. Stone, cob and thatched.

£600

199/285565
HARVEY, Israel, Clothier.   12 June 1770
Workshop in his garden, stone, brick, nogging and tiled £50; Utensils and stk utensils £50.

£100

62/91433
HARVEY, Joshua, Clothier.   31 May 1742
Dwho. and pressho. adj. with a chamber over, thatched £100. Hshld gds and stk in trade in the dwho. £100; Shop and chamber over adj. the dwho., thatched £50; Stk in the pressho. and the shop and chambers over £50.

£300

111/147031
HARVEY, Joshua, Clothier.   11 June 1755
Dwho., pressho. adj. and chamber over £100; Hshld gds and stk therein £100; Large adj. workshop and chamber over £50; Utensils and stk therein £50; Ho., stable and barn adj. in tenure to an apothecary, stone, cob and thatched £100. All above stone, cob and thatched, sit. in South Street, Axminster.

£400

149/202337
PARRATT, Joseph, Clothier.   6 Sept. 1763
Dwho., shops and warerooms over and offices adj., stone, cob and thatched £140; Hshld gds and stk therein £60.

£200

47/74026
RAMSON, Samuel, Clothier.   1 July 1737
Dwho., Warehos and workhos and other offices under one roof, forming a court, stone, timber and thatched £250; Hshld gds, utensils and stk in trade in the said building £250.

£500

96/130045
THOMAS, William, Clothier.   N.S. 7 April 1752
Dwho., workshop and outhos adj. thatched £100; Hshld gds, utensils and stk in trd. therein £100.

£200

149/202666
THOMAS, William, Clothier.   24 Sept. 1763
Dwho. and shops adj. £150; Hshld gds, utensils and stk therein £100;

One ho. in Lyme Street £30; Dyeho., furnace and pump therein £20; All stone, cob and thatched.

£300

131/173943
WARREN, John, Clothier.   26 Feb. 1760
Dwho., workshop and stable and offices adj., stone, cob and thatched £50; Hshld gds and stk therein £50.

£100

149/202326
WOOLEY, Joseph, Clothier.   6 Sept. 1763
Four tenements under one roof. Two outhos and linneys adj. in tenure of himself and others, stone, cob and thatched.

£100

49/75533
WOOLLEY, John, Clothier.   25 Dec. 1737
Thatched ho. known as the 'Rose and Crown' in tenure of Robert Lidden, innholder £80; The stables and outhos thereto belonging, thatched £20; Thatched dwho. £50; Fulling mills and dyeho. under one roof, thatched, £50.

£200

67/96001
SHERIVE, Samuel, Fuller.   23 Aug. 1743
Hshld gds and stk in trd. in his dwho, and warehos under one roof, stone, cob and thatched, £100; Stk in trd. in his burling shop, cob and thatched, £100. Stk in trd., including vats and coppers in his dyeho., distant from the aforesaid buildings, thatched, £100.

£300

149/202322
HAMLIN, Benjamin, Clothworker.   6 Sept. 1763
Ho. in South Street, in tenure, £45; linney rear £5; ho. and linney adj. in Chard Street £30; Hshld gds therein £20. Stone, cob and thatched.

£100

BARNSTAPLE

90/122561
DEAN, John, Clothier.   7 Sept. 1750
Hshld gds and stk in trd. in his dwho. and range of workshops and stable, brick and slated.

£300

145/194492
DEANE, John, Clothier.   14 Dec. 1762
Dwho. and offices adj. and communicating in Holland Street, brick

and slated, £150; Hshld gds and stk therein £150; Utensils and stk in his pressho. and rooms over on the other side of the street. Stone, brick and slated, £100.

£400

67/95245
FOX, Amos, Clothier. 14 June 1743
Dwho., stone, brick, lath plaster and slated £100; Hshld gds and stk in trd. therein £60; Workshops and ware chambers under one roof, stone, slated and thatched, £30; Utensils and stk in trd. therein £10.

£200

120/160284
FOX, Amos, Clothier. 14 Dec. 1757
Dwho., workshop, brewho., stable adj. in Joy Street, stone, brick plaster, slated, £200; Hshld gds, utensils and stk therein £100.

£300

159/216712
ORAM, John Wood, Clothier. 29 Jan. 1765
Ho., workshops and stable adj. at Litchdon in Barnstaple in tenure of Captain Haines, brick and slated.

£300

130/173486
ROBBINS, John, Clothier. 1 Feb. 1760
Dwho., shops and offices under one roof adj., stone, brick, lath, plaster and slated, £90; Hshld gds and stk therein £100; Stable behind, slated, £10.

£200

90/122560
WOOD, John, Clothier. 7 Sept. 1750
Dwho. and offices adj., brick and tiled, £320; Hshld gds and stk in trd. therein £500; Pressho and rooms over, on the left hand, behind the ho., brick and tiled, £50; Utensils and stk in trd. therein £30. Ho. and range of workshops in Litchdon, Devon, in tenure of John Dean, clothier, brick and slated, £300.

£1,200

178/249632
BESLEY, Oliver, Dyer. 7 Oct. 1767
Dwho. and outho. adj. near Molton Bridge. In tenure, brick and slated.

£100

75/103075
FROST, Elizabeth, Stuffmaker. 8 Aug. 1745
Dwho., stone, cob and slated, £200; Hshld gds and stk in trd. therein £200; Dyeho., worsted ho. and stable adj., stone, cob and slated, £20; Utensils and stk in trd. therein £80.

£500

105/139895
GRIBBLE, Robert, Stuffmaker.   6 March 1754
Hshld gds and stk in trd. in his dwho. and workhos adj., stone, brick
and slated.

£200

131/173944
GRIBBLE, Robert, Stuffman and Woolcomber.   26 Feb. 1760
Hshld gds and stk in dwho., workshops and offices adj. in High Street,
stone, brick, cob, slated and tiled.

£200

161/21992
ROBBINS, Walter, Mercer and Yarn Jobber.   4 June 1765
Stk in his warerooms in dwho. in Crediton. Brick, lath, plaster and
thatched.

£200

BOVEY TRACEY

114/152358
COYTE, Samuel, Sergemaker.   19 May 1756
Dwho., stone, lath, plaster and slated, £60; Hshld gds and stk in trd.
therein £80; Parlour, chambers over, stable, tallet and brewho. and
chamber over separate from the house, stone, cob, lath, plaster and
thatched, £30; Hshld gds and stk therein £30.

£200

149/199902
MILLS, Ann and COYTE, Samuel   22 June 1763
Newton Abbot   Bovey Tracey
Mortgagee   Sergemaker, Mortgagee
Dwho. in Bovey Tracey in tenure of Samuel Coyte, stone lath, plaster
and stk.

£100

BOW

118/156510
STEPHENS, William, Sergemaker.   16 March 1757
Dwho., two shops, pantry, stable and offices adj., stone, cob and thatched
£40; Hshld gds and stk therein £60.

£100

BRADNINCH

107/141700
MELHUISH, Richard, Woolstapler.   5 July 1754
Dwho., stable and offices adj., stone, cob and thatched, £50; Hshld gds
and stk therein £50.

£100

162/224774
BLACKHALLER, Robert, Sergemaker.   19 Sept. 1765
Three tenements under one roof with barn in tenure £40; One tenement in tenure £15; One tenement in tenure £15; Two tenements under one roof in tenure £20; One tenement in tenure £10. Stone, cob and thatched.

£100

136/182062
BOWDEN, Henry, Sergemaker.   23 April, 1761
Dwho., offices, combshop, dyeho., poundho., barn and engine ho., stable and linney adj. £150; Hshld gds and stk therein £50; Three tenements under one roof called Underwood £100; One ho., barn, stable and linney and office adj. in tenure of soap boiler in reversion £100. All stone, cob and thatched.

£400

67/96876
ELLIS, Edward, Sergemaker.   3 Nov. 1743
Dwho. and tenements and small stable, with loft over, in tenure of three persons, stone, cob and thatched, £70; Hshld gds and stk in trd. therein £50; A back kitchen, cider ho. and chambers over, behind the above and under one roof, stone, cob and thatched, £30; Two cottages under one roof, stone, cob and thatched, in tenure of two persons, £50.

£200

111/145708
ELLIS, Edward, Sergemaker.   27 Mar. 1755
Ho. and tenements with small loft under same roof in tenure £70; Hshld gds and stk in trd. therein £150; Kitchen, cider ho. and chamber behind the above £30; two cottages under one roof in tenure £50. All stone, cob and thatched.

£300

153/206348
ELLIS, Edward, Sergemaker.   20 Jan. 1764
Ho., outhos, stable and loft over and small cottage in tenure and one cottage untenanted all under one roof £70; Hshld gds in his dwho. £40; Back kitchen, cellar and chambers under one roof £30; Hshld gds therein £10; Two small cottages under one roof in tenure of woolcombers £50. Mud and thatched.

£200

167/232790
PRATT, John, Sergemaker and Maltster.   15 April 1766
Dwho., maltho., combshop, cellar adj. £100; Hshld gds therein £20; Utensils and stk therein £35; Two tenements under one roof adj. in tenure £30 One tenement and offices adj. vacant £15. All stone, cob and thatched.

£200

104/139264
RICHARDS, Charles, Sergemaker.   10 Jan. 1754
Ho., stable, linney and offices adj. £90; Barns and hanging linney £10;
Six tenements under one roof in tenure of Thomas Fry, Thomas
Hayle and others £100.

£200

113/149998
RICHARDS, Charles, Sergemaker.   18 Dec. 1755
Hshld gds and stk in trd. in his dwho., workshops, offices and stable
adj. Stone, cob and thatched.

£200

132/176965
RICHARDS, Charles, Sergemaker and Shopkeeper.   22 July 1760
Hshld gds and stk in his dwho., combshops, warerooms, dyehos, and
offices adj., stone, cob and thatched.

£200

95/129815
WINDSOR, John, Sergemaker and Maltmaker.   N.S. 27 Mar. 1752
Dwho., and maltho., warping shop, wash-ho., pantry, shop and cellar
adj. £140; Hshld gds and stk therein £130; Linney and combshop adj.
£20; One other linney £10; Three tenements under one roof in tenure
of three persons £60; Tenement in tenure of one person £40. All
stone, cob and thatched.

£400

88/120771
WINSOR, John, Sergemaker.   5 April 1750
Hshld gds and stk in trd. in his dwho. and workhos adj. £100; Three
tenements under one roof, in tenures of three persons £60; Tenement
in tenure of one person £40. All stone, cob and thatched.

£200

123/162104
WINSOR, John, Sergemaker.   10 April 1758
Ho. and office adj. in tenure of William Collier and Andrew Burridge
£43; Three tenements under one roof adj. in tenure, stone, cob and
thatched £57.

£100

BURLESCOMBE

92/126657
BROOM, John, Sergemaker.   23 July 1751
Dwho., workho., warehos, and stable under one roof, stone, cob and
thatched £100; Hshld gds and stk in trd. therein £300.

£400

106/141809
BROOM, John, Sergemaker.   9 July, 1754,
Dwho., combshops, yarn shops, dyeho., stable and linneys adj. called
Bowden £100; Hshld gds and stk therein £150; One ho. in two tene-
ments in tenure of Mary Dyer and John Holy £100; One ho., stable
and linney adj. £100; Two barns and four linneys adj. £50; Ho. called
Blacklands, candleho., soapho., cider cellar and stable adj. in tenure of
William Parrack, tallow chandler in Willand [Welland] £100. All
stone, cob and thatched.
                                                £600

132/177270
BROOM, John, Sergemaker.   14 Aug. 1760
Dwho., combshops, yarn shop, dyeho., stables, linneys and maltho.
adj. called Bowdons £150; Hshld gds, utensils and stk therein £150;
Ho. in two tenements in tenure £100; Ho., barn and linney adj. in
tenure of woolcomber £100; Ho. and barn adj. in several tenures £50;
Ho., stable and linney adj. in Kentisbeare in tenure of farmer £100;
Two barns and four linneys adj. £50; Ho., chandleho., soapho. cider
cellar and stable adj. in tenure of tallow chandler £100. Stone, cob
and thatched.
                                                £800

153/206663
QUICK, William, Sergemaker.   3 Feb. 1764
Hshld gds and stk in his dwho., offices adj., stone, cob and thatched.
                                                £200

CHAGFORD
101/135471
BEYNELS, William, Sergemaker.   18 April 1753
Hshld gds and stk in trd. and dwho. and adj. offices, stone, cob and
thatched.
                                                £400

103/138463
LEACH, Edward, Sergemaker.   13 Nov. 1753
Dwho., warehos, stable, barn, shop, linney, one other wareho., and
cellar, all adj. and forming a court, stone, cob and thatched £100;
Hshld gds and stk in trd., hay and corn therein £100.
                                                £200

65/94947
TURNER, Isaac, Sergemaker.   12 May 1743
In Thorverton, Devon, stone, cob and thatched: — tenement in tenure
of William Dennis and George Haywood, with cellars, linney and
hogsty adj. £40; Three tenements under one roof in tenure of three
persons £40; Tenement with stable, outhos and chamber over adj.,

in tenure of James Skinner £15; Three tenements adj. in tenure of three persons £5.

£100

CHUDLEIGH

145/195216
PULLING, John, Sergemaker.　　　　　　　　　　7 Jan. 1763
Dwho. and offices adj. £80; Hshld gds, stocks of cider for sale therein £200; Poundho. and pound engine therein and stable adj. £30; Gds and stk therein £10; Ho. in his own tenure £10; Stk therein £35; One moiety of a ho. adj. the aforesaid in tenure £5; Stk and cider for sale in another dwho. stone, cob and thatched £30.

£400

173/240790
PULLING, John, Sergemaker.　　　　　　　　　24 Dec. 1766
Dwho. and offices adj. £80; Hshld gds therein £60; Utensils and stk therein £100; China and glass and earthenware £6; Wearing apparel £14; Poundho., pound engine and press therein and stable adj. £30; Ho. opposite in own tenure £10; Utensils and stk therein £10; Utensils and stk in ho. and cellar with adj. outhos. £60; Two tenements under one roof in tenure £20. Stone, cob and thatched.

£400

101/134920
WESTCOTT, Elizabeth, Sergemaker.　　　　　　20 March 1753
Dwho., workshop, stable, wash-hos and pighos adj., stone and thatched £120; Five tenements adj. £70; Nearby stable, thatched £10.

£200

173/241428
WESTCOTT, John, Sergemaker.　　　　　　　　8 Jan. 1767
Ho. in tenure to widow, stone, lath and plaster and slated £20; Kitchen and chamber over £20; Cellar and chamber over £10; Two hos in tenements, stone, cob, slated and thatched £40; Stables, tallet and woodho. adj. thatched £10; Woodhos, stable and wash-ho. adj., stone, cob, slated and thatched £50; Utensils and stk in trd. therein £200; Two tenements under one roof containing utensils, stk and gds, cider for sale, stone, cob and thatched £50.

£400

COLYTON

25/42477
BEED, John, Sergemaker.　　　　　　　　　　8 Sept. 1727
Dwho. timber, plaster and thatched £150; Hshld gds and stk in trd. therein £150.

£300

30/50306
BEED, John, Sergemaker.   10 April 1730
Dwho., stone, cob and thatched £90; Hshld gds and stk in trd. therein
£100; Linney and stable adj. to the dwho. £10

£200

126/167543
BURNARD, Thomas, Sergemaker and Maltster.   2 March 1759
Dwho., maltho., millho., gateway and chamber over tenements in
tenure of Joseph Goss, weaver, with combshop under one roof £200;
Hshld gds, utensils and stk in trd. £100. Stone, cob and thatched.

£300

32/54750
CROW, Thomas, Sergemaker.   1 July 1731
Dwho., stone, cob and thatched, £150; Hshld gds and stk therein £50;
Three hos adj., stone, cob and thatched, one at £50, two at £25.

£300

88/120603
PEARCE, John, Sergemaker.   27 March 1750
Hshld gds and stk in trd. in his dwho. and workhos under one roof,
stone, cob and thatched.

£300

25/43434
SLADE, Nathaniel, Sergemaker and Shopkeeper.   26 Dec. 1727
Thatched dwho. £100; Hshld gds and stk therein £200; Another
thatched ho. opposite his dwho, ' wherein he does his sergemaking
business ' £100; Gds and stk therein £100.

£500

26/46566
SLADE, Nathaniel, Sergemaker.   4 Jan. 1728
Dwho., thatched £60; Hshld gds and stk in trd. therein £120; One
other ho., thatched, opposite the dwho, ' wherein he does his sergemaking business ' £60; Gds and stk therein £60.

£300

169/235377
VICARY, Elizabeth, Widow.   9 July 1766
Ho., linneys round the court; outho., linney and garden ho. adj.
£400; Hshld gds £150; Stable £50; Ho., poundho., pound engine and
press and stable all adj. £300; Cartho., barns, stalls and linney adj.
£100. Stone, cob and thatched.

£1,000

38/63222
PRINCE, William, Clothier.   5 March 1733
Dwho., thatched £75; Hshld gds and stk in trd. therein £100; Thatched

workho. opposite his dwho. £75; Utensils and stk in trd. therein £50.

£300

80/109368
PRINCE, William, Clothier.   3 Sept. 1747
Stk in trd. and hshld gds in his dwho., thatched £400; Gds and stk in
trd. in his ho. wherein he carries on the clothing trd., stone, timber
and slated £100.

£500

74/104547
SLADE, John, Clothier.   10 March 1745
Dwho. and offices adj. £100; Hshld gds and stk in trd. therein £200;
Ho. and offices adj. in reversion, in Colyton in tenure of William
Yeovatt, apothecary £50; Ho. in reversion in Colyton, in tenure of
William Prince £50.

£400

101/135792
SLADE, John, Clothier.   18 May 1753
Dwho. £100; Hshld gds and stk £100; Stk in nearby workhos £200;
Ho. and office of William Prince (tenant) £50; One Ho. in tenancy of
William Yeovat (apothecary) £50, all stone, cob and thatched and
situated in Colyton.

£500

170/237121
SPURWAY, John, Clothier.   11 Sept. 1766
Dwho., office and stable adj. £200; Hshld gds £30; Workshop, warerooms over, dyehos adj. £40; Utensils and stk therein £30, all stone,
cob and thatched.

£300

154/210908
WEST, James, Clothier.   18 July 1764
Hshld gds, utensils and stk in his dwho., shops and warehos, under
one roof, stone, cob and thatched.

£200

CREDITON
169/234756
ANSLEY, William, Sergemaker.   24 June 1766
Dwho. of Anchor Inn, tenements under same roof and range on left
behind, stable adj. in tenure, stone, brick, slated and thatched £360;
Range behind on right in tenure, £40.

£400

176/246223
ANSTEY, William, Sergemaker.   10 June 1767

Dwho. £110; three dwellings in tenure £90, brick, cob and slated.

£200

199/287357
BADLEY, George, Sergemaker.   26 July 1770
Hshld gds in his dwho. and workshop adj., stone, brick, cob and slated
and thatched £30; Utensils and stk therein £70.

£100

168/234019
BASS, Samuel, Sergemaker.   27 May 1766
Hshld gds in his dwho., shops and chamber under one roof £50;
Utensils and stk therein £150.

£200

195/278962
BASS, Samuel, Sergemaker.   28 Dec. 1769
Intended dwho., workshops, warerooms, outhos, and chain linneys
adj. not finished, stone, brick, cob, slated or tiled £400; Hshld gds
therein £50; Utensils and stk not hazardous therein £150.

£600

172/242217
BEER, Roger, Sergemaker.   27 Jan. 1767
Four tenements under one roof, cider cellar and little linney adj. in
tenure of himself and others, stone, cob and thatched.

£100

172/242875
BICKNELL, John, Sergeweaver.   17 Feb. 1767
Two tenements under one roof in tenure of himself and J. Slater,
weaver, stone, brick, cob and thatched.

£100

104/139669
BISHOP, Elias, Sergemaker.   12 Feb. 1754
Ten small tenements and woodhos adj. in tenure of John Maredon
and others, stone, cob and thatched.

£200

36/59359
BORTON, Mark, Sergemaker.   14 Nov. 1732
Stone, cob and thatched ho. in occupation of Charles Lawrence, cur-
rier, £200; Linney or workshop behind £100.

£300

36/59757
BORTON, Mark, Sergemaker.   11 Jan. 1732
Dwho., stable, woodho. and cellar, all under one roof £100; Two hos,
£15 on each £30; Ho. in occupation of Alexander Warren, victualler

£60; Four houses, £15 on each £60; Ho. in occupation of Charles Lawrence, currier £60; Two linneys behind said ho. £20 on each £40; Ho. in occupation of James Ven, Senior, shoemaker £30; Shop and chambers over £20.

£400

23/41060

BUCKINGHAM, John, Sergemaker and Maltster. 13 March, 1726
Dwho. containing seven under rooms, two linneys, eight chambers 'used and employed in the sergemaking trade' £350; Hshld gds, utensils and stk therein £250; Four under rooms, five chambers, one stable and hayloft over the same, millho., kiln and one linney 'used and employed in the Malt trade' £150; Utensils and stk therein £250.

£1,000

37/60239

BUCKINGHAM, John Jnr., Sergemaker. 21 March 1732
Dwho.,* thatched £150; Hshld gds and stk therein £20; One stable and lofts £30; Three linneys only, in equal proportion £30; Maltho. £100; Stk therein £30; Four tenements occupied by two weavers and others, £100; Two tenements in occupation of two weavers £40.

£500

 * In Dean St.

42/67338

BUCKINGHAM, John Jnr., Sergemaker. 27 June 1735
Dwho., cellar, linneys etc., all together, stone, cob and thatched £100; Hshld gds, utensils and stk in trd. therein £100.

£200

54/83397

BUTLER, Robert, Sergemaker. 25 March 1740
Hshld gds and stk in trd. in his dwho. and warehos, under one roof, cob and thatched £250; Three cob and thatched tenements £20; Four cob and thatched tenements £30.

£300

70/100365

BUTLER, Robert, Sergemaker. 11 Oct. 1744
Dwho., great warehouse and chamber over, a tenement under same roof, in tenure of Robert Woodnut £300; Hshld gds and stk in trd. therein £150; Barn £20; Two chain linneys, £10 on each £20; Stock therein, £5 in each, £10; Three tenements adj. £100.

£600

88/120272

BUTLER, Robert, Sergemaker. 7 March 1749
Four thatched tenements in tenures of four persons, £30 on each, £120; Another thatched tenement £40; Four thatched tenements in tenures of four persons, £30 on each, £120; Two thatched tenements

in tenures of a currier £40; Two brick, cob and tiled tenements, one in tenure of a mason and one in tenure of a weaver, £40 on each, £80; Two brick, cob and tiled tenements, one in tenure of a James Shute, weaver and one in tenure of John Hoare, weaver £40; Two stone, cob and thatched tenements in tenure of two persons £60.

£500

114/150917
BUTLER, Robert, Sergemaker. 13 Feb. 1756
Dwho., great warehos with chambers over and tenements under one roof, now in tenure £300; Hshld goods and stk therein £150; Barn only £20; Two chain linneys £20; Stk in each linney £10; Five tenements opposite the dwho. under one roof adj. in tenure and new built tenement vacant £130; Four tenements under one roof in tenure £120; Four tenements under one roof in tenure £130; Ho. and two stables adj. in tenure £70; Two tenements under one roof in tenure, stone, cob and thatched £50.

£1,000

168/234582
BUTLER, Robert, Sergemaker. 18 June 1766
Dwho., great and little wareho., rooms over, stables, woodho., cellar, barn and three tenements, linney and two stables £500; Hshld gds therein £100; Utensils and stk therein £200; China and glass therein £10; Two linneys adj. £30; Utensils and stk therein £10; A range of six tenements, stables and outhos under one roof in tenure £150; Four tenements and one behind in tenure under one roof £150; Four tenements and outhos behind in tenure under one roof £150; Ho. in tenure of Samuel Haines, sergemaker £45; Outhos near above, stone, cob and thatched £5; Tenement in tenure, stone, cob and tiled £80; Chain linney behind, pantiled £20.

£1,400

66/96711
CLEAVE, John, Sergemaker. 19 Oct. 1743
Dwho. £25; Ho. with cellar, shop and chamber over, in the tenure of Widow Paddon £55; Brewho. in said Paddon's tenure £10; Stable and wood linney £5; Chain linney £5. All stone, cob and thatched.

£100

104/139669
CLEAVE, Richard, Sergemaker. 12 Feb. 1754
Seventeen small tenements under one roof in tenure of William Davey and others, stone, cob and thatched.

£200

139/185138
CLEAVE, Richard, Sergemaker. 9 Oct. 1761
Three tenements, cellar, shop, chambers over, brewho., stable and wood linney under one roof in tenure of himself, a staymaker and

spinster £140; Hshld gds, stk and cider for sale £50; chain linney £10. Stone, cob and thatched.

£200

93/63086
COOK, William, Sergemaker.   12 Feb. 1733
Dwho. £70; Stable adj. £10; Linney at a small distance £20; Ho. in occupation of Samuel Ruddall, blacksmith and William Downey, weaver £100. All thatched.

£200

93/126579
DAVY, George, Sergemaker.   16 July 1751
Press shop, warerooms, burling shops with drying lofts over, all under one roof, cob, timber and thatched £100; Utensils and stk in trd. therein £200.

£300

54/82626
DICKER, William, Sergemaker.   25 Dec. 1739
Ho., cellar, and brewho. adj. in tenure of Thomas Ringwell £80; Barn, two linneys and a little ho. in tenure of James Francis, farmer £50; Linney near the above £10; Hshld gds and stk in trd. in his dwho. £60.

£200

202/293246
DOLBEARE, Bernard, Sergemaker.   11 Jan. 1771
Dwho., office, and workshops adj. in the West Town, stone, brick, thatched £50; Utensils and stk £450.

£500

79/108915
ELLACOTT, Robert, Sergemaker.   9 July 1747
Dwho., brick and slated £200; Hshld gds and stk in trd. therein £400; Stone, cob and thatched ho. in Sandford, in tenements £70; One other tenement near the above £30.

£700

72/100933
FROST, John, Sergemaker.   14 Dec. 1744
Two stone, cob and tiled tenements, under one roof, with ground room and chamber £250; One thatched and tiled tenement in his own tenure £35; Thatched woodho. £2 10s.; Thatched woodho. and stable £2 10s.; Chain linney £10.

£300

66/96712
GOSLAND, John, Sergemaker.   19 Oct. 1743
Stone, cob and slated ho. in occupation of himself and several others

£170; Stone, cob and thatched tenement in tenure of John Woolcot £20; Thatched stable and chain linney, £5 on each, £10.

£200

136/182852
HAINE, Samuel, Woolstapler.   2 June 1761
Stk in trd., gds in trust or on commission in his wareho., stone, cob and thatched.

£200

155/209532
HAINE, Samuel, Sergemaker.   14 June 1764
Intended dwho., chain linney on the left hand behind, cellar, linney, wareho. and stable adj. on the right hand not finished. Brick, cob and pantiled.

£200

168/234573
HAINE, Samuel, Sergemaker.   18 June 1766
Ho., poundho., pound engine and press therein, barn, stable, outho., brewho., cellar, sty and hanging linney adj. called Hanington in tenure £237; Linney £13; Ho. pump and cheese wring, linney, stable and sty adj. in tenure £80; Outho., poundho., pound engine and press therein, linney adj. £40; Barn with linney adj. £30. All stone, cob and thatched.

£400

168/234585
HAINE, Samuel, Sergemaker.   18 June 1766
Dwho., warehos, stable, chain linney adj., brick, slated and tiled £400; Hshld gds therein £100; Plate therein £20; Stk and gds in trust therein £480.

£1,000

53/81299
HAMLIN, Stephen, Sergemaker.   12 July 1739
Ho. in two tenements in tenure of himself and Joseph Parry, weaver, cob and thatched £70; One other tenement in tenure of Samuel Underhill, sergemaker, cob, thatched and slated.

£100

88/119542
HARRIS, Charles, Sergemaker.   11 Jan. 1749
Hshld gds and stk in trd. in his dwho. and warehos under one roof, brick, cob and tiled.

£200

25/44071
HARRIS, James, Sergemaker.   19 Feb. 1727
Dwho., thatched £100; Gds and merchandise therein £200.

£300

168/234576
HATCH, Josiah, Plushmaker, Sergemaker &   18 June 1766
   Shopkeeper.
Hshld gds in his dwho. in West Town of Crediton, stone, cob and
pantiled £30; Utensils and stk therein £70.

£100

116/152973
HOOKER, Samuel, Sergemaker.   1 July 1756
Dwho., stone, brick, lath, plaster and slated £300; Two tenements,
brewho. and stables in tenure, stone, cob and thatched £100; Ho. and
office adj. in tenure £50; Ho. and office adj. in tenure £50; Both brick
and slated; Three tenements under one roof in tenure, stone, cob and
thatched £100.

£600

93/127660
HOOKER, Stephen, Sergemaker.   10 Oct. 1751
Hshld gds and stk in trd. in his dwho., stone, cob and thatched.

£100

99/132973
HOOKER, Stephen, Sergemaker.   N.S. 1 Nov. 1752
Hshld gds and stk in trd. in his dwho. and chamber over the brewho.
of Benjamin Hooker adj., stone, cob and thatched £200; Stk in trd. in
the dwho. of Daniel Buckingham, cordwainer, in parish of St. Mary
Major, Exeter £100.

£300

153/206397
HUXHAM, William, Sergemaker.   24 Jan. 1764
Hshld gds and stk in his dwho., stone, brick and tiled.

£200

158/216245
HUXHAM, William, Sergemaker.   15 Jan. 1765
Dwho., cellars and stable adj., stone, cob and thatched £100; Hshld
gds and stk therein £200.

£300

195/278788
HUXHAM, William, Sergemaker.   22 Dec. 1769
Intended dwho. not yet finished £300; Hshld gds therein £180;
Utensils and stk therein £100; Wearing apparel therein £20; Work-
shops, warerooms, stable and chain linney adj. near the above £150;
Utensils and stk therein £250. All stone, brick, cob, slated and tiled.

£1,000

174/245151
JOHNSON, William, Sergeweaver.   29 April 1767

Ho. and bakeho. adj. on the Green in tenure of himself and others, £90; Cellar and stable adj. £10. All stone, brick, cob and thatched.

£100

55/83567
JOPE, Thomas, Sergemaker. 3 April 1740
Cob and thatched hos: — Two hos in tenures of a butcher and tailor, £40 on each, £80; Two hos in tenures of a spinster £30; Ho. £40; Hshld gds and stk in trd. in his dwho. in Crediton £50.

£200

99/132976
KINGDON, Edmund, Sergemaker and Maltster. N.S. 1 Nov. 1752
Hshld gds, utensils and stk in trd. in his dwho. and maltho., stone, cob and thatched £190; Utensils and stk in his thatched millho. £10.

£200

71/99691
MARE, Samuel, Sergemaker. 25 July 1744
Dwho., cellar and stable under one roof, stone, cob and thatched £150; Hshld gds and stk in trd. therein £50.

£200

88/121155
MARE, Samuel, Sergemaker. 2 May 1750
Dwho., cellar and stable under one roof £145; Hshld gds and stk in trd. therein £50; Chain linney in his garden £5.

£200

123/162824
MARE, Samuel, Sergemaker. 25 May 1758
A range of tenements in tenure of weavers. Stone, cob and thatched.

£100

67/96596
MAY, John, Sergemaker. 13 Oct. 1743
Stone, cob and thatched: — Dwho., back kitchen, sizeho., weaving shop under one roof, with chambers over £80; Chain linney on the left hand £5; Chain linney on the right hand £10; Stable and loft over and behind the dwho. £5; Tenements in tenure of a tailor £10; One tenement in tenure of staymaker on the right hand £10; Three tenements in tenure of three persons £30; One tenement in tenure of a weaver £10; Hshld gds in his dwho. £40.

£200

71/99688
MELHUISH, Samuel, Sergemaker and Maltster. 25 July 1744
Dwho. £70; Hshld gds and stk in trd. therein £25; Woodho. and warping Shop over behind £10; Brewho. adj. £10; Millho. and maltho. under one roof, near £60; Utensils and stk in trd. therein £75; Five

tenements under one roof £60; One ho. in tenure of victualler £30; Another ho. £40; Ho. in tenure of a perukemaker and two others £70; Ho. in tenure of Sylvanus Russell, weaver £10; Ho. in two tenements in tenure of John Carterbrook and Robert Farsman, weavers £40; Tenement not finished £20; Tenement in tenure of William Flood, weaver £20; Ho. in tenure of victualler with a brewho. £60. All stone, cob and thatched.

£600

88/119013
MELHUISH, Samuel, Sergemaker and Maltster.   12 Dec. 1749
Dwho., brick and slated, in the West Town £170; Hshld gds and stk in trd. therein £100; Brick and slated ho. in tenure of a mason £30; Shop and working chamber behind his dwho. £10; Stk in trd. therein £20; Brewho. and chamber over £15; Gds and stk therein £15; Millho. and maltho. £60; Utensils and stk therein £75; Five tenements under one roof £60; One empty tenement £15; Ho. in tenure of two persons £40; Ho. in tenure of himself and others £70; Tenement behind the above £10; Ho. in tenure of two persons £40. All in the West Town. Ho. in the East side in tenure of three persons and a brewho. and small offices adj. £70. All stone, cob and thatched.

£800

105/139749
MELHUISH, Samuel, Sergemaker.   21 Feb. 1754
Dwho., brick and slated £180; Hshld gds and stk therein £100; Ho. in tenure of John Tichell, brick and slated £20; Shop and warping chamber behind dwho., thatched £15; Stk therein £50; Thatched brewho. and chamber £15; Gds. and stk therein £15; Millho. and maltho. adj. £60; Utensils and stk therein £100; Five tenements under one roof in the tenure of B. Bird, joiner, and others £70; One tenement in tenure of James Hubber £15; Ho. near the Meeting Ho. in tenure of Hamlins and Pinsent £40; One ho. in two tenements in tenure of Mathews and Westaway £40; One ho. in tenure of Samuel Chilcott, Rebecca Phillips and Zachary Scott with brewho. and offices adj. £80.

£800

111/147034
MELHUISH, Samuel, Sergemaker.   11 June 1735
Inn (Red Lyon) and tenements under one roof, stone, brick and slated £200; Four tenements, stone, cob and slated, two vacant £100; Slaughter ho., ostlery and outhos £30, plaster and stone. Two stables, stone, cob, timber and slated £20; Adj. formho. and office in tenure, stone, cob and thatched £120; Linney and stable barn and adj. outhos £30.

£500

55/82369
MELHUISH, Thomas, Sergemaker.   20 Nov. 1739
Tenement in his own possession £50; Chain linney and stable in the

garden £5; Three tenements in tenures of Joseph Melhuish, John Clapworthy and Caesar Phelp, weavers, in equal proportions £45; One tenement and stable in tenure of Richard Gribble, ropemaker £35; Two tenements in tenures of four persons £40; One tenement in tenure of two persons £15; One tenement in tenures of two persons £10.

£200

101/135052
MELHUISH, Thomas, Sergemaker.   30 March 1753
Tenement £50; Linney and stable adj. £5; Three adj. tenements £45. All stone and thatched, in Bowden Hill.

£100

87/117330
MILFORD, Richard, Sergemaker.   12 Aug. 1749
Dwho. in the West Town, brick and slated £170; Hshld gds and stk in trd. therein £30; Range of workshops, brewho. and stable on the left hand behind the dwho., brick, cob, slated and thatched £130; Utensils and stk therein £45; Thatched chain linney £20; Stk therein £5; Stk in trd. in wareroom in a vacant ho. adj. the Baptist Meeting Ho. in Exeter, stone, timber and slated £100.

£500

93/125263
MILFORD, Richard, Sergemaker.   29 March 1751
Dwho., brick and slated £160; Hshld gds and stk in trd. therein £40; Range of workshops, brewho. and stable on the left hand, brick, cob, slated and thatched £120; Gds, utensils and stk in trd. therein £60; Chain linney £15; Stk therein £5; Ho. in two tenements in tenure of John Milford, sergemaker, and Thomas Dennis, woolcomber £210; Large linney £10; Barn, poundho. and stable adj. £40; Small outho. £10; Dyeho. and furnace therein £25; Small ho. near above £5. All stone, cob and thatched.

£700

110/146726
MILFORD, Richard, Sergemaker.   17 May 1755
Stk in dwho. and warehos adj. in Tokenho. Yard, brick.

£300

81/111134
MILTON, Walter, Sergemaker and Victualler.   26 Feb. 1747
Hshld gds and stk in trd. in his dwho., foreshop and wareho. and brewho. and two cellars under one roof and drinking room in the East Town of Crediton, brick, cob and thatched.

£200

148/199618
NELSFORD, John, Sergemaker.   7 June 1763

Four tenements under one roof adj. in tenure, stone, cob and thatched.

£100

50/78207

PADDON, Benjamin, Sergemaker.   21 Sept. 1738
Part thatched dwho. £140; Thatched stable and woodho. near £20;
One other ho. in his tenure, part thatched £40.

£200

62/92675

PADDON, Mary, Sergemaker.   5 Oct. 1742
Dwho. part thatched £130; Hshld gds and stk in trd. therein £60;
Stable and woodho. adj., thatched £10.

£200

67/96802

PADDON, Mary, Widow and Sergemaker.   26 Oct. 1743
Hshld gds and stk in trd. in her dwho., cellar, shop and chamber over,
under one roof £190; Her stk in trd. in her chain linney £10.

£200

67/96867

PADDON, Mary, Widow and Sergemaker.   2 Nov. 1743
Hshld gds and stk in trd. in her dwho., stone, cob and thatched £40;
Stk in trd. in her yarn wareho. and chambers over, stone, cob and
thatched £150; Stk in trd. in her chain linney, stone, cob and thatched
£10; Stk in trd. in a room in the vacant ho. in Exeter £100.

£300

72/101761

PADDON, Mary Jnr., Sergemaker.   20 March 1744
Dwho., brick and slated £200; hshld gds and stk in trd. therein £100;
Two back offices only, behind the above, tiled £40; Gds and stk in trd.
therein £30; Chain linney, thatched £20; Gds and stk in trd. therein
£10; Stk in trd. in a wareho. in a vacant ho. in St. Mary's parish,
Exeter, stone, timber and slated £100.

£500

43/68345

PADDON, Thomas, Sergemaker.   7 Oct. 1735
Thatched dwho., part in his own occupation, part in the occupation
of Sarah Hillingford, spinster, part in occupation of John Haydon,
weaver £80; Hshld gds and stk in trd. therein £120; Workshop,
wareho. and two tenements (one in occupation of John Collins, weaver
and Joseph Saunders, maltster), thatched, under one roof £40; Stk in
his said workshop and wareho. £50; Woodho., stable and loft £10.

£300

70/100243

PADDON, Thomas, Sergemaker.   2 Oct. 1744

Dwho., brick and slated £400; Hshld gds and stk in trd. therein £400; Brick, cob and tiled outho. in the yard £20; Gds and stk therein £60; Thatched chain linney £20.

£900

87/116864

PADDON, Thomas, Sergemaker.   29 June 1749

Hshld gds and stk in trd. in dwho., workshop and rooms over in the East town of Crediton, stone, cob and thatched £190; Stk in his chain linney, thatched £10.

£200

67/96597

PADDON, Thomas, Jnr., Sergemaker.   13 Oct. 1743

Stk in trd. in the dwho. of John May and in the back kitchen, size ho. and weaving shop, all under one roof, stone, cob and thatched £140; Stk in trd. in his thatched linney on the right hand side £10; Stk in a chamber in a vacant ho. in Exeter, stone, timber and slated £50.

£200

67/96801

PADDON, Thomas, Snr., Sergemaker.   26 Oct. 1743

Hshld gds and stk in trd. in his dwho. £100; Stk in trd. in his wareho. and chambers over, under one roof, behind the dwho. of Walter Milton £150; Stk in trd. in his warechambers under one roof £50.

£300

89/119729

PARR, Yeates, Sergemaker.   24 Jan. 1749

Hshld gds and stk in trd. in his dwho., cellar and stable adj. in the West Town, stone, brick and thatched £170; Stk in his workshop and loft over, behind the above, brick, cob and tiled £20; Stk in his thatched chain linney £10.

£200

137/182365

PARR, Yeates, Sergemaker.   6 May 1761

Hshld gds and stk in trd. in his dwho., combshops, working shops and offices adj. £270; Gds and stk in his barn and stable adj. £30. Stone, cob and thatched.

£300

152/206403

PARR, Yeates, Sergemaker.   24 Jan. 1764

Hshld gds and stk in his dwho., combshops, warerooms, drying loft and offices adj. £300; Utensils, stk (cider included) in his cellar, barn and linney adj. the above. All stone, cob and thatched £100.

£400

36/59710
PHILLIP, Samuel, Sergemaker.   6 Jan. 1732
Dwho., brewho., cellars and chambers, two stables, one hayloft, two
cider cellars and four linneys, thatched £150; Three other small tenements £50.

£200

200/288826
PRICKMAN, Robert, Sergeweaver.   11 Sept. 1770
Ho. when finished will be in tenure of himself and a collarmaker
£140; Hshld gds therein £20; Utensils and stk therein £40. Brick, cob
and tiled.

£200

73/101941
READ, John, Sergemaker.   2 April 1745
Dwho. and small offices adj. on the left £90; Hshld gds and stk in trd.
therein £50; Ho. in tenure of a shoemaker £70; Three tenements under
one roof; one in tenure of Benjamin Leach, tanner, £25; One in
tenure of Richard Potter, perukemaker £35; One in tenure of Robert
Burges, shoemaker £30. All stone, brick, cob and plastered.

£300

71/100672
REED, John, Sergemaker.   13 Nov. 1744
Dwho., stone, cob and thatched £80; Hshld gds and stk in trd. therein
£80; Woolho. only, stone, cob and thatched £10; Stk in trd. therein
£20; Comb shop £5; Chain linney, distant, thatched £15; Ho. in
tenure of a shoemaker £70; Two hos £35 each, £70; Ho. in tenure of
William Thomas, a weaver £50.

£400

74/103347
REED, John, Sergemaker.   18 Sept. 1745
Nine tenements under one roof in tenure of weavers and a ropemaker,
stone, cob and thatched.

£200

78/107021
REED, John, Sergemaker.   18 Dec. 1746
Intended dwho. and warerooms under the same roof, brick, lath,
plaster and tiled £150; Hshld gds, utensils and stk in trd. therein
£150.

£300

119/156440
REED, John, Sergemaker.   10 March 1757
Hshld gds and stk in trd. in his dwho., brick, cob and tiled.

£300

106/141810
REED, John, Jnr., Sergemaker. 9 July 1754
Dwho. in West Town of Crediton £150; Hshld gds and stk £150;
Cellar and shops over, workshop, brewho., woodho., and linney adj.
on the left hand behind the above £50; Stk therein £50.

£400

137/181141
REED, John, Snr., Sergemaker. 12 March 1761
Hshld gds and stk therein in his dwho. £250; Ho. fronting the street
with offices adj. in tenure of shoemaker £90; Ho. adj. in tenure of
shagmaker £70; Three tenements under one roof behind the above
in tenure of carpenter, shoemaker and widow £90. All situated in the
West Town of Crediton, stone, brick, lath and plaster.

£500

66/96710
REID, John, Sergemaker. 19 Oct. 1743
Dwho., stone, cob and slated £60; Hshld gds and stk in trd. therein
£100; One stone, cob and slated ho. adj. in tenure of John Tray, shoemaker £50; One ho. adj. intended for a baker £35; One empty
ho. adj., stone, cob and slated £30; Thatched wareho. separate £5;
Thatched chain linney £15; Stone, cob and slated weaving shop £5.

£300

51/78051
REMMETT, John, Sergemaker. 28 Aug. 1738
Hshld gds and stk in trd. in his dwho., cellar and stable, cob part
tiled/thatched £80; Stk in trd. in his linney £20; Stk in trd. in his
wareho. behind Widow Reynells in the Sergemarket in Exeter £10.

£200

67/96590
REMMETT, John, Sergemaker. 12 Oct. 1743
Hshld gds and stk in trd. in his dwho. £80; Hshld gds and stk in trd.
in his wareho. and chambers over £10; Stk in trd. in his linney adj.
£10; Stk in trd. in his second linney £10. All stone, cob and thatched.
Stk in trd. in a vacant ho. in Exeter, stone, timber and slated £100.

£300

70/99459
REMMETT, John, Sergemaker. 5 July 1744
Hshld gds and stk in trd. in his dwho., warping shop, sorting shop
with warerooms, stone, cob, slated and thatched £160; Gds and stk in
his brewho. £5; Gds and stk in his cellar and stable adj. £15; Gds and
stk in his chain linney £20; Stk in trd. in a room in a vacant ho. in
the Sergemarket, Exeter, stone, timber and slated £100.

£300

86/117196

REMMETT, John, Sergemaker.   26 July 1749

Dwho. in the West Town of Crediton, brick and tiled £360; Hshld gds and stk in trd. therein £200; Ho. in the court and yarn chamber over, brick, cob and tiled £80; Gds and stk therein £90; A little thatched ho. near the same £10; Gds and stk therein £10; Thatched chain linney £30; Gds and stk therein £20; Stk in trd. in his wareroom in a vacant ho. in the Sergemarket in St. Mary Major Parish, Exeter £100.

£900

126/166227

REMMETT, John, Sergemaker.   22 Dec. 1758

Ho. in tenure of W. Nicholls, stone, brick and tiled £100; One ho. in tenure of H. Morgan, stone, cob and thatched £15; Four tenements adj. in tenure thatched £40; Seven tenements adj. under one roof in tenure, thatched £45.

£200

133/176737

REMMETT, John, Sergemaker, in trust for   10 July 1760
     William Shepherd, Minor.

Ho. and offices adj. in Narrow Street in tenure £140; Barn, linney and strawho. adj. £50; Stable £10. Stone, cob and thatched.

£200

135/178248

REMMETT, John, Sergemaker.   10 Oct. 1760

Dwho. with an additional new building communicating in the West Town, brick, stone and slated £450; Hshld gds and stk therein £210; One ho. and room over separate in the court, thatched £80; Hshld gds and stk therein £90; Stable, woodho. and loft over separate £30, stone, cob and slated; Gds and stk therein £10; Chain linney, thatched £20; Gds and stk therein £10; Stk in his wareroom in a vacant ho. in South-gate Street in the City of Exeter, stone, timber and slated £100.

£1,000

168/23458

REMMET, John, Sergemaker.   18 June 1766

Seventeen tenements in a court adj. Dean Street in tenure £190; Woodho. £5; Six tenements in court in tenure £90; Woodho. £3; Two dwellings under one roof on Bowden Hill in tenure £40; Woodho. £2; Ho. behind, above in tenure £19; Woodho. £1; Ho. behind White Hart Inn £20. All above stone, cob and thatched. Utensils and stk and cider for sale in cellar £10. Ho. in the Narrow Street in tenure, stone, brick and tiled £100; Ho. behind and separate in tenure, stone, cob and thatched £20.

£500

54/83737
RISDON, William, Sergemaker.   17 April 1740
Dwho., wareho. and workshop in his own tenure and a small tenement
with a workshop and woodho. in tenure of John Hall, weaver, all adj.,
cob and thatched £55; Hshld gds, utensils and stk in trd. in that part
in his own tenure £100; Three tenements adj. in tenure of three
weavers £45.

£200

59/88636
RISDON, William, Sergemaker.   27 Aug 1741
Dwho., workshop and chambers over, stable and haylofts over and
woodho., with a small tenement and workshop and woodho. in the
tenure of James Hole, weaver £50; Hshld gds and stk in trd. in that
part in his own tenure £90; Chain linney behind the dwho. £10;
Three tenements under one roof adj. to his dwho. in occupation of
Robert Morrish, John White and Philip London, weavers £50; Two
tenements under one roof with workshop, woodho. and offices adj.
the same in tenure of James Reade £50; Ho., barn and stable all adj.
in Venny Tedburn, Devon, in tenure of John Tucker, farmer, stone,
brick, cob and thatched £45; Thatched linney near the above £10.

£300

68/98245
RISDON, William, Sergemaker.   8 March 1743
Stable, loft over dwho., barn and hanging linney under one roof in
tenure of John Tucker, farmer £90; Linney and shippen adj. in the
court £10; Dwho., workshop, woolchamber over and one tenement
under same roof and a weaving shop when finished £100; Hshld gds,
utensils and stk in trd. therein £120; Stable adj. backwards £5; Chain
linney not finished £20; Three tenements under one roof adj. his
dwho. with a workshop behind the first tenement £55.

£400

103/138068
RISDON, William, Sergemaker.   18 Oct. 1753
Six tenements under one roof with six small woodhos and little linney
adj. in the tenure of Daniel Osgood, one void, Joseph Berry, Nathaniel
Slee, James Gregworthy and Richard Brooks £250; Three tenements
under one roof in the tenure of Robert Loll, Grace Durgay and one
void £150. All stone, cob and thatched.

£400

110/147213
RONE, John, Sergeweaver.   20 June 1755
Three tenements fronting street, two behind, stone, cob and thatched.
£100

162/222726
ROWE, John, Sergemaker.   26 July 1765

Hshld gds and stk in his dwho., shop and cellar adj.,* brick, cob, lath, plaster and thatched £200; Three tenements under one roof in tenure £60; Two tenements under one roof behind the above in tenure £40.

£300

* In West Town.

77/105129
SAUNDERS, Christopher, Sergemaker.   23 May 1746
The George Inn in Crediton, in the tenures of John Mager, innholder, and May Weeks, shopkeeper, with a brewho., two stables, slaughter ho. and linney under one roof, stone, brick, lath plastered and thatched £300; Two tenements under one roof in tenures of John Tucker, carpenter and John Jellacombe, weaver, stone, cob and thatched £50; The Deanery divided into tenements in occupation of Roger Welsford, sergemaker and others, slated and thatched £100; Range of eight buildings behind, stone, cob and thatched £70; Four tenements under one roof, stone cob and thatched £30; Dwho. and offices in Crediton East Town, stone, cob and thatched £50.

£600

130/172916
SAUNDERS, Christopher, Sergemaker.   12 Jan. 1760
Two tenements under one roof, stable and two linneys adj. in tenure of himself £60; Hshld gds and stk in dwho., shops, yarn chambers over above £100; Three tenements under one roof in tenure of three persons £30; Two tenements and linney adj. in tenure of two persons £25; Two tenements under one roof in tenure of two persons £25; Two tenements and linney adj. in tenure of two persons £20; Four tenements and two linneys adj. in tenure of two persons £50; Two tenements and linney adj. in tenure of two persons £20; Two tenements and two linneys adj. in tenure of two persons £40; Two tenements and linney adj. in tenure of two persons £30. All cob and thatched.

£400

70/99540
SHEPHERD, John, Sergemaker.   11 July 1744
Ho., brewho., warping shops and warerooms over and adj. in tenure of John Remmett, sergemaker, brick, cob, slated and thatched £280; Chain linney, cellar and stable adj., thatched, behind the above £20.

£300

133/176736
SHEPHERD, John, Sergemaker.   10 July 1760
Eight tenements adj. in Westwood in tenure £100; One ho., offices and chain linney adj. in tenure of sergemaker £150; Three tenements adj. called Winswood in tenure £50. Stone, cob and thatched.

£300

169/235328

SHEPHERD, John, Sergemaker.   9 July 1766
Dwho., offices and chain linney adj. in Narrow Street £170; Hshld gds
£30; Utensils and stk therein £40; Stable £10; Seven tenements under
one roof in tenure in Westwood £100; Ho. in three tenements £50.
Stone, cob and thatched.

£400

132/176550

SHEPHERD, Samuel, Sergemaker.   3 July 1760
Dwho., brewho., warping shops, warerooms over £280; Hshld gds and
stk therein £60; Linney, cellar and stable adj. £20; Four tenements
adj. in tenure of four persons £40. Stone, cob and thatched.

£400

148/199616

SHEPHERD, Samuel, Sergemaker.   7 June 1766
Dwho. and range of offices adj., stone, cob and tiled £400; Hshld gds
and stk therein £100; Stable separate, thatched £20; Cellar, stable,
linney and offices adj., thatched £30; Four tenements under one roof
adj. in Chiddenbrook in tenure, one empty, thatched £50.

£600

29/48284

SHUTE, Thomas, Sergemaker and Shopkeeper.   23 July 1729
Hshld gds in dwho., thatched.

£200

49/74336

SHUTE, Thomas, Sergemaker and Shopkeeper.   26 July 1737
Hshld gds and stk in trd. in his dwho., wareho. and loft over on the
East Side his shop and in the warehos, loft and workshops on the left
hand behind the above £380; Stk in the linney in the garden £20.

£400

67/96594

SHUTE, Thomas, Sergemaker.   13 Oct. 1743
Hshld gds and stk in trd. in dwho. and chambers adj. under one roof
£130; Stk in trd. in two linneys, £10 in each, £20; Stk in trd. in ho.
and chambers behind Mr. Wilford's shop £150; Hshld gds and stk in
trd. in his shop and wareho. with chambers over, adj. to Mr. Stephen
Shute's £100. All stone, cob and thatched. Stk in trd. in his chamber
in a vacant ho. in Exeter, timber and slated £100.

£500

70/99458

SHUTE, Thomas, Sergemaker and Shopkeeper.   5 July 1744
Hshld gds and stk in his dwho. and warping shop, sorting shop with
warerooms, stone, cob and thatched £370; Stk and gds in a stable
and cellar adj. £15; Gds and stk in a chain linney only £15; Stk in trd.

in his room in a vacant ho. in the Sergemarket, Exeter, in St. Mary's
Parish, timber and slated £100.

£500

SHUTE, Thomas, Sergemaker.   104/138833
                                                         14 Dec. 1753
Two barns and shippens, stone, cob and thatched £80; Spinning linney, thatched £20.

£100

SHUTE, Thomas, Sergemaker.   136/181398
                                                         26 March 1761
Nine tenements under one roof not yet finished £150; Two barns,
sheep pen and strawho. adj., thatched £50.

£200

SHUTE, Thomas, Sergemaker.   138/183688
                                                         14 July 1761
Gds in trd. in the wareho. adj. and communicating, brick and timber.

£400

SHUTE, Thomas, Sergemaker.   170/238523
                                                         18 Oct. 1766
Dwho., shops, warehos and cellars adj. £200; Stable and wood linney
£10; Chain linney £15; Two dwellings, wood linney and cellar adj.
in tenure £40; Two dwellings under one roof in tenure, £25. Stone,
cob and thatched.

£300

SHUTE, Thomas, Sergemaker.   174/244625
                                                         10 April 1767
Dwho., warping shop, wareho. and rooms over £210; Hshld gds therein £100; Wearing apparel therein £20; Utensils and stk £650; Stable,
cellar and woodho. adj. £10; Utensils and stk therein £15; Chain linney £25; Utensils and stk therein £15; Summerho. £10; Two hos,
linney and cellar in tenure £50; Two hos in tenure £45; Nine tenements in Spinning Walk in tenure of weavers £180; Two barns,
strawhos adj. £70. All stone, cob and thatched. Stk in warerooms in
vacant ho. in Southgate Street [? Exeter], stone, timber and slated
£100.

£1,500

SHUTE, Thomas, Sergemaker.   176/247499
                                                         16 July 1767
Stk in his dwho. and warehos adj. and communicating, brick and
timber, in Little Winchester Street. London.

£200

SHUTE, Thomas, Sergemaker.   204/295245
                                                         12 March 1771

Dwho. and wareho. communicating and offices £240; Hshld gds therein £100; Printed books therein £10; Wearing apparel therein £20; Utensils and stk therein £490; Kitchen and warerooms £40; Utensil and stk therein £80; Chain linney in the garden, part tiled £30; Utensils and stk therein £20; Stable and cellar and woodho. adj. £10; Utensils and stk therein £10; Nine tenements under one roof in Spinning Walk in tenure £180; Two barns adj. £60; Three tenements under one roof £60; Stk in a ho. in Southgate Street [? Exeter] £50, stone, timber and slated.

£1,400

87/118547

SHUTE, Thomas and WELSFORD, Roger,   2 Nov. 1749
    Sergemakers.
Stk. in trd in the dwho. of Joan Badcock, widow, in South Molton, Devon, stone, cob, plaster and slated.

£200

101/136138

SHUTE, Thomas and WELSFORD, Roger,   30 June 1753
    Sergemakers.
Stk in trd in adj. warehos, brick built.

£400

105/140514

SHUTE, Thomas and WELSFORD, Roger,   11 April 1754
    Sergemakers.
Stk. in trd. in three warehos adj. known by letters A, B and C in Worm Street, London, brick.

£1,000

108/144279

SHUTE, Thomas and WELSFORD, Roger,   11 Jan. 1755
    Sergemakers.
Stk in trd. in seven warehos communicating, brick and timber situated at Little Whithaven Street, London Walls.

£1,000

120/158490

SKINNER, Thomas, Sergemaker.   21 July 1757
Hshld gds and stk in trd. in dwho., wareho. and offices adj., stone, cob and slated.

£300

94/128979

SMALE, Augustine, Sergemaker.   N.S. 16 Jan. 1752
Dwho., brewho., wash-ho. and chambers over, adj., brick and slated £400; Hshld gds and stk in trd. therein £600.

£1,000

138/186055
SMALE, Augustine, Sergemaker and Shopkeeper.　27 Nov. 1761
Dwho., brewho. and chambers over, brick nogging and slated £250;
Hshld gds and stk therein £350; Maltho. in tenure and chain linney
adj. behind the above, stone, cob and thatched £60; Stable thatched
£10. The above in the West Town of Crediton. Stk in dwho. on Bull
Hill [Street], Exeter, stone, timber and slated £30.

£700

194/279962
SMALE, Augustine, Sergemaker and Shopkeeper　12 Jan. 1770
Dwho. and brewho. adj. and chamber over, brick and slated £300;
Hshld gds therein £100; Utensils and stk therein £250; Stk in his
wareho. in Mermaid Lane £50.

£700

55/84360
SPRAGUE, Richard, Sergemaker.　24 June 1740
Ho. in tenure of Samuel Robert, victualler £30; Five tenements in
tenures of five weavers £40; Two tenements in tenures of a weaver
and tailor £30.

£100

54/82905
TAPP, Robert, Sergemaker.　25 Jan. 1739
Stone, cob and thatched: — Tenement, working shop, woodho., cellars
and linney adj., in his own tenure £80; Hshld gds and stk in trd.
therein £50; Tenement £20; Tenement and workho. in tenure of
John Fulford, weaver £20; Tenement not finished £20; A range of
woodhos, workshops and cellars £10.

£200

129/171020
TREDDLE, George, Junior.　19 Oct. 1759
Dwho. and offices adj., tenement adj. forming a small court in tenure
of Ben Turner, woolcomber £190; Hshld gds and stk therein £100;
Stable (separate) £10; Two tenements in tenure £30; One tenement
in tenure £10; Three tenements under one roof £30; One tenement
in tenure of Samuel Collier, weaver, and another in tenure of John
Taylor, weaver, £30.

£400

53/81489
TREMLET, Robert, Sergemaker.　7 Aug. 1739
Dwho., stable and loft over, under one roof £70; Hshld gds and stk in
trd. in his dwho. £90; Chain linney £10; Stk in trd. therein £10; Tenement adj. to the above in tenure of Samuel Kansbear, weaver, £20.

£200

130/173488

TUCKER, Peter, Sergemaker. 1 Feb. 1760
Dwho. Duke William now in two tenements, maltho., brewho., bakeho., stables and offices adj. in tenure of Thomas Potter, victualler and baker and H. Harris, maltster £250; One tenement opposite in tenure of shopkeeper £60; Two tenements adj. in tenure of himself and others £200; Hshld gds and stk therein £40; Three tenements and stable on Threashers' Causeway in tenure of himself and others £40; One tenement in tenure £10; One tenement finished and six unfinished under one roof in tenure £200; One ho., stable and offices in Moretonhampstead in his own tenure, part slated £60; Five tenements, stable and offices in Moreton Ho. in Chagford in tenure £20; Stable and offices adj. £20; All stone, cob and thatched £20.

£1,000

153/208704

TUCKER, Peter, Sergemaker. 24 April 1764
Dwho. of the Duke William in two tenements, maltho., brewho., bakeho., stables and offices adj. in tenure of maltster and innholder £250; Tenement opposite the above in tenure of shopkeeper £50; Five tenements under one roof adj. stable, brewho., offices and chain linney adj. when some additions are finished in tenure of himself and others £200; Hshld gds and stk therein £40. All in West Town of Crediton. Four tenements under one roof in Threashers' Causeway in Crediton in tenure £40; A college of five tenements, stable, livery and offices adj. in Moretonhampstead in tenure £100; Ho. called Hornlake in Chaggord in tenure of farmer £20. All stone, cob and thatched.

£700

86/11697

VICARY, Samuel, Sergemaker. 21 June 1749
Dwho. £80; Chain linney behind £20; Tenement in tenure of David Vicary, sergemaker, £20; His hshld gds and stk in his dwho. £80.

£200

102/137007

VICARY, Samuel, Sergemaker. 14 Aug. 1753
Dwho. and offices adj., brick nogging and tiled £300; Hshld gds and stks in trd. £200.

£500

38/62421

WEEKES, Nathaniel, Maltster and Sergemaker. 21 Nov. 1733
Hshld gds and stk in trd. in his dwho., part thatched £100; Utensils and stk in trd. in his maltho. £100.

£200

25/44070

WELSFORD, Giles, Sergemaker. 19 Feb. 1727
Thatched dwho. £100; Goods and merchandise therein £300.

£400

51/78052
WELSFORD, Giles, Jnr., Sergemaker.   28 Aug. 1738
Hshld. gds and stk in trd. in his dwho. and chain linney, all under
one roof, cob and thatched £100; Stk in trd. in his wareho. adj. to the
Baptist Meeting Ho. in the Sergemarket, Exeter £100.

£200

58/86825
WELSFORD, Giles, Snr., Sergemaker.   11 Feb. 1740
Stk in trd. in his warechamber in a vacant ho. in Exeter, stone, timber
and slated.

£300

158/217357
WELSFORD, John, Sergemaker.   26 Feb. 1765
Hshld gds and stk in his dwho. and shops under one roof, stone, cob
and tiled £150; Stk in his chain linney in the garden, thatched £10;
Stk in dwho. in Southgate Street, Exeter, stone, timber and slated £40.

£200

206/298502
WELSFORD, John, Sergemaker.   18 June 1771
Utensils and stk in trd. in his wareho., cellar and warerooms at the
end of the yard distant from his dwho. in the West Town of Crediton,
stone, cob and thatched £170; Beer, cider and casks therein £10;
Utensils and stk in his chain linney, thatched £20.

£200

85/115718
WELSFORD, Richard, Sergemaker.   23 March 1748
Hshld gds and stk in trd. in his dwho., warerooms and shop under one
roof and linney adj.

£200

93/127661
WELSFORD, Richard, Sergemaker.   10 Oct. 1751
Hshld gds and stk in trd. in his dwho., warerooms and shop under one
roof, stone, cob and thatched £200; Stk in trd. in a wareroom in a
vacant ho. in parish of St. Mary Major, Exeter, stone, timber and
slated £100.

£300

202/292212
WELSFORD, Richard, Sergemaker.   18 Dec. 1770
Hshld gds in his dwho. and workshop adj., brick, cob, tiled, brick
nogging £50; Utensils and stk of gds in trust or on commission £50;
Utensils and stk and gds in trust or on commission in his wareho. and
room over, shop adj. behind and separate from ho., thatched £100.

£200

68/97127
WELSFORD, Roger, Sergemaker.   30 Nov. 1743
Hshld gds and stk in trd. in his dwho £50; Stk in trd. in his wareho.,
being part of the Old Deanery £150; Stk in trd. in his warping shop
and chambers over £90; Stk in trd. in his chain linney £10; Tenement
in tenure of John Gribble £50; Two empty tenements £50. All stone,
cob and thatched. Stk in trd. in a chamber in a vacant ho. in Exeter
in St. Mary's Parish £100.

£500

71/100086
WELSFORD, Roger, Sergemaker.   18 Sept. 1744
Hshld gds and stk in trd. in his dwho., brick, cob and tiled £270; Gds
and stk in trd. in the cellar, brewho. and stable at a distance, stone,
cob and thatched £20; Gds and stk in his thatched chain linney £10;
A stone, cob and thatched tenement £50; Two stone, cob and thatched
tenements £50; Stk in trd. in his chamber in a vacant ho. in St. Mary's
Parish, Exeter, stone, timber and slated £100.

£500

99/132535
WELSFORD, Roger, Sergemaker.   N.S. 12 Oct. 1752
Two tenements in the West Town, cob and tiled, in tenures of two
persons £100; Two cob, timber, plaster and tiled tenements still
unfinished £80; One thatched tenement in tenure £20.

£200

138/183687
WELSFORD, Roger, Sergeworker.   13 July 1761
Gds in trd. in the wareho. adj. and communicating, brick and timber.
£500

201/288633
WELSFORD, Roger, Sergemaker.   4 Sept. 1770
Utensils, stk and gds in trust in his wareho. adj. his dwho. in Narrow
Street, stone, cob, tiled.

£500

39/63427
WORTH, Joseph, Sergemaker.   3 April 1734
Dwho. thatched £50; Hshld gds and stk in trd. therein £70; The
backho. adj. thatched £50; Gds and stk therein £30.

£200

49/74337
YEATHERD, Joshua, Sergemaker.   26 July 1737
Brick, timber and slated ho. in occupation of Mary Yeatherd, widow,
£100; Brick, timber and slated ho. in occupation of Joshua Sprey,
apothecary, £100; Dwho. and offices, thatched £100.

£300

71/100170
YEATHERD, Joshua, Sergemaker.   27 Sept. 1744
Two empty hos, brick and slated, £150 on each £300; Dwho., brick
and slated, behind £300; Two shops and chambers over, brick and
thatched £70; Chain linney, brick and thatched £30; Two stone, cob
and thatched tenements £100.
                                                         £800

86/118344
YEATHERD, Joshua, Sergemaker.   18 Oct. 1749
Hshld gds and stk in trd. in his dwho., brick and slated £100; Stk
in trd. in his shops and chambers over, behind the aforesaid, brick and
thatched £190; Stk in trd. in his chain linney, thatched £10.

                                                         £300

123/162026
YEATHERD, Joshua, Sergemaker and Shopkeeper.   25 May 1758
Dwho., brick and slated £150; Hshld gds and stk in trd. £300; Ho.
adj. in tenure £150; Hos in tenure £300; Hshld gds and stk in trd.
£100; Two shops, stables over and chambers adj., stone, cob, slated
and tiled £70; Gds and stk in trd. £190; Thatched linney £30; Stk
£10; Two tenements in tenure, stone, cob and thatched £100.
                                                       £1,400

169/235380
YEATHERD, Joshua, Sergemaker.   9 July 1766
Ho. and offices adj. called the Gateho. in Washford Pyne in tenure
£80; Linneys, barn and stable adj. £20; Stone, cob and thatched.
                                                         £100

194/278084
YEATHERD, Joshua, Sergemaker and Shopkeeper.   5 Dec. 1770
Dwho. fronting the street, stone, brick and slated £500; Hshld gds
therein £150; Utensils and stk therein £230.

                                                         £900

203/291981
YEATHERD, Mary, Sergemaker and Shopkeeper.   11 Dec. 1770
Dwho., stone, brick and slated £500; Hshld gds therein £100; Utensils
and stk therein £300; Ho. and stable adj. in tenure of victualler, stone,
brick, cob and tiled £150; Brewho., cellar and chamber over adj. in
own tenure, stone, brick, cob and tiled £50.

                                                       £1,100

160/221664
YEATHERD, Samuel, Sergemaker.   8 July 1765
Hshld gds and stk in his dwho., thatched £70; Stk in his shop and
yarn chamber above, thatched £80; Stk in linney, thatched £10; Stk
in warerooms and in a vacant ho. in Southgate Street in Exeter. Brick,
lath, plaster and slated £40.
                                                         £200

169/234757
YEATHERD, Samuel, Sergemaker.   24 June 1766
Hshld gds in his dwho. £70; Utensils and stk in his two shops, two
chambers and garret over, under same roof, thatched £130; Stk in
warerooms in Southgate Street, Exeter, brick, lath, plaster and slated
£100.
                                                              £300

                                                   179/251979
BUTLER, Robert, Clothier.   18 Dec. 1767
Stk in dwho. and warehos communicating of Messrs. Burford and Sons,
Barge Yard, Bucklesbury, London.
                                                              £600

                                                   108/144716
DAVEY, George, Clothier.   23 Jan. 1753
Prince Frederick Aleho. and tenement adj. in the tenure of John
Langaman, victualler and John Wear, weaver, near the Church Gate
in the East Town of Crediton £80; Two tenements adj. in the tenure
of Nathaniel Mortimer and one vacant £40; Three tenements next
Dean Street adj. in the tenure of Trowbridge Taylor, Elizabeth Taylor,
widow, and one vacant. All stone, cob and thatched £80.
                                                              £200

                                                   153/206398
DAVY, George, Clothier.   24 Jan. 1764
Ho. and water millho. called the Four Mills with the working utensils
and running tackle in tenure, stone, brick, cob and tiled £200; Four
tenements under one roof in tenure, stone, cob and thatched £100.
                                                              £300

                                                   94/127900
SHUTE, Stephen, Tanner and Clothier.   23 Oct. 1751
Stk in a wareho., No. 7., at Cottons Wharf in Southwark, timber, £700;
Stk in the dwho. of James Lyne, packer, in Sherborne Lane, Brick,
£1,000; Stk in the dwho. of John Tremlett, warehouseman, in Cateaton
Street, brick, £300.
                                                              £2,000

                                                   96/130717
SHUTE, Stephen, Tanner and Clothier.   N.S. 30 May, 1752
Stk in trd. in two drying lofts and a pressroom, finishing room, burling
room, packing room under the said lofts, cob, timber and tiled £400;
Stk in the millho., separate from the aforesaid, thatched £50; Stk in
his wareho. adj. his dwho. in East Town of Crediton, thatched £50.
                                                              £500

                                                   97/131433
SHUTE, Stephen, Tanner and Clothier.   N.S. 10 July, 1752
Stk in a wareho., No. 24., at Cottons Wharf, near the Bridgeyard,

brick £1,000; Stk in the brick dwho. of James Lyon, packer £350; Stk in the brick dwho. of John Tremlett, warehouseman £450.

£1,800

126/136935

SHUTE, Stephen, Tanner and Clothier.   6 Aug. 1753

Stk in a wareho. in the dwho. of Mr. John Savill in Winchester Street, London, brick £800; Stk in a wareho. in the dwho. of Edward Sumpter in Bell Yard, Church Street, brick £800; Stk in Long Ell Wareho. at Cottons Wharf, brick £500.

£1,600

126/166309

SHUTE, Stephen, Tanner and Clothier.   28 Dec. 1758

Dwho., brick and slated £350; Hshld gds and stk £150; Two warehos and brewho. under one roof £60; Gds and stk £140; Stable and two linneys adj. £40; Stk £40; Drying lofts £40; Stk £20; Chain linney £15; Stk £10; Four turf frames £20; Turf £8; Six tenements and barn under one roof, barn in own possession, tenements in tenure £150; Stk in barn £100; Four tenements and gatehos under one roof in tenure £90; Three tenements under one roof £90; Ho., stable, brewho., office adj. under one roof in tenure £120; Pound ho., pound and engine £60; Double barn £30; Two single barns, ho. and stable under one roof £27; Barn and linney adj. £10.

£1,570

[This policy may be incomplete as the page has decayed.]

104/138759

DAVY, George, Fuller.   6 Dec. 1753

Four tenements and stable under one roof in tenure of himself and others, stone, cob and thatched £150; Dwho. and gallery adj. farther on left not finished, brick and tiled £250; Hshld gds and stk in trd. and gds in trust or on commission £100; Press shop, furnished rooms, packing shop and wareho. with two drying lofts over shop unfinished £150; All adj., stone, brick, timber, cob and tiled. Utensils, stk and gds in trust or on commission £500; Linneys unfinished, stable, wood-hos, dyehos, adj., brick, cob and tiled £100; Utensils and stk in trd., horses and gds in trust or on commission £100; Millho., and calender ho. under one roof separate from above, stone, cob and thatched £50; Utensils, stk and gds in trust or on commission £100.

£1,500

CULLOMPTON

194/279307

WHITBY, Robert, Woolstapler.   3 Jan. 1770

Dwho., brewho., wash-ho., cellars and warerooms, wool lofts and linneys adj., stone, cob, slated and thatched.

£200

198/285796
WHITBY, Robert, Woolstapler.   19 June 1770
Dwho., brewho., wareho., cellars, warerooms, wool lofts etc., stone,
cob, slated and thatched £200; Hshld gds therein £100; Utensils and
stk therein £300.

£600

169/236346
WHITBY, Robert, Junior, Woolstapler.   12 Aug. 1766
Hshld gds in his dwho., thatched £50; Utensils and stk in his wareho
£50.

£100

116/154151
ASH, Nathaniel, Sergemaker.   7 Oct. 1756
Tenements under one roof forming a court in tenure £90; Hshld gds
and stk therein £20; Tenements and outho. adj. in tenure known by
the Sign of Bishop Blaize £65; Dwho., blacksmith's shop in tenure
£25; All cob and thatched.

£200

40/65016
BIDWELL, John, Sergemaker.   4 Oct. 1734
Hshld gds, utensils and stk in trd. in his dwho., stone, cob and
thatched.

£200

53/79885
BIDWELL, William, Sergemaker.   23 Feb. 1738
Hshld gds, utensils, stk in trd. in his dwho., stone, brick and slated.

£400

66/96388
BIDWELL, William, Sergemaker.   29 Sept. 1743
Hshld gds and stk in trd. in his dwho., stone, brick and slated £700;
Stk in his stable and wareho. adj. and loft over in his court, separate
from his dwho., cob and thatched £100.

£800

74/104548
BIDWELL, William, Sergemaker.   10 March 1745
Dwho. and small office adj., stone and slated £250; Hshld gds, utensils
and stk in trd. therein £250.

£500

111/146152
BLISS, Humphrey, Sergemaker.   15 April 1755
Three tenements, combshop, warping shop, sorting chamber, workho.
and cellar under, stone, cob and thatched £100; Hshld gds and stk in
trd. therein £100.

£200

68/98330
BROWN, William, Sergemaker.   16 March 1743
Ho., barn, stables and linneys adj. under a roof, wherein he intends soon to live £150; Hshld gds and stk in trd. therein £100; Poundho. and pound therein, pressho. and cellar under one roof £20; Ho., late in tenure of Solomon Wilby £30. All stone, cob and thatched.

£300

92/126383
BROWN, William, Sergemaker.   4 July 1751
Dwho., milkho., three cellars, wool combing shop, six chambers over the same, a porch, one barn, two rooms used as a yarn shop and warping shop, outhos, and stables, all adj., brick, stone, cob and thatched £200; Hshld gds, utensils and stk in trd., unthrashed corn included, therein £100.

£300

132/174823
BROWN, William, Sergemaker and Maltmaker.   9 April 1760
Utensils and stk in trd. in maltho., brick, stone, cob and thatched.

£100

132/176003
BROWN, William, Sergemaker.   11 June 1760
Buildings and gds and stk, stone, cob and thatched and his dwho. and workshops adj. £180; Hshld gds and stk therein £200; Yarnshop, warping shop, dyeho. etc. £15; Stk therein £10; Stable and linney adj. £10; Stk therein £5; Barn and stk therein £15; Ho., brewho., cellar, weaving shops and outho. adj. called Selways in tenure of John Perry, victualler £110; Gds and stk therein his property £10; Poundho. and pound engine therein £10; Four tenements and offices adj. £60; One tenement and offices adj. in tenure of a gunsmith £50; Three tenements and outhos adj. called Fosters £40; Three tenements and offices adj. called Shortland £60; One tenement £10; One tenement and offices adj. called Thornes £35; One tenement in tenure of James Tayler, weaver £25; One tenement in tenure of John Padger, comber £25; Two tenements in tenures of two persons under one roof £30; Three tenements in tenures under one roof £40; Three tenements under one roof £40; One tenement £20.

£1,000

74/104555
BROWN, William, Jnr., Sergemaker.   11 March 1745
Dwho. and comb shop and offices adj. and chambers over and a stable adj. £95; Cellar and office adj. £5; Ho. divided into tenements, one in tenure of Stephen Tozer, woolcomber £100. All stone, cob and thatched.

£200

97/130564

BROWN, William, Jnr., Sergemaker.   N.S. 13 May 1752
Dwho., stone, brick, cob and thatched £130; Hshld gds and stk in
trd. therein £60; Three outhos, linneys and stables separate, thatched
£10; Gds and stk in trd. in his father's dwho., chambers, outhos,
combing shop, sorting chambers, warping shops etc., all adj., stone,
cob and thatched.   **£300**

56/84667

BROWN, William, Snr., Sergemaker.   4 July 1740
Dwho. divided into two tenements £40; One tenement in tenure of a
weaver £40; One empty tenement £20; Hshld gds, utensils and stk
in trd. in his new dwho., comb shop, stable, under one roof £200.

£300

74/104554

BROWN, William, Snr., Sergemaker.   10 March 1745
Stone, cob and thatched ho., late in tenure of John Lewis £85; Barn,
stable and offices adj., stone, cob and thatched £15.

£100

82/112442

BROWN, William, Snr., Sergemaker.   15 June 1748
Dwho. and offices under one roof, £150; Hshld gds and stk in trd.
therein £85; Barn adj. the above £20; Gds and stk therein £5; Stables,
linneys, poundhos adj. £20; Yarn shop and pump ho. £10; Gds and
stk therein £10.   £300

74/104556

BROWN, William Snr., BROWN, William Jnr.,   11 March 1745
      Sergemakers.
Hshld gds and stk in trd. in the late dwho. of John Lewis £47. 10s.;
Stk in the barn £5; Hshld gds, utensils and stk in trd. in their dwho.,
combshop and offices adj., with chambers over and in a stable £47. 10s.

£100

56/84666

MAY, John of Thorverton, Gent.   4 July 1740
BROWN, William of Cullumpton, Sergemaker.
As Trustees for William Brown, a minor, in Cullumpton. Brick, stone,
cob and thatched:— Ho., combshop and stable under one roof, in
tenure of William Brown, Snr. £170; Small building on the left £10;
Poundho. and press therein £20; Two tenements under one roof in
tenure of a gunsmith and a shoemaker £60; Ho. in tenure of two
weavers and a comber £70; Ho. in tenure of a weaver £20; Ho. in
tenements in tenure of two weavers and a woolcomber £50.
                                                    £400

71/100164
BUSELL, Constance, Widow and Sergemaker.   26 Sept. 1744
Dwho. and tenement under the same roof, in tenure of Charles Cooke, comber, with a slated comb shop adj. £70; Dyeho., woodho., cellar and chamber and a tenement in tenure of Paul Rogers, comber, stable and cowho. adj. £30; Ho., linney and shop under one roof, in tenure of John [Gease?], attorney-at-law £50; Two tenements in tenures of Thomas Frost, Jnr., sergemaker and Bernard Kendall, comber, dyeho., yarnshop and chamber over, under one roof £50. Stone, cob and thatched.

£200

148/199625
BUSSELL, John, Sergemaker.   7 June 1763
Two tenements under one roof and offices adj. in tenure £70; Tenement adj. near the above in tenure £30; Two tenements under one roof, warerooms and offices adj. in tenure £50; Hshld gds and stk therein £50; Stone, cob and thatched.

£200

132/177274
CHANNON, Robert, Silverton, Yeoman.   14 Aug. 1760
CHANNON, John, Cullumpton, Sergemaker.
Ho., cellars and offices adj. called Cook's Place, Silverton in the occupation of R. Channon £70; Barn and linneys £10; Poundho., pound and engine therein and stable and sheep pen adj. £20. Stone, cob and thatched.

£100

59/88115
CLAPP, William, Sergemaker.   1 July 1741
Stone, cob and thatched ho. in tenure of Thomas Jeffries, sadler.

£100

33/54838
CODNER, John, Sergemaker.   8 July 1731
Six thatched hos £100; Dwho. stone, cob and thatched £150; Barn behind the ho., thatched £25; An empty tenement and stable adj. thatched £25.

£300

128/170815
CRIDDLE, William, Sergemaker.   14 Oct. 1759
Buildings, stone, cob and thatched. Ho. in tenure £50; Two tenements in tenure £30; Two tenements in tenure £20.

£100

161/220633
CRIDDLE, William, Sergemaker.   19 June 1765
Ho., brewho., stables, outhos, and offices adj. in tenure, part thatched

£200; Ho., the George Inn, with stables etc. in tenure £115; Brewho. £5; Hshld gds and brewing utensils in the above buildings £30; Three tenements called Blakes in tenure of himself and others £80; Barn and linney adj. called Godfreys in his tenure £50; Stk therein £20; Three tenements called Thorne in tenure of a weaver and others £30; Hshld gds and stk in his dwho. £70. Stone, cob and thatched.

£600

119/158281
ELLACOTT, Robert, Sergemaker.   8 July 1757
Ho., tenement, under one roof, brewho., chamber over, stable, comb-shop, chamber, warping shop, chamber over and dyeshop adj. Stone, brick, cob, slated and thatched £100; Hshld gds and stk therein £200; Five tenements, maltho., barn, stable and linney called Kendall £50: Three tenements under one roof, stable, linney adj. Stone, cob and thatched £50.

£400

138/184007
ELLACOTT, Robert, Sergemaker.   28 July 1761
Ho., brewho., and stable adj. in tenure of victualler. Stone, cob and thatched.

£100

140/188109
ELLACOTT, Robert, Sergemaker.   25 March 1762
Hshld gds and stk in dwho., workshops, warerooms and offices adj. £190; Gds and stk in stable and outho. adj. at the end of the court. £10. Stone, cob and thatched.

£200

154/210911
ELLACOTT, Robert, Sergemaker and Maltster.   18 July 1764
Dwho., tenement under same roof in tenure of widow, brewho., chamber over, stable, combshop, chamber over, warping shop, chamber over and dyeho. adj., stone, brick, cob, slated and thatched £100; Hshld gds and stk therein £200; Five tenements, barn, maltho., stable and linneys adj. in tenure of himself and others. Stone, cob and thatched £350; Utensils and stk in the maltho. and barn £100; Three tenements under one roof, stable, linneys and pig looses [open pigsties] adj. in tenure. Stone, cob and thatched £50.

£500

87/116991
ELLACOTT, Robert, Jnr., Sergemaker.   7 July 1749
Dwho. and tenements under one roof in tenure of James Vossner, with a brewho. and stable adj., stone, brick, cob and thatched £100; Hshld gds and stk in trd. therein £100.

£200

67/96151
ELLICOTT, Robert, Jnr., Sergemaker.   13 Sept. 1743
Hshld gds and stk in trd. in his dwho., cob, timber and thatched.

£100

205/295736
ENDICOTT, Abraham, Sergemaker.   26 March 1771
Maltho., cistern and dry [? ho.]* therein in tenure of maltster £60;
Ho. in tenure of shoemaker £20; Ho. in tenure of labourer £20. All in
Bradninch, stone, cob and thatched.

£100
[*omission in register.]

53/81304
FINNYMORE, John, Sergemaker and Maltster.   12 July 1739
Dwho. £150; Maltho. £100; Brewho. and stable adj. £50.

£300

39/61862
FINNYMORE, Thomas, Sergemaker and Maltster.   27 Sept. 1733
Hshld gds, stk in trd. in his dwho., maltho., and brewho., all under
one roof, thatched.

£300

157/215486
FOWLER, James, Sergemaker.   28 Dec. 1764
Ho., cellar etc., yarn shop, wash-ho., dyeho., four chambers over wareho., combshop and linney. Stone, cob, slated, tiled and thatched £200;
Hshld gds, utensils and stk therein £240; College of hos adj. in tenure
of several persons. Stone, cob and thatched £80; Seven tenements
under one roof in tenure £80.

£600

70/100789
FOWLER, John, Sergemaker.   29 Nov. 1744
Hshld gds and stk in trd. in his dwho., comb shops and wool chambers
over offices, barn and stable adj., forming a square court £250; Tenement £50; Five adj. tenements £50; One tenement £10; Four tenements
£40. All stone, cob, and thatched.

£400

74/104161
FOWLER, John, Sergemaker.   9 Jan. 1745
Hshld gds and stk in trd in his dwho., comb shop and wool chambers
over with offices, barn and stable adj. forming a square court £100;
College of tenements adj. in tenure of Nicholas Tucker and others
£40; One tenement in tenure of John Sawyer, Jnr. £10; Five tenements
in tenures of five persons £50. All stone, cob and thatched.

£200

82/112516

22 June, 1748

FOWLER, John, Sergemaker.
In reversion on his dwho., shop and wool chambers over with offices, barn and stable adj. forming a square, stone, cob and thatched.

£200

105/139033

27 Dec. 1753

FOWLER, John, Sergemaker.
Dwho. and offices adj. £200; Hshld gds and stk therein £140; College of hos at North end of town in tenure of Samuel May, Joseph Watson and others £40; Tenement near above £10; Seven tenements under one roof near above in tenure of others £50; One square court of tenements near the Church in tenure of Ralph Fowler and Adam Fryer £60. All stone, cob and thatched.

£500

121/160508

29 Dec. 1757

FOWLER, John, Sergemaker.
Dwho. and office adj. £200; Hshld gds and stk therein £140; Ho. near the college in tenure £10; A square court of tenements near the Church in tenure £50. Stone, cob and thatched.

£400

119/158072

29 June 1757

FRANK, John, Sergemaker.
Dwho., combshop, stable, warpshop, two cellars and loft under one roof, stone, cob and thatched £140; Hshld gds and stk therein £150; Dyeho. tiled £10.

£300

66/95075

27 May 1743

FROST, Thomas, Sergemaker.
Ho., pantry, comb shop and warping shop adj., cob and thatched, in tenure of Christopher Seaman £100; Dwho., pantry, cellar, linney and woodho. adj., cob and thatched £60; Hshld gds therein £40.

£200

153/206603

16 Feb. 1764

GOODHIND, Richard, Sergemaker.
Hshld gds and stk in his dwho., combshops, warehos., stable and offices adj., stone, cob and thatched.

£200

67/96879

3 Nov. 1743

MATTHEWS, William, Sergemaker.
Dwho., wash-ho., cellars, yarn shop, combshops, two chambers in tenure of a maltmaker, wash-ho. and one other combshop and woolshop and chamber with four tenements in tenures of an exciseman, two weavers and a roper, all forming a square court £95; Maltho. with a leaden cistern, in tenure of aforesaid maltster, Thomas Stone, £60;

Linney, stable and two woodhos adj. each other £15; Linney intended to be built £10; Dyeho. and roof running to dyeho. over the gateway £20. All stone, brick, cob and thatched.

£200

84/115216

MATTHEWS, William, Sergemaker.   2 Feb. 1748

Dwho., wash-ho., cellar, yarn shop, combshop, two chambers over, in tenure of Thomas Stone, maltmaker, wareho., one other comb shop and wool chamber over with four tenements in tenures of an exciseman, weaver, husbandman and a weaver, all under one roof, forming a court £95; Maltho. adj. with a leaden cistern and hutch in tenure of Thomas Stone, maltster £60; Linney, stable and two woodhos under one roof £15; Linney further back £10; Dyeho. and roof running to the dwho. £20. Stone, brick, cob and thatched. Two tenements under one roof £40; Two tenements under one roof £30; Two tenements under one roof £30.

£300

123/163396

MATTHEWS, William, Sergemaker.   30 June 1758

Ho. in his own possession, dyeho and woodho., cellar, linney, yarnshop, wash-ho., combshop, maltshop, chambers over gateway, linneys, stables and two tenements in tenure £295; Hshld gds and stk included, cistern in maltho. and copper in dyeho. £100; Weaving shop £5; Two tenements in tenure £40; Two tenements in tenure £30; Two tenements in tenure £30; All stone, cob and thatched.

£500

149/202757

MAWDITT, Thomas, Sergemaker.   28 Sept. 1763

Dwho., cellar, poundho., pound engine and press therein and offices adj. in the parish of Bradninch, in tenure, £175; Barn and outho. adj. £50; Large linney and cellar adj. £50; Stable £10; Linney £5; Double linney £10; Ho. and offices adj. in village of Westcott £150; Barn and hanging linney £20; Barn and stable adj. £20; Large linney £10.

£500

108/143986

NORMAN, John, Sergemaker.   11 Dec. 1754

Dwho. and outhos adj. in the tenure of Berroni Peters, surgeon £150; Ho. only in the tenure of Mary Hunter £25; Ho. and offices adj. in the tenure of Bartholomew Coombe, fellmonger, £100; One ho. and outho. adj. in the tenure of James Smith £25. Brick, stone, cob, lath, plaster, slated, and thatched.

£300

67/96589

REYNOLDS, Christopher, Sergemaker.   13 Oct. 1743

Hshld gds and stk in trd. in his dwho., warping shop, yarn shop and

wool chamber and cellars under one roof, stone, cob and thatched
£120; Stk in trd. in two comb shops and chamber over and linney adj.,
stone, cob and thatched £80.

£200

205/295421
SEAMAN, Joseph, Sergemaker.   19 March 1771
Hshld gds in his dwho., workshops and offices adj., stone, cob and
thatched £50; Utensils and stk therein £50.

£100

134/178023
SEARLE, Samuel, Sergemaker and Woolstapler   2 Oct. 1760
  and Dryer.
Hshld gds and stk in trd. in his dwho. and brewho. adj. situated aforesaid, stone and thatched £110; Stk in two stables adj. and loft over
in the backyard, stone and thatched £80; Utensils and stk in his dyeho. and linney, thatched £10.

£200

136/181756
TRUMP, Charles, Sergemaker.   10 April 1761
Dwho., cellar and offices adj., brick, slated and thatched.

£100

141/189004
TRUMP, Charles, Sergemaker.   14 April 1762
Ho. and cellar under one roof £150; Barn and linneys adj. £50. Stone,
cob and thatched.

£200

129/169375
UPCOTT, Nehemiah, Sergemaker.   29 June 1759
Ho., offices, back stable, linneys and outhos adj. in tenure of Roger
Parker, weaver. Stone, cob and thatched.

£100

155/211119
UPCOTT, Nehemiah, Sergemaker.   31 July 1764
Hshld gds and stk in his dwho., yarn shops, comb shops, warehos and
offices adj. called Shortlands. Stone, cob and thatched.

£400

169/234760
VESEY, Hugh, Sergemaker.   25 June 1766
Hshld gds in his dwho., office, barn, stable, cellar, yarn shop, wool
chamber over, all under one roof adj. £50; Utensils and stk therein
£150. Stone, cob and thatched.

£200

141/189819
WHITBY, Richard and Robert, Sergemakers.   1 June 1762
Hshld gds and stk in their dwho., workshop and offices adj., stone, lath, plaster, slated and thatched £70; Stk in trd. in comb shop, yarn shop, wool chamber and cellar and linneys adj. £30.

£100

89/120925
WHITBY, Thomas, Sergemaker.   14 April 1750
Hshld gds and stk in trd. in his dwho., wool chambers, comb shop, warping shop, yarn shop and wash-house adj. £70; His ho., two cellars, stable and linney adj. near the Shambles, in tenure of John Selwood £30.

£100

111/145709
WHITBY, Thomas, Sergemaker.   27 March 1755
Ho. in tenure of shopkeeper £40; Three tenements under one roof in tenure of weavers £45; One tenement in tenure of a weaver £15; Hshld gds and stk in new dwho., cellar, yarn shops, comb shops and offices adj. £100. Stone, cob and thatched.

£200

58/87574
FINNYMORE, William, Clothier   5 May 1741
Dwho., shop, barn and stable adj., cob and thatched £90; Hshld gds, utensils and stk in trd. therein £50; Maltho., two shops and chambers adj. and near or adj. the above, cob and thatched £50; His utensils and stk in trd. therein £10.

£200

CULMSTOCK
[see also Hillmore]

102/136669
BRADFORD, Stephen, Sergemaker.   17 July 1753
Stk. in trd. in his dwho., comb shop, tending shop and office adj. £270; Utensils and stk in trd. in his wash-ho. and rooms over and linney adj. £30. Stone, cob and thatched.

£300

148/199753
FRY, Robert, Sergemaker.   16 June 1763
Hshld gds and stk in his dwho., tending shop, comb shops, stable, stall and linney, dyeho., cellar, barn and outhos adj. Stone, cob and thatched.

£200

168/234871
FRY, Robert, Sergemaker and Tanner.   27 June 1766
Dwho. £100; Utensils and stk in his wareho., shops, wool chamber,

warping chamber under one roof £205; Utensils and stk in outho., cellar and comb shop adj. £40; Utensils and stk, stable, hall, linney, dyeho. £25; stk in his barn, separate £10; Ricks and stacks in his rick yard £20; All stone, cob and thatched.

£400

160/220428
RADFORD, Stephen, Sergemaker and Shopkeeper. 15 June 1765
Dwho., comb shops, tending ho., chambers over, stable, dyeho. etc. Stone cob and thatched, £200; Hshld gds, utensils and stk therein £300.

£500

101/136144
WEBBER, Thomas, Jnr., Sergemaker. 20 June 1753
Dwho., tending shop with comb shop and office adj. and hshld gds and stock, stone, cob and thatched.

£100

66/96709
WYNE, Thomas, Sergemaker. 19 Oct. 1743
Dwho., rooms and offices adj. each other £300; Hshld gds and stk in trd. therein £30; Sorting ho. and room adj. £50; Stk in trd. therein £130; Comb shop and rooms adj. £30; Stk in trd. therein £40; Barn £20. All stone, cob and thatched.

£600

EXETER

24/43367
BURY, Edward, Wool Merchant. 25 Dec. 1727
Hshld gds and stk in trd. in his dwho. £150; Stk in warehos adj. his dwho. £350.

£500

212/309100
FRYER, William, Merchant and Dyer. 24 March 1772
Dwho., offices and outhos adj., stone, brick, plaster and slated £400; Hshld gds £500; China and glass £100; Plate £100; Utensils, stk and gds therein £1,200; Ho. in own tenure, brick, plaster and slated £200; Cellar, room over, ware rooms, stable and offices, weather boarded £400; Pressho. rooms adj. and little office £350; Ho. room over the Gateway in Tudor Street [*Todders Lane*] in tenure of J. Dunsford, pressman £250; Ho. and wareho. under it, stone, brick and slated £200; Utensils, stk and gds therein £500; Ho. fronting the Island, wareho., scarlet dyeho. on the right hand, dyeho. at the end, wareho. and dyeho. brick, stone, timber and slate £400; Utensils, stk and gds therein £1,500. All in the Island in the West Gate of the city.

£6,100

123/162429
PASSAVANT, Claudius, Merchant.   27 April 1758
Dwho. £800; Hshld gds and stk in trd. £1,000; Binding shop, press
hos, warerooms with lofts and warehos over £350; Utensils and stk
in trd. and gds in trust or on commission £3,000; Presshos with room
over in tenure £100; Utensils, stk in trd. and gds in trust or on commission £300; Dwho. in tenure £150; Drying linney in the Friars,
stone, brick, timber and slated £300; Stk in trd. and gds in trust or on
commission £500.

£6,500

123/162430
PASSAVANT, Claudius, Merchant.   27 April 1758
Coach hos, warehos, counting ho. under one roof, brick and slated
£400; Stk in trd. and gds in trust or on commission £1,000; Burling
shop and saddle ho. £50; Gds and stk therein £100; Stable adj., stone,
cob and slated £100; Range of offices consisting of staircase, cellar,
engine ho., coal ho., burling shop and garden shop, timber and slated
£150; Gds and stk £100; Greenho. and small office adj. in garden,
brick, cob and slated £100.

£2,000

123/162431
PASSAVANT, Claudius, Merchant.   27 April 1758
Cellar and lofts over and adj. £300; Stk in trd. and gds in trust or on
commission £1,000.

£1,300

123/162432
PASSAVANT, Claudius, Merchant.   28 April 1758
Stk and gds in trust or on commission in the public wareho. on the
quay of Topsham, Devon, stone, lath, plaster and slated £1,000; Stk
and gds in trust or on commission £1,000 in public wareho. near quay
in Topsham.

£2,000

130/174245
DEWEY, Thomas, Woolstapler.   18 March 1760
Hshld gds in his dwho., stone, timber and slated £50; Stk in trd. in
dwho. in Southernhay, stone, cob and thatched £150.

£200

140/188116
DEWEY, Thomas, Woolstapler.   9 March 1762
Hshld gds and stk in dwho., warehos and lofts over, all adj. in
Southernhay East [*Broad Southernhay Lane*], stone, timber and
slated.

£300

115/152117
KENNAWAY, William, Wool Merchant.   27 April 1750
Stk in his wareho. on the Holloway, brick and slated.

£300

104/138751
KENNAWAY, William, Wool Merchant.   6 Dec. 1753
Stk in trd. in his wareho. and lofts over on left and in court leading
to Holloway without South Gate in parish of Holy Trinity £250; Stk
in wareho on right hand of court £50.

£300

136/183250
KENNAWAY, William, Woolstapler.   25 June 1761
Dwho. in the Holloway, brick, timber and slated £195; One office in
the Court, slated £5.

£200

158/215763
KENNAWAY, William, Wool Merchant.   4 Jan. 1765
Intended dwho. and offices adj. leading to the Holloway, brick, lath,
plaster and slated.

£500

101/134679
KENNAWAY, William, Jnr., Woolstapler   28 Feb. 1753
Hshld gds and stk in trd. in dwho. in the Holloway without the South
Gate, and new dwho. Brick, timber and slated.

£700

136/183251
KENNAWAY, William, Jnr., Woolstapler.   25 June 1761
In trust for the Rev. Samuel Stavely ho. in Back Lane in tenure, stone,
brick and lath and plaster and slated £150; Stable adj. in tenure of
broker and innholder, stone, timber and slated £50.

£200

158/216059
ALLEN, Francis, Sergemaker.   11 Jan. 1765
Two dwellings under one roof and offices adj. in Paris Street in tenure
of himself and others, stone, brick, cob, timber and slated £150; Hshld
gds and stk therein £50; Ho. in Paris Street in tenure, stone, cob
and thatched £80; Tenement behind in tenure, thatched, £20.

£300

111/146623
BARTLETT, Edward, Sergemaker.   13 May 1755
Dwho. £160; Hshld gds and stk therein £180; One tenement and
brewho. adj. in own occupation £40; Utensils, gds and stk in trd.
therein £20; Ho. in tenure of shopkeeper £20; Two tenements and

brewhos, stable and tenement at end of the Great Court near the West Gate in tenure to victualler and two combers £80. All stone, brick, timber and slated.

£500

115/1524458
BARTLETT, Edward, Sergemaker.   27 May 1756
Ho., maltho and linney with a tallet over called Honeyland in tenure £140; Linney, tallet over barn, ciderho. and chambers over, stable, linney and tallet over and hanging linney behind £60. Stone, cob and thatched.

£200

155/209816
BARTLETT, Edward, Sergemaker.   20 June 1764
Dwho. in Fore Street in St. John's £210; Hshld gds and utensils and stk therein £180; Tenement and brewho. adj. behind the above in his own occupation £40; Gds, utensils and stk therein £20; Ho. near the West Gate (All Hallows on the Walls) in tenure of cheesemonger £50. All stone, brick, timber and slated.

£500

152/206062
BOND, Samuel, Sergemaker.   12 Jan. 1764
Hshld gds and stk in his dwho. without the West Gate, stone, brick, lath, plaster and tiled.

£200

28/48829
BOUCHER, Joseph, Sergemaker.   4 Oct. 1729
Dwho. without the East Gate, thatched £100; Hshld gds and stk therein £80; Backho. behind, thatched £100; Hshld gds and stk therein £20.

£300

43/68790
BOUCHIER, Joseph, Sergemaker.   14 Nov. 1735
Ho. in tenure of Mary Rawlings, thatched £40; Ho. in tenure of Thomas Barens, baker, with a stable and bakeho. adj. £80; Another tenement in said Barens' possession £70; Small tenement in a court behind the last £10; all being thatched hos without the East Gate in tenure.

£200

70/99105
BOUCHIER, Joseph, Sergemaker and Shopkeeper.   7 June 1744
Dwho. with a warping shop adj. without the East Gate £150; Hshld gds and stk in trd. therein £150; Dwho. behind the above with small offices adj. £100; Hshld gds and stk therein £100.

£500

178/251594
BOUCHIER, John, Sergemaker.   8 Dec. 1767
Dwho., workrooms, washrooms and warerooms adj. in the parish of
St. Sidwell without the East Gate, stone, brick and slated £50; Utensils
and stk therein £200; Utensils and stk in his workshop and wool
chambers over, separate from above, stone, brick, slated and thatched
£50.
                                                           £300

198/284928
BRIGHT, Benjamin, Sergemaker.   23 May 1770
Dwho. in Northgate Street, brick and slated £300; Hshld gds therein
£50; Utensils and stk therein £150.
                                                           £500

176/246365
BROWNE, Hugh, Sergemaker.   17 June 1767
Hshld gds in his dwho., shops, warerooms and lodging rooms adj. and
communicating in St. Sidwell's without the East Gate, brick, brick
panelled, cob and slated £50; Utensils and stk in a range of offices on
the right of the entrance, brick, timber and pantiled £30; Utensils and
stk in the dwho., shops, warehos and lodging rooms aforesaid £320.
                                                           £400

120/159931
CADBURY, Joel, Sergemaker.   16 Nov. 1757
Dwho., brick and slated £110; Hshld gds and stk in trd. therein £90;
One ho. adj. with wareho. and workshops therein, kitchen, cellar,
Taylors Hall adj. in Goldsmith Lane, stone, brick, lath, plaster and
slated £150; Hshld gds, utensils and stk in trd. £250.
                                                           £600

179/252136
CADBURY, Joel, Sergemaker.   23 Dec. 1767
Dwho., brick and slated £200; Hshld gds therein £100; Ho. adj. as
wareroom and workshop, kitchen, cellar, Taylors Hall and offices adj.
in Goldsmith Lane, stone, brick, lath and plaster and slated £200;
Utensils and stk therein £500.
                                                         £1,000

44/71043
CADBURY, John, Sergemaker.   27 July 1736
Dwho., brick, cob, timber and slated in two tenements without the
North Gate £270; Gds and stk in trd. in his dyeho., woodho. and
cellar £30.
                                                           £300

125/165728
CARPENTER, William and DUGDILE, William,   17 Nov. 1758
    Sergemakers.

Hshld gds and stk in trd. in their dwho., in Guinea Street, stone, timber and slated.

£200

154/211634

CHARLOCK, Thomas, Sergemaker and Shopkeeper.   21 Aug. 1764

Hshld gds and utensils and stk in his dwho. in St. Sidwells without the East Gate, brick, lath, plaster and slated £170; Utensils and stk in his wash-ho., shop, communicating behind, separate from the house, brick slated and thatched £30.

£200

138/186438

COKER, Richard, Sergemaker.   17 Dec. 1761

Hshld gds and stks in his dwho., standing shops, workshops and dye-hos adj. leading to the Holloway without the South Gate of Exeter (Holy Trinity), stone, timber and slated.

£200

153/208701

COKER, Richard, Sergemaker.   24 April 1764

Hshld gds and stk in his dwho. and offices communicating in Southern-hay (Holy Trinity), stone, cob, brick and thatched £60; Gds and stk in his offices, combshops and woolchambers in the right hand behind the above, brick, lath, plaster and pantiled and slated £120; Utensils and stk in his dyeho. at the end of his garden, pantiled £20.

£200

101/135474

COULBRIDGE, William, Sergemaker.   18 April 1753

Two tenements under one roof and adj. brewho. in Exe Island £190; Wareho. and cellar behind £10. Brick, timber, and slated.

£200

71/99233

DACIE, Robert, Sergemaker.   21 June 1744

Stone, plaster and slated ho. without the North Gate in tenure of Matthew Welden, pressman £170; Brick and slated pressho. £30.

£200

153/206253

DUNSFORD, James, Sergemaker.   18 Jan. 1764

Three tenements, stable adj. in Preston Street in St. Mary Major in tenure with stable in his own possession, stone, timber and slated.

£100

164/226359

EUSTACE, John, Sergemaker.   25 Oct. 1765

Dwho., offices, dyeho. on the left, workshop, weaverooms behind and office on the right forming a court in St. Sidwells, outside the East

Gate, part tiled, part thatched £150; Hshld gds utensils and stk therein £150.

£300

195/280718
1 Feb. 1770

EUSTACE, John, Sergemaker.
Hshld gds in his dwho. and range of offices on the left hand behind
adj., stone, brick, timber and slated £50; Utensils and stk therein £50;
Utensils and stk in his cellar, maltho., millho. and linneys adj. in the
right and at the bottom of the court behind the ho., stone, cob and
thatched £200; Ho., offices and dyeho. on the left, workshops, warerooms and offices on the right adj. and forming a court, at present
empty, stone, cob and thatched £200. All in St. Sidwells without the
East Gate.

£500

25/43433
26 Dec. 1727

FOLLETT, Roger, Sergemaker.
Ho. in St. Sidwells Parish, brick and tiled, in occupation of Edward
Follett, sergemaker £200; Backhos belonging to the same, timber and
plaster and mostly tiled £100.

£300

97/130910
15 June 1752

FORD, John, Sergemaker.
Four hos, brick, plaster and slated.

£300

101/134677
28 Feb. 1753

FROST, Matthew, Sergemaker.
Hshld gds and stk in trd. and dwho. in the Fore Street £200; Utensils
and stk in trd. in his shop behind dwho. and room over adj. court,
brick, stone and slated £100.

£300

180/255158
15 March 1768

FRY, Thomas, Sergemaker.
Hshld gds in his dwho. in Fore Street, stone, timber and slated £50;
Utensils and stk therein £250; Utensils and stk in wareho., stable and
lofts in Idle Lane, stone, brick, lath, plaster and slated £230: Horses
therein £70.

£600

161/219408
13 May 1765

HANDLEIGH, John, Sergemaker.
Dwho., workshops, wareho., rooms over and stable adj. in Magdalen
Street, stone, timber, cob, slated and thatched £100; Hshld gds, utensils
and stk therein £100; Ho. and offices adj. in tenure of a fuller and
others, brick, lath, plaster and slated £100.

£300

                                                        194/278466
HANDLEIGH, John, Sergemaker.   14 Dec. 1769
Ho. in the Holloway, in tenure £200; Hshld gds therein £30; Utensils
and stk therein £10; Range of offices, brick, lath and plaster and slated
£15; Utensils and stk therein £45.
                                                        £300

                                                        73/101204
HARWOOD, Richard, Sergemaker.   10 Jan. 1744
Ho. in two tenements without the East Gate in tenures of Richard
Penny, farrier, and himself, stone, brick, lath, plaster and slated.
                                                        £200

                                                        161/220704
HARWARD, Richard, Sergemaker.   20 June 1765
Dwho., stone, cob and thatched £60; Hshld gds and stk therein £40.
                                                        £100

                                                        162/223452
HEATH, James, Victualler and Sergemaker.   9 Aug. 1765
Hshld gds and stk in his dwho., cellars and offices adj. by the Antilope
without the East Gate, stone, cob, timber and thatched £190; Gds and
stk in his brewho. behind £10.
                                                        £200

                                                        85/113917–8
HOLMES, John, Sergemaker.   20 Oct. 1748
Two tenements £25 each, one ho. at £100, ho. at £150; in Exeter
£300; Ho., milkho., cellars stables, barn, pigsties adj. in Poughill,
Devon, empty, stone, thatched and cob £270; Cellars, apple chambers
and offices adj., stone, cob and thatched £30.
                                                        £300

                                                        136/181758
HOLMES, William, Sergemaker.   10 April 1761
Ho., bakeho. and office adj. in tenure of farmer in Upton Hellions
£100; Barn, stable and linney adj. £30; Another barn £20; Linney
adj., all stone, cob and thatched £10; Cellar and linney adj. £10;
Three cottages at a small distance adj. £30, in tenure of husbandman.
                                                        £200

                                                        199/284707
HOLMES, William, Sergemaker.   15 May 1770
Utensils and stk in his wareho. in Idle Lane, stone, brick and lath
plastering.
                                                        £600

                                                        25/43792
JACKSON, Jane, Sergemaker.   19 Jan. 1727
Dwho. £300; Hshld gds. £100; Stk in trd. in the dwho. £300; Backho.
and rooms over £100; Stk therein £200. In Holy Trinity parish.
                                                        £1,000

85/114661
KENNAWAY, Robert, Sergemaker. 29 Dec. 1748
Hshld gds and stk in trd. in his dwho. in Idle Lane, brick and tiled
£100; Utensils and stk in trd. in his dyeho., comb shop and rooms
over, brick, timber and slated £200.   **£300**

88/121860
KENNAWAY, Robert, Sergemaker. 6 July 1750
Hshld gds, utensils and stk in trd. in his dwho. and offices on the
left and in the wash-ho., dyeho. and warerooms on the right hand all
adj. without the South Gate, stone, brick, lath, plaster and tiled.
                                                               £300

126/167153
KENNAWAY, Robert, Sergemaker and Maltmaker. 1 Feb. 1759
Hshld gds and stk in his dwho. and office, wash-ho., warerooms, dyeho.,
chambers over, stone, brick, lath, plaster and tiled £200; Utensils and
stk in maltho., near the above, leading to the Holloway, £200; Utensils
and stk in maltho. in a court in Coomb Street [*Rocks Lane*] £100.
                                                               £500

157/212605
KENNAWAY, William, Sergemaker. 4 Oct. 1764
Hshld gds and stk in his dwho. leading to the Holloway £100; Hshld
gds and stk in adj. ho. used as wareho., combshop and offices £100. All
stone, brick, lath, plaster and slated.   **£200**

114/151530
KENNAWAY, William and Robert, Sergemakers. 24 March 1756
Stk. and warerooms adj. in Magdalen Street, brick, cob, slated and
thatched.   **£200**

29/48530
MARKS, John, Sergemaker and Maltster. 20 Aug. 1729
Hshld gds and stk in trd. in his dwho., stone, cob and timber, slated
£200; Utensils and stk in his maltho., stone, brick and slated £200.
                                                               £400

56/85713
MEDLAND, Nicholas, Sergemaker. 17 Oct. 1740
Dwho. in Coombe Street [*Rocks Lane*] in tenure of Anthony Nash,
victualler, and several others, stone, brick and slated £190; offices,
stone, timber and slated £10.   **£200**

110/146425
MOORE, John, Sergemaker. 1 May 1755
Stk in trd. in workshop and wareroom in two tenements made into
one, without the South Gate. Stone, brick and slated.   **£300**

116/153324
MOORE, John, Sergemaker.   20 July 1756
Hshld gds and stk in trd. in his dwho., combshop, wash-ho., with
chambers over and dyeho. adj. and forming a small court without the
South Gate of the City. Stone, timber and slated.

£300

154/213170
NENNING, John, Sergemaker.   18 Sept. 1764
Dwho., comb shop, warerooms over, coal ho. and dye linney adj.
in Tudor Street [*Tudors Lane*] in the Island without the West Gate
of the City, stone, brick, timber and slated £150; Hshld gds and utensils and stk therein £150.

£300

30/50217
PALMER, Robert, Saymaker.   3 April 1730
Dwho., part in the tenure of Widow Rice, cob and thatched £200;
Maltho. adj., in tenure of Abraham Radford, brick and slated £150;
Brick and slated ho. in parish of St. Thomas the Apostle in tenure
of Samuel Truslade, baker £150.

£500

178/250882
PIDGLEY, John, Sergemaker.   11 Nov. 1767
Hshld gds in his dwho., wash-ho. and workshop adj. in Mermaid Lane,
stone, timber and slated £40; Utensils and stk therein £160.

£200

176/247809
PIKE, Christopher, Sergemaker.   28 July 1767
Hos and ranges behind in tenements in St. Sidwells without the East
Gate of the City in tenure of himself and a sergemaker and a weaver.
Brick and slated.

£300

104/139667
PIKE, Edward, Sergemaker.   12 Feb. 1754
Hshld gds and stk in trd. in his dwho., sorting shop, tending shop and
warehos all adj., brick, lath, plaster and slated in Magdalen Street,
parish of Holy Trinity.

£200

67/96054
ROBINS, Francis, Sergemaker.   30 Aug. 1743
Hshld gds and stk in trd. in his dwho. in Preston Street, brick, timber
and slated £280; Utensils and stk in trd. in the dyeho., brick, timber
and slated £20.

£300

96/131625

ROBINS, Francis, Sergemaker.   N.S. 21 July 1752
Dwho. and offices adj. in Preston Street, stone, timber and slated £200;
Hshld gds and stk in trd. therein £400.   £600

33/54842

SPLATT, Jacob, Sergemaker.   8 July 1731
Dwho., cob and thatched £160; Stable, woodho. and tallet over it, cob
and thatched £20; Wash-ho. and coalho., thatched £10; Hshld gds and
stk in trd. in his dwho. £100; Stone, cob and thatched ho. adj. his
dwho. in tenures of Auchelus Holworthy and John Brow, combers,
and John Bayley, cordwainer and Widow Pinn £110.   £400

174/243783

STOODLY, Charles, Sergemaker.   24 March 1767
Dwho. leading to Bartholemew's Yard from West Gate, brick and
slated £400; Hshld gds therein £50; Utensils and stk therein £50;
Shop and warerooms over, stone, brick, lath, plaster and slated £100;
Utensils and stk therein £300.   £900

91/124376

TREMLET, Anthony, Sergemaker.   11 Jan. 1750
Dwho. and tenement under the same roof in tenure of Abraham
Harris, woolcomber, without the North Gate stone, cob and slated
£100; Hshld gds and stk in trd. therein £200; Maltho. behind the
above in his own occupation, stone, cob and thatched £50; Four tenements under one roof, adj. the said maltho., thatched £50.   £400

26/44347

TREMLET, Samuel, Sergemaker.   29 March 1728
Dwho., brick, cob and tiled, with a tenement under the roof, occupied
by Thomas Shanon, labourer, £200; Hshld gds and stk in his dwho.
£200; Maltho. belonging to the dwho. with three tenements in tenure,
all thatched £50; Stk in maltho. £50.   £500

33/54127

TRIMLETT, Samuel, Sergemaker.   5 May 1731
Dwho., stone, cob and thatched known as the New Inn, without the
North Gate £150; Cellar and chamber over it, in the yard £10; Brew-
ho. and stable £30; Linney £10.   £200

85/114663

TUCKER, John, Sergemaker.   29 Dec. 1748
Hshld gds, stk in trd. and gds on trust in his dwho. and wash-ho. adj.
in Ewings Lane, stone, brick, lath plastered.   £200

180/253222
TUCKER, Richard, Shuttle and Staymaker and   15 Jan. 1768
    Sergemaker.
Hshld gds in his dwho. in Mermaid Lane, stone, brick, timber and
slated £50; Utensils and stk therein £150.

£200

157/214250
WESTCOTT, Robert, Sergemaker.   22 Nov. 1764
Hshld gds, utensils and stk in his dwho., combshops, workshops and
dyeho., all adj. in Coombe Street [*Rocks Lane*], stone, timber and
slated.

£200

104/138801
WILCOCKS, Henry, Sergemaker.   11 Dec. 1753
Dwho. and office, workshop and room over, without the South Gate,
brick, timber and slated £200; Hshld gds and stk in trd. £400.

£600

25/43785
WILLCOCKS, Henry, Sergemaker.   19 Jan. 1727
Hshld gds and stk in his brick dwho. £250; Stk in his timber and
plaster workshop adj. £250.

£500

137/181401
WILLIAMS, William, Sergemaker.   26 March 1761
Ho. without the West Gate in tenure, stone, timber and slated £100;
Maltho. adj., stone, brick and slated £60; Slaughterho. adj. in tenure
of butcher, timber and tiled £20; Stable, woodho. and cellar adj. in
the Court on the right hand, stone, timber and slated £20.

£200

178/252297
REMMETT, Robert Butler, Clothier.   29 Dec. 1767
Stk in his wareho. communicating at Messrs Burfoots and Sons in
Barge Yard, Bucklersbury, London, brick built.

£600

41/65913
ALLEN, Joseph, Fuller.   15 Jan 1734
Dwho. in the Friars, cob, timber and slated £125; Hshld gds and stk
therein £125; Pressing ho. and packing chambers, all under one roof,
brick, timber and slated £100; Utensils and stk therein £150.

£500

80/109640
ALLEN, Joseph, Fuller.   29 Sept. 1747
Dwho. including a small cellar, in Holloway, brick, timber and slated

£150; Hshld gds, stk in trd. and gds on trust therein £100; Workshop behind the above, brick nogging and slated £50; Utensils and stk in trd. and gds on trust therein £200; Utensils, stk in trd. and gds on trust in his workshop on the right hand adj. (late the school of Andrew Glass), stone, brick and slated £300.

£800

102/136946
ALLEN, Joseph, Fuller.   7 Aug. 1753
Dwho. and offices, without the South Gate, brick, nogging and slated £200; Hshld gds, stk in trd. and gds in trust or on commission £360; Presshos behind the above, brick nogging and slated, £50; Utensils and stk in trd. and gds in trust or on commission £190.

£800

149/199908
ALLEN, Joseph, Fuller and Maltster.   22 June 1763
Ho. and workshop communicating and offices adj. leading to the Holloway in tenure, brick, brick nogging and slated £300; Ho. and maltho. adj. in his own occupation, part slated and part thatched £100; Hshld gds, utensils and stk and gds in trust or in commission therein £100.

£500

83/112248
BARTLETT, Thomas, Fuller.   24 May 1748
Hshld gds, stk in trd. and gds on trust in his dwho. and workshops adj. in Coombe Street [*Rock Lane*], stone, timber and slated.

£500

149/199909
BASTARD, Thomas, Fuller.   22 June 1763
KENNAWAY, Robert, Maltster.
Executors in trust to the last will of Rebeckah Govat, deceased, for the benefits and interest of Thomas Bastard, a minor.
Ho. in the parish of St. Sidwells in tenure £100; Ho. behind the above in tenure £100, stone, timber and slated.

£200

143/191105
BATTERSBY, John, Fuller.   17 July 1762
Utensils, stk in trd. and gds on trust in pressho., wareho., rooms over and adj. each other in Coombe Street [*Rocks Lane*], stone, brick and slated.

£600

58/86823
BAWDEN, Benjamin, Fuller.   11 Feb. 1740
Stk in trd. in his cellars under a vacant ho. in Fore Street, brick, timber and slated.

£200

68/98707
BAWDEN, Benjamin, Fuller.   12 April 1744
Hshld gds, stk in trd. and gds in trust in his dwho., pressho., chambers
over, packing chambers over, packing chambers and burling loft adj.,
in Fore Street, brick, timber, slated £550; Stk in trd. and gds in trust
in his drying linney in the garden, stone, timber and slated £50; Stk
in trd. in cellar under dwho. of Exeter shopkeeper £100.

£700

83/112249
BAWDEN, Benjamin, Fuller.   24 May 1748
Hshld gds, stk in trd. and gds on trust in his dwho., packing chambers
and burling shop adj. in Fore Street in parish of St. John, brick, timber
and slated £450; Stk in trd. and gds on trust in his drying linney,
slated £50.

£500

83/112250
BAWDEN, Benjamin, Jnr.   24 May 1748
Utensils, stk in trd. and gds on trust in his two press hos adj. with a
finishing room over, within the foredoor of Benjamin Bowden Snr. in
Fore Street in St. John's parish, brick, timber and slated.

£200

92/127159
BAWDEN, Benjamin, Snr., and   5 Sept. 1751
      BAWDEN, Benjamin Jnr., Fullers.
Hshld gds, utensils, stk in trd. and gds on trust in their dwho., packing
chambers, burling shops and two presshos, with a finishing room over,
all adj. in Fore Street, brick, timber and slated £750; Their stk in trd.
and gds on trust in their drying linney, slated £50; Stk in trd. and gds
on trust in the cellar £200.

£1,000

50/78942
BAWDON, Benjamin, Fuller.   23 Nov. 1738
Hshld gds in stk in trd. in his dwho., packing chamber and burling
shops in Fore Street £450; Stk in his drying linney in his garden behind
the dwho. £50.

£500

118/156169
BICKFORD, Timothy, Fuller.   10 Feb. 1757
Dwho., back kitchen, linney, office, packing room and drying loft,
intended to be lengthened, in Magdalen Street without the South Gate
£200; Hshld gds, stk in trd. and gds in trust on commission therein
£250; Two tenements in Friars without the South Gate, in tenure £50.
Stone, timber and slated.

£500

136/183249
25 June, 1761

BOWRING, Benjamin, Fuller.
Ho. in tenure of gent. and shopkeeper, stone, timber and slated £240;
Offices adj. each other behind £40; Stable and loft over, brick and
slated £20. All situated without the East Gate.

£300

136/183248
25 June 1761

BOWRING, Nathaniel, Fuller.
Ho. and offices adj. in tenure £100; One ho. adj. in tenure, brick,
slated and thatched £180; One ho., stable and office under one roof,
thatched £20. All situated without the East Gate.

£300

176/247285
16 July 1767

BOWRING, Nathaniel, Fuller.
Ho. and offices adj. in St. Sidwell's without the East Gate in tenure of
himself and exciseman, brick, timber and slated £150; Hshld gds
therein £50.

£200

134/178021
2 Oct. 1760

BROOK, Nicholas, Fuller, Exeter.
REED, John, Sergemaker, Crediton.
Their hshld gds in the dwho., kitchen and offices on the right hand
behind, of Nicholas Brook, stone, brick, plaster and slated £100; Utensils and stk in trd and gds in travel or on commission within offices,
presshos, warerooms over, packing chambers and loft area on the left
hand, brick, lath, plaster, slated £400. Situated in Exe Island.

£500

100/35936
5 June 1753

BROOKE, James, Fuller.
Hshld gds, stk in trd. and gds on trust in his dwho. and offices adj. in
Exe Island, stone, brick, plaster and slated £100; Utensils, gds, stk in
trd. and gds on trust in his offices, pressho. and warerooms over the
packing chamber, brick and cob £400.

£500

101/136254
27 June 1753

BURNELL, John, Fuller.
Hshld gds and stk in trd. in dwho. next to City Gate in St. Edmund's
parish, stone, timber and slated.

£200

62/92624
30 Sept. 1742

BURNETT, Christopher, Tucker.
Utensils and stk in trd. and gds in trust in his wareho. and packing
chambers, under one roof without the West Gate, stone, brick, timber
and slated.

£800

69/97748
BURNETT, Christopher, Tucker and Shopkeeper.   20 Jan. 1743
Hshld gds and stk in trd. in his dwho. without the West Gate, stone,
brick and slated £200; Utensils, stk in trd. and gds on trust in his
wareho. and packing chamber over, under one roof £400, stone, brick,
plaster and tiled.

£600

83/111955
BURNETT, Christopher, Tucker.   26 April 1748
Dwho., pressroom, warerooms adj. in Ewings Lane, stone, timber and
slated £250; Hshld gds, utensils, stk in trd. and gds on trust therein
£400; Dyeho. intended to be converted into a dryho. and lengthened,
stone, timber and slated £50.

£700

92/127194
BURNETT, Christopher, Tucker.   10 Sept. 1751
Dwho. and pressrooms and warerooms adj. in Ewings Lane £300; Hshld
gds, stk in trd. and gds on trust therein £400; Drying linney behind and
adj. £200; Stk in trd. and gds on trust therein £100. All stone, timber
and slated.

£1,000

129/170569
BURNETT, Christopher, Fuller.   28 Sept. 1759
Dwho., packing rooms, burling rooms and warerooms adj. in Ewings
Lane without the West Gate of the city £300; Hshld gds, utensils, stk
in trd. and gds in trust or on commission £1,000; Dryho. behind and
adj. £200; Gds, stk and gds on trust therein £1,000. Stone, timber and
slated.

£2,500

43/66613
BURY, John, Fuller.   28 March 1735
Hshld gds and stk in trd. in his dwho. in the Holloway, brick and
slated £200; Stk in his wareho., brick, timber and slated £300; Stk in
his other wareho., brick, timber and slated £100.

£600

145/195222
BURY, Thomas, Fuller.   8 Jan. 1763
Hshld gds, stk and gds on trust and on commission in his dwho.,
burling shops, warerooms and offices adj. near the Town Walls, stone,
brick and timber and slated £160; Stk and gds on trust and on commission in his backing ho. and loft over behind the above, brick, timber and slated £40.

£200

152/206051
BURY, Thomas, Fuller.   12 Jan. 1764
Hshld gds, stk and gds in trust or commission in his dwho., burling

shops, warerooms over the offices adj. near the town walls in St. Mary Major £400; Stk and gds in his packing ho. and loft over £200; Stk and gds in trust or on commission in his drying loft over the Quay [Key] Mills £100. All stone, brick, timber and slated.

£700

202/292207
CLARK, Joseph, Fuller. 19 Dec. 1770
Hshld gds in his dwho. in Magdalen Street, stone, brick, slated £100; Utensils and stk of gds in trust or on commission £100; Utensils and stk or gds in trust or on commission in office, packing burling and other shops adj. behind. Stone, brick, lath, plaster and slated. Two dwho. under one roof in Quay [Key] Lane in tenure, stone, timber and slated £100.

£800

158/216554
CLARK, Joseph and MAYNE, Samuel, 23 Jan. 1765
Fullers and Pressmen.
Utensils, stk and gds on trust in the pressho., finishing rooms, under one roof in the Friars, stone, timber and slated.

£300

178/251599
CLARKE, Joseph, Fuller. 8 Dec. 1767
Dwho. in Magdalen Street without the South Gate £50; Utensils, stk and gds in trust and on commission in the pressho., packing shops, finishing rooms and wisking rooms adj. Brick, timber and slated £350.

£400

194/279761
CLARKE, Joseph, Fuller. 12 Jan. 1770
Hshld gds in his dwho. in Magdalen Street, stone, brick and slated £100; Utensils, stk and gds in trust and on commission in his press shop, packing shop, finishing room adj. and behind the above. Stone, brick, timber and slated £450; Ho. in two tenements in Quay [Key] Lane in tenure, stone, timber and slated £50.

£600

172/241114
CLARKE, Joseph and MAYNE, Samuel, 1 Jan. 1767
Fuller and Pressman.
Utensils, stk and gds in trust or on a commission in pressho., packing shop, finishing room adj. behind dwho. in Magdalen Street, stone, timber and slated £450; Hshld gds, property of Joseph Clarke, in his dwho. £50.

£500

63/92525
COSSERATT, Nathaniel Elias, Fuller. 22 Sept. 1742
Hshld gds and stk in trd. in his dwho. in Mint Lane, stone and slated

£100; Gds, utensils and stk in trd. in a parlour and dining room over, cellar, brewho., burling shop and pressho., all adj. brick, timber and slated £200.

£300

85/113915
COSSERATT, Nathaniel Elias, Fuller.   20 Oct. 1748
Hshld gds and stk in trd. and gds on trust in his dwho. in the Mint, stone and slated £200; Hshld gds, utensils and stk in trd. and gds on trust in his parlour and dining rooms over cellar, brewho., burling shops and presshos all adj., behind his dwho., stone, brick, timber and slated £400.

£600

25/42475
CROKER, Richard, Fuller.   8 Sept. 1727
Gds and stk in his burling shop, packing chamber in the chambers over them, tiled, Holy Trinity parish £500; Two brick hos in St. Martin's parish, one in occupation of Samuel Stephens, apothecary £250, one in occupation of Richard Greenfield, coffee ho. keeper £250.

£1,000

44/69154
DARK, Nicholas, Fuller and Hotpresser.   1 Jan. 1735
Hshld gds and stk in trd. in his dwho. in Stepcott Hill, brick, timber and tiled £400; Utensils and stk in trd. in his packing chamber adj. the ho., stone, timber and slated £100.

£500

55/84361
DARK, Nicholas, Fuller and Hotpresser.   24 June 1740
Dwho. and packing chamber adj., running over the wareho. of Thomas Helegist, on Stepcott Hill, brick, timber and slated £300; Hshld gds, utensils, stk in trd. and gds on commission therein £600; Press shop intended to be built in the garden behind the above, timber and slated £30; His utensils, stk in trd. and gds on commission therein £70.

£1,000

70/99550
DARK, Nicholas, Fuller.   11 July 1744
Dwho. and packing chamber adj., running over the dwho. of Thomas Kete, on Stepcott Hill, brick, timber and slated £500; Hshld gds, utensils and stk in trd., gds on trust therein £100; Pressho. behind the above, timber and slated £40; Utensils, stk in trd. and gds on trust therein £60.

£700

50/77008
DIX, Samuel, Fuller.   3 May 1738
Hshld gds, stk in trd. or on commission in his brick and slated dwho.

in Idle Lane £100; Stk in trd., utensils, or on commission in his stone, lath, plaster and slated wareho. adj. the dwho. £400.

£500

67/95246
DIX, Samuel, Fuller.   15 June 1743
Hshld gds, stk in trd. and gds in trust in his dwho. and warehos and packing chambers, adj. and under one roof in Idle Lane, lath, plaster, stone, brick £200; Pressho., wareho. and burling shop, brick, stone, slated £25; Utensils, stk in trust and gds on trust therein £50; Pressing rooms and packing room opposite the last mentioned, stone, brick and slated £25; Hshld utensils, gds on trust and stk in trd. therein £25.

£500

71/100061
DIX, Samuel, Fuller.   13 Sept. 1744
Dwho., pressho., packing chamber and warerooms adj. in Idle Lane, stone, brick, timber and slated.

£200

109/143308
DIX, Samuel, Fuller.   26 Oct. 1754
Dwho. part brick and slated, pressho., packing chambers and warerooms in Idle Lane adj., lath, plaster and slated £200; Hshld gds, utensils, stk in trd. £200; Behind new brick part of dwho., burling shops, warehos and pressho. and packing room, brick, stone and slated £50. Utensils, stk and gds therein £550.

£1,000

122/163103
DIX, Samuel, Fuller.   14 June 1758
Ho. in Idle Lane in tenure of Elizabeth Bastard, brick and slated.

£200

115/152120
FORCE, John, Fuller and Pressman.   27 April 1756
Hshld gds, utensils, stk in trd. and gds on trust and on commission in his dwho., press shop and finishing rooms adj. and forming a court in Rack Lane in the City, brick, lath, plaster and slated.

£300

169/236348
FORCE, John, Fuller and Pressman.   12 Aug. 1766
Hshld gds in his dwho., pressho. over and offices adj. fronting the Town Walls at the foot of Rack Lane £100; Utensils and stk and gds in trust or on commission £900; Utensils and stk and gds in trust or on commission in pressho. in his court behind £400. Brick, stone, lath, plaster and slated.

£1,400

58/87217
FOSTER, Samuel, Fuller.   1 April 1741
Hshld gds and stk in trd. and utensils in his dwho. in Ewings Lane,
brick, timber and slated.

£200

111/147027
GLANVILL, John, Fuller.   10 June 1755
Dwho. without the South Gate, in tenure to a merchant, brick and
slated £160; Warehos. and packing chambers, brick, lath, plaster and
slated £40.

£200

108/143289
HAKENWELL, Charles, Fuller and   25 Oct. 1754
    Victualler.
Hshld gds and stk in trd. in his dwho., brewho., cellars, drinking
rooms and chambers over leading to the Holloway without the South
Gate of the City. Stone, timber, bricks and slated.

£200

136/181394
HAYDON, Benjamin, Fuller.   26 March 1761
Dwho., brewho. and rooms over adj. and communicating in Coombe
Street [Rocks Lane], stone, lath, plaster £300; Hshld gds, utensils and
gds on trust or on commission therein £400.

£700

175/246119
HAYDON, Benjamin, Fuller.   2 June 1767
Dwho., pressho. and rooms over, adj. in Coombe Street [Rocks Lane],
stone, timber and slated £350; Hshld gds therein £100; Utensils and
stk therein £550.

£1,000

88/121061
HAYMAN, George, Fuller.   26 April 1750
Hshld gds and stk in trd. and gds on trust in his dwho., workshops and
warerooms adj. in Coombe Street [Rocks Lane], stone, brick, timber
and tiled £200; Stk in trd. and gds on trust in his packing room behind
the above, stone, brick, timber and slated £100.

£300

100/134827
HAYMAN, George, Fuller.   15 March 1753
Dwho., working shops and packing rooms over adj. each other in
tenure, in St. Mary Major parish £200; Hshld gds, stk in trd. and gds
on trust therein £200; Ho. in tenure in Back Lane £100.

£500

52/81036
HILLMAN, David Jnr., Fuller. 24 June 1739
Dwho. in the Friars, brick, timber and slated £70; Hshld gds and stk
in trd. therein £50; Workshop and wareho. adj. each other behind the
ho., brick, timber and slated £30; Utensils and stk in trd. therein £50.

£200

69/98079
HILLMAN, David, Jnr., Fuller. 16 Feb. 1743
Dwho. in the Friars, brick, timber and slated £70; Hshld gds and stk in
trd. therein £50; Wareho. and workshop adj. behind his ho., brick,
timber and tiled £50; Utensils and stk in trd. therein £430.

£600

145/194001
HILLMAN, Joseph, Fuller. 16 Nov. 1762
Dwho. and offices adj. in the Holloway without the South Gate, stone,
brick and slated £150; Hshld gds, stk and gds in trust and on commission therein £50.

£200

31/51307
HUTCHINGS, Thomas, Fuller. 17 Aug. 1730
Hshld gds and stk in trd. in his dwho. the corner of Idle Lane, brick
and slated £300; Stk in his pressho. adj. £200.

£500

101/134672
JEFFERY, Edmund, Fuller and Hotpresser. 28 Feb. 1753
Hshld gds, stk in trd. and gds in trust or on commission. His dwho.,
pressho. and rooms adj. and communicating in Baker Lane, in parish
of St. Mary, stone, timber and slated.

£300

132/176553
KANOWSLEY, Robert, Fuller. 4 July 1760
Two tenements, workshops and offices behind in Quay [Key] Lane in
tenure of himself and another, stone, timber and slated £100; Hshld
gds, stk and gds in trust or on commission therein £100.

£200

74/103648
LEGG, Edward, Tucker and Hotpresser. 16 Oct. 1745
Hshld gds, utensils and stk in trd. and gds on trust in his dwho.,
presshos and warerooms over the Holloway, stone, timber and slated.

£300

93/125542
LEGG, John, Fuller and Pressman. 16 April 1751
Hshld gds, utensils, stk in trd. and gds on trust in his dwho., pressho.

and finishing chamber over, adj. on Stepcott Hill, stone, brick, timber and slated £190; His gds, utensils, stk in trd. and gds on trust in his brewho. behind £10.

£200

107/141911

LORING, William, Fuller.   16 July 1754
Hshld gds, stk in trd. and gds in trust in dwho. on Stepcott Hill, stone, timber and slated £200; Utensils, stk in trd. and gds in trust in workshop in garden behind, timber and slated £100.

£300

109/144587

LUKE, John, Fuller.   17 Jan. 1755
Four tenements, stable and brewho. and cellar intended to be converted into tenement adj. the bottom of the Holloway, brick cob, small part lath, plaster and slated.

£200

134/178586

MANN, William, Tucker.   22 Oct. 1760
Ho., millho., grist mill with all their running tackle, linney and offices adj. in the tenure of John Bussell, miller £124; Tenement, linney and stable near the above in the tenure of the said John Bussell £20; One ho., cellar, linney and offices under one roof in the tenure of John Fryer, apothecary, £100; Two linneys on the right and left hand of the above £6; Ho. in tenure of John Pearce, farmer, £40; Barn, stable and linney adj. £10. All stone, cob and thatched.

£300

195/280569

MANN, William, Tucker.   27 Jan. 1770
Ho., maltho., grist mills with all their running tackle and offices adj. in tenure of miller £130; Tenement, linney and stable adj. near the same in tenure £20; Ho. and offices adj. in tenure of farmer £40; Barn, linney and outhos. adj. £10; All in Kenton; stone, cob and thatched.

£200

148/199622

MOOR, Ann, Widow and Fuller.   7 June 1763
Stk and gds in trust or on commission in her drying linney leading to Holloway, brick, timber and slated.

£800

179/251315

MOOR, Ann, Widow and Fuller.   25 Nov. 1767
Stk and gds in trust in her drying linney in the Holloway, £1,000; Stk and gds in trust in Mr. Passavant's drying linney in the Friars £400. Brick, timber and tiled.

£1,400

91/122790
MOOR, Philip, Tucker.   28 Sept. 1750
Stone, brick and slated hos without the South Gate, in tenure of
Browne, woolcomber and Benjamin Haydon, fuller, £50 on each, £100;
Dwho., stone, brick and slated £160; Hshld gds, stk in trd. and gds on
trust therein £100; Range of workshops on the right hand behind,
brick, timber and tiled £140; Utensils, stk in trd. and gds on trust
therein £300; Fulling mills in Topsham, stone, cob and thatched £35;
Gds, stk in trd. and gds on trust therein £30; Burling shop near,
thatched £15; Gds, stk in trd. and gds on trust therein £20.

£900

100/134742
MOOR, Philip, Tucker.   6 March 1753
His two stone, brick and slated hos in tenure, £50 on each, £100; His
brick, stone and slated dwho. £160; Hshld gds, stk in trd. and gds on
trust therein £100; A range of workshops on the right hand, behind,
brick, timber and slated £140; Utensils, stk and gds on trust therein
£900. Above in Holy Trinity parish. Fulling mills adj. each other in
Topsham, stone, cob and thatched £35; Stk in trd and gds on trust
therein £30; A thatched burling shop near the above £15; Stk in trd.
and gds on trust therein £20.

£1,500

29/48191
PARSON, Nicholas, Fuller.   12 July 1729
Hshld gds and stk in his dwho., stone and slated, behind the Guildhall,
£500; Ho., brick and slated, tenure of Peter Prickman, fuller £100;
Gds and stk therein £100.

£700

151/205833
PAYNE, William, Fuller.   6 Jan. 1764
Ho. in two tenements, woodho. and offices adj. leading to the Holloway
within the South Gate (Holy Trinity), in tenure, stone, cob and
thatched £50; Hshld gds therein £50.

£100

161/221156
PHILLIP, John, Fuller.   28 June 1765
Ho., burling shops, wareroom etc. near Town Walls in parish of St.
Mary in tenure of a fuller £170; Packing ho. and loft over £30. All
stone, brick, timber and slated.

£200

50/77006
PIERCE, Samuel, Fuller.   3 May 1738
Hshld gds and stk in trd. in his brick built and slated dwho. without
the South Gate £300; Utensils and stk in trd. in his packing room,
timber and slated behind his dwho. £500; Stk in trd. in his timber and
slated burling shop £100.

£900

82/112837

PIERCE, Samuel, Tucker.   14 July 1748

Dwho., pressho., warerooms over in the Holloway, stone, timber and tiled £200; Hshld gds, utensils and stk in trd. therein £500.

£700

99/134108

PIERCE, Samuel, Fuller.   18 Jan. 1753

Dwho., two tenements under the same roof in the tenure of a barber and carpenter with burling shops, packing room, cellars and stable adj., stone, brick, plaster and tiled without the South Gate £300; Hshld gds and stk therein £300.

£600

194/279308

POPE, Alexander, Fuller.   3 Jan. 1770

Intended dwho. in Southgate Street, stone, timber and slated £120; Hshld gds therein £60; Wearing apparel therein £20.

£200

118/155875

POPE, James, Fuller.   20 Jan. 1757

Hshld gds, stk in trd. and gds in trust and on commission in his dwho. in the Holloway without the South Gate, brick and slated £300; Stk in trd. and gds in trust on commission in his wareho., packing chamber and shop adj., brick, timber and slated £200.

£500

198/285799

POPE, Sarah, Fuller.   20 June 1770

Hshld gds in her dwho., offices, warerooms, packing, burling and shearing rooms, stone, brick, lath, plaster and slated £120; Wearing apparel therein £30; Utensils, stk etc. therein £300; Utensils, stk etc. in drying linney, behind, back £50.

£500

132/177207

PUNCHARD, Isaac, Fuller.   8 Aug. 1760

Three tenements under one roof in Frog Lane, in tenure of journeymen dyers and shoemaker, stone, timber and slated.

£100

170/237129

PUNCHARD, Isaac William, Fuller.   11 Sept. 1766

Utensils, stk and gds in trust or on commission in wareho., packing rooms and rooms over in the Island, brick and slated £100; In warerooms £100; In little office £20; In drying lofts and rooms £80. Brick, timber and slated.

£300

135/179947
PYNE, George, Fuller.   8 Jan. 1761
Two tenements and maltho. adj. without the West Gate of the City in
tenure of himself and others with the kiln and cistern therein, stone,
brick and slated £100; Hshld gds in that he occupies £100.
£200

50/77007
RICE, James, Fuller.   3 May 1738
Dwho. and workshop on St. David's Hill, stone, cob and thatched, part
in his own possession and part in possession of a labourer.
£200

91/122300
RICE, James, Fuller.   10 Aug. 1750
Dwho. and workshop and tenement under the same roof on St. David's
Hill, stone, cob and thatched.
£200

97/132258
RICE, James, Fuller.   N.S. 29 Sept. 1752
Dwho. and tenements under one roof, workshop adj. on St David's Hill
£200; Hshld gds and stk therein £50; Tenements under one roof in
tenure of three weavers, £100; Drying linney £50. All stone, cob and
thatched.
£400

104/140007
RICE, James, Fuller.   15 March 1754
Dwho. and tenement under same roof, workshop and offices adj. on St.
David's Hill £200; Hshld gds, utensils and stk and gds in trust or on
commission £50; Three tenements under one roof adj. in tenure of
Thomas Hore, Joseph Hawkins and Humphrey Chappell, weavers
£100; Four tenements under one roof unfinished £200; Drying linney
in his garden £50.
£600

149/199907
RICE, James, Fuller.   22 June 1763
Ho. and tenement under one roof in tenure, workshop and offices adj.
in his own tenure £180; Utensils and stk and gds in trust or on commission in that part he occupies £50; Two tenements in possession
under one roof in tenure of weavers £90 Four tenements under one
roof in tenure of himself and others £180.
£500

204/294833
ROWDEN, Philip, Fuller.   26 Feb. 1771
Hshld gds in his dwho., brick, lath and plaster and slated £70; Wearing
apparel therein £15; Utensils and stk therein £15.
£100

76/106547
SHORT, Arthur, Fuller. 23 Oct. 1746
Hshld gds, utensils and stk in trd. in his wareho., workshops and lofts over in Coombe Street [*Rocks Lane*], cob and slated £180; Stk in two warehos behind the above, stone, cob and slated £20; Stk in his wareho. in Coombe Street [*Rocks Lane*] behind the dwho. of [?] Jenkins, carpenter, stone, timber and slated £100.

£300

89/121249
SHORT, Arthur, Fuller. 12 May 1750
Hshld gds, utensils and stk in trd. in his dwho., warehos, workshops and lofts over adj. each other in Coombe Street [*Rocks Lane*], stone, cob and slated £360; Stk in trd. in his two warehos adj. each other, behind the above, stone, cob and slated £40; On his stk in trd. in a wareho. behind the dwho. of [?] Jenkins, carpenter, stone, timber and slated £200.

£600

94/127837
SHORT, Arthur, Fuller and Dealer. 18 Oct. 1751
Dwho. and wareho. and lofts over in Coombe Street [*Rocks Lane*], stone, brick and slated £240; Hshld gds and stk in trd. therein £380; wareho. behind the dwho. of [?] Jenkins, carpenter, stone, timber and therein £120.

£800

31/52159
SOMMERS, Richard, Fuller. 11 Nov. 1730
Dwho. in Rack Lane, brick, timber and slated £500; His hshld gds and stk in trd. therein £500.

£1,000

199/284705
SPEAR, William, Fuller. 15 May 1770
All stone, brick, timber and slated. Ho., grist mills and tucking millho under one roof or adj. called Cricklepit Mills with the going gear of materials therein without the West Gate in tenure of miller and merchants £180; Stable near £20; Ho., offices and tenement adj. each other in St. Thomas the Apostle in tenure of cheesemonger £200.

£400

174/244241
SPEARE, Arthur, Fuller. 2 April 1767
Dwho. in Northgate Street £100; Ho. and brewho. adj. in parish of St. Mary in tenure £100. All stone, timber and slated.

£200

153/207868
SPEARE, Arthur and William, Fullers. 28 March 1764

Ho. and cellars adj. called Waye in Whitestone in tenure of farmer, stone, cob and thatched.   £100

131/172553
2 Jan. 1760
SPREY, Benjamin, Fuller.
Stk in trd. in wareho. in Pack warehos at Kayes Wharf adj. Bridge Yard, Southwark, brick £400; Stk in trd. in wareho. at Mr. Hilditch's £400; Stk in wareho. adj., brick and timber £500.   £1,300

31/50925
29 June 1730
SPRY, Benjamin, Fuller.
Hshld gds and furniture in his dwho., brick and slated £100; Stk in trd. in his two warehos, one over the other in his yard, behind the dwho., brick, timber, plaster and slated £400.   £500

100/130830
15 March 1753
SPRY, Benjamin, Snr., Fuller.
SPRY, Benjamin, Jnr., Plushmaker.
Hshld gds and stk in trd. on his own account in the fulling and tucking trade and in partnership with his son in the plush trade in his dwho., packing chambers adj. £600; Stk in trd. in his paved court and under a small linney including two leaden cisterns, stone, brick and slated £100; Stk in trd. in the dwho. of Thomas Dear, plushmaker, in Butcher Row, stone, timber and slated £200.
                                                  £900

194/278609
18 Dec. 1769
SPYING, Thomas, Fuller and Presser.
Hshld gds in his dwho. and packing room over Mrs. Forster's ho. adj. on Stepcott Hill, stone, brick, timber and slated £100; Utensils, stk and gds therein in trust and on commission £250; Utensils, stk and gds in trust and on commission in his pressho. adj. and communicating, behind the above, brick, timber and slated £250.
                                                  £600

200/289503
3 Oct. 1770
TOTHILL, Robert, Fuller and Shopkeeper.
Hshld gds in his dwho. £50; Utensils, stk and gds in trust and on commission therein £80; Utensils, stk and gds in his workho. behind £20; Ho. in the Friars in tenure £50. All brick, timber and slated.
                                                  £200

79/107301
9 Jan. 1746
WARDALL, Matthew, Fuller and Pressman.
Hshld gds, stk in trd. and gds on trust in his dwho. only without the North Gate, brick, cob, lath and plaster £300; Utensils, stk in trd. and gds on trust in his pressho. only, near his ho., stone, brick and slated £100.   £400

139/185953
WORTHY, Jonathan, Fuller.   19 Nov. 1761
Ho., poundho., pound and engine therein and barn in tenure in Stoke
Canon £80; Tenement, stable and cellar adj. £20. Stone, cob and
thatched.

£100

162/224226
ASBORNE, Thomas, Dyer.   3 Sept. 1765
Dwho., dyeho. in Ewings Lane £300; Hshld gds, stk in trd. and trust
therein £100; One ho. under the town walls £200; Stk and gds in trust
therein £100. Stone, timber and slated.

£700

108/143514
BARTLETT, John, Dyer.   7 Nov. 1754
Utensils, stk in trd. and gds in trust on commission in his brewho.,
dyeho. and bridgeho. adj. in the court of Frog Lane without the West
Gate £250; Stk in trd. and gds on commission in his wareho. £100;
Hshld gds, stk in trd. and gds in trust on commission in his dwho. and
cellars in Frog Lane £50. All stone, timber and slated.

£400

126/166310
BARTLETT, John, Dyer.   28 Dec. 1758
Hshld gds, stk in trd. and gds in trust or on commission in his dwho.,
stone, brick and slated £190; Hshld gds, stk in trd. and gds in trust or
on commission in his ho. behind, stone, brick, brick and nogging and
slated £10; Utensils, gds, stk in trust or on commission in his wareho.,
dyeho., bridgeho., in Frog Lane, stone, timber and slated £300.

£500

39/62353
BASS, John, Dyer.   13 Nov. 1733
Hshld gds, utensils and stk in trd. in his dwho. in Ewings Lane, stone,
timber and slated.

£300

111/146566
COLLINS, James, Dyer.   8 May 1755
Hshld gds, stk in trd. and gds on trust in following buildings: In
dwho. and adj. office in the Island, brick and slated £700; Dyehos
under one roof opposite dwho. £100; Warerooms, dyeho. and adj.
wareroom, stone, brick, timber and slated £400; Stk in wareho. on
other side of street £500.

£1,700

139/184614
COLLINS, James, Dyer.   15 Sept. 1761
Dwho. situated on the Island without West Gate £250; Hshld gds, stk

in trd., gds on trust therein £400; Dyeho. and scarlet dyeho. under one roof, brick, plaster and slated £100; Utensils, stk, gds in trust therein £100; Dyeho. and warerooms adj. £50; Utensils and stk and gds on trust therein £300; Stk in wareho. on other side of street £200.

£1,400

95/128865

COOMBE, William, Maltster and Dyer.   N.S. 9 Jan. 1752
Dwho. called Axis Estate, timber and slated in Frog Lane £100; Dyeho. behind the above, brick, timber and slated £100; Utensils, stk in trd. and gds in trust therein £200.

£400

31/52154

COSSERATT, Bernard, Jnr., Dyer.   11 Nov. 1730
Stk in trd. and hshld gds in his dwho. in the Island, brick and slated £300; Stk in trd in a wareho. in the yard before his ho., brick and slated £200.

£500

234/347054

FLEMING, John, Dyer.   6 Dec. 1774
Hshld gds in dwho., dyeho. and outhos adj. in Frog Lane, stone, lath, plaster and slated £100; Utensils, stk and gds £700; Wareho., brick and slated £150; Utensils, stk and gds therein £150.

£1,100

84/114910

FLOUD, Henry, Dyer.   12 Jan. 1748
Hshld gds, stk in trd. and gds on trust in his dwho. and office adj. without the West Gate, stone, brick, timber and slated £150; Gds, utensils, stk in trd. and gds on trust in his dyeho. behind his dwho., stone, brick, timber and slated £150.

£300

95/128048

FLOUD, Henry, Dyer.   N.S. 5 Nov. 1751
Hshld gds, utensils and stk in trd., gds on trust in his dwho., wareho. and dyeho. adj. in Frog Lane, stone, brick, lath, plaster and slated £350; Utensils, stk in trd. and gds on trust in his dyeho., stone and slated £50.

£400

104/139266

FLOUD, Henry, Dyer.   10 Jan. 1754
Ho. in tenure of himself and John Bartlett, dyer, Widow Collins and Nathaniel Saunders, dyer, with wareho. and dyeho. adj., in Frog Lane, stone, brick, lath, plaster and slated £180; Hshld gds, utensils, stk in trd. and gds in trust or in commission £350; Dyehos opposite, stone and slated £20; Utensils and stk in trd. and gds in trust or in commission £50.

£600

108/143515
FLOUD, Henry, Dyer.   7 Nov. 1754
Ho. in the tenure of himself, John Bartlett, dyer, Widow Collins and
Nathaniel Saunders, dyer, wareho., dyeho. adj. in Frog Lane without
the West Gate, stone, brick, lath and plaster and slated £180; Hshld
gds, utensils and stk in trd., gds in trust on commission £1,000; Dyeho.
opposite, stone and slated £20; Utensils, stk in trd. and gds in trust on
commission in a stable on the opposite side of the street, stone, cob
and thatched. £100.

£1,400

118/157426
FLOUD, Henry, Dyer.   6 May 1757
Ho., wareho., dyeho., linney adj. in Frog Lane without the West Gate
in tenure £200; Hshld gds, stk and gds in trust or commission therein
£900; Two dyehos and outhos opposite the dwho., stone, brick, timber,
slated and tiled £100; Utensils, gds and stk in trust or commission
therein £200; Ho. vacant in Guinea Lane £100; Stk and gds in trust
and on commission in his stable, thatched £100.

£1,600

129/170044
FLOUD, Henry, Dyer.   7 Aug. 1759
Ho. which when finished will be part in his possession and part under
tenants. Warehos, dyeho., linney adj., stone, brick, plaster and slated
£300; Hshld gds, utensils and stk and gds in trust or commission therein
£900; Two dyehos, warehos and outhos opposite the dwho., stone,
brick, timber and slated and tiled £100; Utensils, stk and gds on trust
in commission therein £200; Stk in wareho. in a dwho., timber and
slated £200; Stk of gds in trust or commission in his stable, thatched
£100; Ho. in Guinea Lane in tenure, stone, timber and slated £100.

£1,900

170/238521
FLOUD, Henry, Dyer.   18 Oct. 1766
Hshld gds in his dwho., dyehos and wareho., stone, timber, slated £100;
Utensils, stk and gds in trust or on commission in dwho. without the
West Gate £300.

£400.

174/244821
FLOUD, Henry, Dyer.   16 April 1767
Utensils and stk in his warehos in Frog Lane, stone, cob and thatched.

£100

238/352072
FLOUD, Henry, Dyer.   7 April 1775
Three tenements, dwho., ware rooms, chambers over and dyeho. in the
court in Frog Lane in tenure of himself and others, brick, timber and
slated £400; Hshld gds £200; Utensils, stk and gds therein £400; New

buildings in Frog Lane, stone plaster and slated £100; Utensils, stk and gds £200.

£1,300

54/83040
FRYER, Elizabeth, Dyer.   11 Feb. 1739
Hshld gds, utensils and stk in trd. in her dwho. in the Island, stone, brick and slated £600; Utensils and stk in trd. in her dyeho. and warehos adj., stone, brick, timber and slated £400.

£1,100

95/129242
FRYER, Elizabeth and her son   N.S. 4 Feb. 1752
  William Fryer, Dyers.
Their hshld gds and stk in trd. in their dwho. and offices adj. on the left hand, stone, brick, plaster and slated £1,500; Stk in their wareho., further back on the left, stone, cob, timber and slated £500; Utensils and stk in trd. and gds on trust in their several warehos and dyehos at the entrance and at the end of the court, distant from the dwho. in Exe Island, stone, brick, timber and slated £1,500.

£3,500

109/144450
FRYER, Elizabeth and unnamed partner, Dyers.   10 Jan. 1755
Dwho. fronting the Island, warehos and scarlet dyeho. on right. Dyeho. at end and wareho. and dyeho. on right, brick, timber and slated £400; Stk in trd. and gds in trust therein £2,000; Stk in trd. and gds on trust in warehos behind dwho., slated and brick £800; Stk in trd. and gds on trust in dwho. £2,000; Stk in trd. in warehos and warehos over dwho. £700.

£5,900

106/142144
GILES, William, Dyer.   2 Aug. 1754
Tenement in tenure £50; Two tenements near the above under one roof £80 all in Exe Island; Hshld gds in his dwho. £40; Two tenements in North Gate £30.

£200

126/167544
MANNING, John, Dyer.   2 March 1759
Hshld gds, utensils and stk in trd. and gds in trust or on commission in his dwho., scarlet dyeho. adj. in Exe Island, brick and slated £200; Utensils and stk in trd. and gds in trust or on commission in great dyeho., brick and slated £400; Stk in trd. and gds in trust or on commission in wareho opposite dwho. £100; Gds and stk in trd. and gds in trust or on commission in his brewho., wash-ho. and warerooms adj., brick, lath, plaster and slated £300.

£1,000

79/108916
MICHELL, Samuel, Dyer.   9 July 1747
Hshld gds, stk in trd. and gds on trust in his dwho. in Exe Island
£100; Utensils and stk in trd. and gds on trust in his dyeho. and offices
adj. the aforesaid £300, all stone and brick.

£400

90/124043
MICHELL, Samuel, Dyer.   21 Dec. 1750
Hshld gds and stk in trd. and gds on trust in his dwho. in Exe Island
£300; Utensils and stk in trd. and gds on trust in his dyeho. and offices
adj. £300.

£600

50/78206
OSBORNE, Thomas, Dyer.   21 Sept. 1738
Cob and thatched ho. in Alphington in tenure of three persons £80;
Stable adj. £5; Cellar and bakeho. to it £15.

£100

112/148644
OSBORNE, Thomas, Dyer.   24 Sept. 1755
Dwho. and adj. dyeho. in Ewings Lane, stone, timber and slated £300;
Hshld gds, utensils and stk in trd. therein £100; Gds on trust and stk
in trust in warehos adj., stone, timber and slated £200.

£600

91/124757
POTTER, Richard, Dyer.   14 Feb. 1750
Hshld gds, stk in trd. and gds in trust in his dwho. and scarlet dyeho.
adj. in Exe Island £200; Utensils, stk in trd. and gds on trust in the
great dyeho. £400; Stk in trd. and gds on trust in his wareho. opposite
his dwho. £50; Stk in trd. and gds on trust in his warehos and lofts
over, on the left hand of the entrance £350; All brick, stone, some lath,
plaster and slated: Ho., brewho. and office adj. behind the front roof in
tenure of Thomas Baily, victualler, £200. Brick, lath, plaster and
slated.

£1,200

135/178245
SAUNDERS, Nathaniel, Dyer.   10 Oct. 1760
Hshld gds, stk and gds in trust or on commission in his cellar, dwho.
and dyehos adj. in Frog Lane without the West Gate £350; Stk in his
warerooms in the dwho. of Dyer, fisherman, opposite £50. Stone, brick,
timber and slated.

£400

148/202101
SAUNDERS, Nathaniel, Dyer.   30 Aug. 1763
Hshld gds, stk and gds in trust or on commission in his cellar, loft over,
dwho. and two dyehos all adj. in Frog Lane, brick, timber and slated

£300; Stk and gds in trust and on commission in his warerooms in one ho. in *Tombling Court,* stone, brick, timber and slated £200.

£500

170/238520

SAUNDERS, Nathaniel, Dyer. 18 Oct. 1766

Three tenements under one roof in the Island, brick and slated £200; One tenement adj., brick, lath, plaster and slated £70; One tenement behind £30.

£300

174/243784

SAUNDERS, Nathaniel, Dyer. 24 March 1767

Dwho. in Ewings Lane, stone, brick and slated £250; Hshld gds therein £100; Utensils, stk etc. therein £200; Tenements and dyeho. adj. in tenure of himself and under tenant, brick, lath, plaster and slated £150; Utensils, stk etc. therein £200; Utensils, stk etc. in warehos £400, brick and slated.

£1,300

203/291989

STOKES, John, Dyer. 11 Dec. 1770

Intended dwho., dyeho., linney, brick and slated and new built ho. adj. £500; Hshld gds therein £160; Musical instruments therein £40; Utensils, stk and gds in trust therein £100; Great dyeho., brick and lath £50; Utensils, stk and gds in trust therein £50; Wareho., brick and slated £30; Utensils, stk and gds in trust therein £150; Stable and wareho. adj. and warerooms over, brick and slated, lath and plaster £50; Utensils, stk and gds in trust therein £70.

£1,200

245/264162

STOKES, John, Dyer. 19 Jan. 1776

Dwho., scarlet dyeho., little linney, new built ho. adj. £500; Hshld gds therein, £200; Utensils, stk and gds therein £100; Great dyeho. on the right in the court, brick and slated, £50; Wareho. and sorting ho. in the court, £30; Utensils, stk and gds therein £150; Stable, wareho. and ware rooms on the left, brick and slated, £50; Utensils, stk and gds therein £70; Ho., additional building, offices and press ho. adj. in Frog Lane, in tenure, stone, brick, timber and slated £300.

£1,500

245/364163

STOKES, John, Dyer. 19 Jan. 1776

Ho. in Fore Street in tenure £250; Ho. adj. [sic] in St. Martins Lane in tenure £250; Ho. in Fore Street in tenure £250; Three dwellings and offices £250; Ho. in Northgate Street in tenure £200; Ho., workshop and offices adj. in Northgate Street £300.

£1,500

72/100938
TREWMAN, John, Dyer.　　　　　　　　　14 Dec. 1744
Dwho. and wareho. adj. in Ewings Lane, stone, timber and slated
£300; Hshld gds and stk in trd. therein £200; Dyeho. behind the above
with the coppers therein, stone, timber and slated £100.

£600

104/139666
TURNER, Zachary, Dyer.　　　　　　　　12 Feb. 1754
Hshld gds in his dwho., stone, timber and slated £50; Hos in tenure of
John Stripcott, dyer and others in the Island, stone, timber and slated
£150.

£200

152/206061
TURNER, Zachary, Dyer and Maltster.　　　　12 Jan. 1764
Hshld gds in his dwho., stone, timber and slated £50; One ho. in
tenure, stone, timber and slated £150. The above in the Island. Utensils and stk in his maltho. in the parish of St. Mary, timber and slated
£200. All within the West Gate of Exeter.

£400

195/277674
TURNER, Zachary, Dyer and Maltster.　　　　24 Nov. 1769
Ho. in Ewings Lane without the West Gate, now empty £100; Maltho.
adj. £100; Utensils and stk therein £100. All plaster, brick and slated.

£300

204/293922
TURNER, Zachary, Dyer and Maltster.　　　　29 Jan. 1771
Dwho., stone, timber and slated £200; Hshld gds therein £100; Uten-
sils and stk in his maltho., timber and slated £200; Ho. in tenure £170;
Workshop behind £30.

£700

204/293923
TURNER, Zachary, Dyer and Maltster.　　　　29 Jan. 1771
Utensils and stk in his maltho., brick and plaster and slated.

£100

68/97524
WILMOT, Henry, Dyer.　　　　　　　　　5 Jan. 1743
Stone and slated wareho. in the Island £50; Stk in trd. therein £150.

£200

90/122144
WILMOT, Henry, Dyer.　　　　　　　　26 July 1750
Hshld gds, stk in trd. and gds on trust in his dwho. in the Island,
brick and slated £200; Utensils, stk in trd. and gds on trust in his
dyeho. under one roof, brick and slated £200; Utensils, stk in trd. and

gds on trust in his warerooms and dyeho., westward, stone, brick, timber and slated £100; Wareho. on the other side, stone, brick and slated £50; Stk in trd. therein £450.   £1,000

98/133159
WILMOT, Henry, Dyer.   N.S. 14 Nov. 1752
Hshld gds, stk in trd. and gds in trust in his dwho., brick and slated £1,000; Utensils and stk in dyehos opposite dwho. £100; Utensils, stk in trd. and gds in trust in his warerooms, dyeho., west of the dwho., stone, brick, timber and slated £400; Wareho. in St. Edmund's parish, brick and slated £100; Stk in trd. therein £900.
£2,500

151/205088
WILMOT, Henry, Dyer.   13 Dec. 1763
Dwho. fronting the Island, stable and brewho. adj. on the right hand without the West Gate, brick and slated £300; Hshld gds, stk therein £100; Ground rooms, rooms over on the left hand, stone and slated and ground rooms and rooms over at the end of the first Court being the old building, stone, a small part lath plaster and slated £100; Gds, stk and gds in trust or on commission therein £100; Wareho. on the left hand in the second court, new built, brick and slated £100; Gds and stk therein and gds on trust or in commission £600; Range of warehos and scarlet dyeho. on the right hand, stone, timber and slated £100; Utensils, stk and gds in trust or on commission therein £500; Dyeho. at end of court, stone, timber and slated £100; Utensils, stk and gds on trust or commission therein £100; Groundrooms and loft over the bridge, stone, timber and slated £50; Stk and gds in trust or on commission therein £230; Garden ho. and greenho. adj., brick and slated £25; Stk and gds in trust or on commission therein £25; Tenement fronting the Island now or late in the tenure of a tailor, stone, timber and slated £30; Garden ho. and tenement adj. in the Island in tenure of merchant, brick and slated £20; Tenement in the Island now or late in tenure, stone and slated £20.   £2,500

178/251074
WILMOT, Henry, Dyer.   16 Dec. 1767
Ho., wareho. and offices adj. [in] the Island without the West Gate, in tenure, stone, brick, lath, plaster and slated.
£300

226/333908
WILMOT, Henry, Dyer.   14 Dec. 1773
Dwho. fronting the Island, stable and brewho. £400; Hshld gds £200; Ground rooms and rooms over near the end of the first court £200; Hshld gds £150; Wareho. in second court £200; Utensils, stk and gds £600; Range of warehos, right hand of said court, £200; Utensils, stk and gds £500; Dyeho. at end of court £300; Utensils, stk and gds therein £200; Ground room and loft £50; Utensils, stk and gds therein

£200; New dyeho. over the water £150; Utensils, stk and gds therein £200; Cellar and lofts fronting the Island £100; Ho. leased out fronting the Island £50; Garden ho. leased out £50; Ho. leased out £50.

£3,800

194/278603
WILMOTT, Henry, Dyer.   18 Dec. 1769
Dwho. fronting the Island, stable and brewho. adj., brick and slated £500; Hshld gds therein £270; Ground rooms and rooms over, stone and slate and ground rooms over and adj., stone, a small part lath, plaster and slated £300, at the end of the First Court being the Old Building; Hshld gds therein £200; Wareho. on the left in the Second Court, new built, brick and slated £200; Utensils, stk and gds in trust and on commission therein £600; Range of warehos and scarlet dyeho. adj., stone, timber and slated £300; Utensils, stk and gds in trust and on commission £500; Dyeho. on the end of the court, stone, timber and slated £300; Utensils, stk and gds in trust and on commission therein £100; Ground rooms, loft over the bridge, stone, timber and slated £50; Utensils, stk and gds in trust and on commission £250; Ho. fronting the Island, cellars and offices adj. in tenure £300; Tenements fronting the Island now or late in tenure, stone, timber and slated £50; Gardenho. and tenement adj. in tenure, brick and slated £50; Tenement in tenure, stone and slated £30.

£4,000

203/291986
WILLMOTT, Henry, Dyer.   11 Dec. 1770
Cellar and dyeho. adj., stone, brick, brick *kagged* [? nogging] and tiled £540; Tenement in Coombe Street[*Rock Lane*] in tenure, stone, cob and slated £60.

£600

135/179949
BLIGHT, Caleb, Pressman.   8 Jan. 1761
Utensils and stk and gds in trust or on commission in his pressho. on the right hand of the entrance of the Court in the Holloway without the South Gate of the city £30; Utensils, stk and gds in trust or on commission in the shop on the left hand £20; Hshld gds, stk and gds in trust or on commission in his dwho. £100; Utensils, stk and gds in trust or on commission £50. Stone, timber and slated.

£200

180/253545
CAMPION, Daniel, Pressman.   21 Jan. 1768
Ho., brewho., cellars and offices adj., vacant £200; Ho. in Frog Lane in tenure £100; Tenement and stable adj. in his own tenure £100. All stone, timber and slated.

£400

199/284706
DARE, James, Pressman.   15 May 1770
Hshld gds in his dwho., press shop and offices adj. in Preston Street,

brick, lath, plaster and slated £100; Utensils, stk of gds in trust or on commission therein £900.

£1,000

152/207276
DUNSFORD, John, Pressman.   5 March 1764
Three tenements under one roof and offices adj. in Moretonhampstead in tenure of victualler, stone and thatched.

£200

155/212339
DUNSFORD, John, Pressman.   25 Sept. 1764
Hshld gds, utensils, stk and gds in trust or on commission in his dwho., pressho. and outhos adj. in Frog Lane without the West Gate, stone, brick and slated.

£300

201/288255
HORABIN, William, Pressman.   22 Aug. 1770
Hshld gds in his dwho., warerooms under one roof on the right hand in a court without the West Gate, stone, brick and slate £200; Utensils, stk and gds in trust therein £500; Utensils, stk and gds in trust in his press shop and room over adj. each other on left hand side of court, stone, brick, slated £500.

£1,200

178/251600
MAYNE, Samuel, Pressman.   8 Dec. 1767
Utensils, stk and gds in trust and on commission in his pressho., finishing rooms adj. behind the dwho. of Joseph Clarke in Magdalen Street, stone, brick, timber and slated.

£400

203/291204
MAYNE, Samuel, Pressman.   15 Nov. 1770
Hshld gds in dwho., brick and thatched £100; Utensils and stk and gds in trust in his pressho., finishing rooms adj., brick, lath, plaster and slated £600.

£700

104/139670
NEWBOROUGH, Mary, Hotpresser.   12 Feb. 1754
Hshld gds, utensils, stks in trd. and gds in trust or on commission in her dwho., pressho. and room adj. near the Town Walls in Parish of St. Mary's, stone, timber, slated £650; Utensils, stk in trd. and gds in trust or on commission in her linney, tiled £150.

£800

119/156439
VOSPER, Elizabeth, Presser.   10 March 1757
Dwho. in the Friars without the South Gate £110; Hshld gds, stk and

gds in trd. therein £120; Press shop £20; Utensils, stk and gds in trust therein £150. Brick, timber and tiled.

£400

143/192776

MASTER, WARDENS, Assistants and Commonalty   29 Sept. 1762
of the Corporation of Weavers, Fullers and
Shearmen of Exeter.

Hall, called Tuckers Hall in Fore Street, stone, slated £100; Gds and furniture therein £20; A tenement in tenure of perukemaker and others £110; Tenement adj. and behind in tenure of a carpenter and supervisor of excise £215; Brewho. belonging £10; Tenement consisting of dwho. and packing room in tenure of a fuller £345; Linney, dryho. and burling shop adj. £135; Two presshos adj. £55; Gardenho. behind in tenure, brick and slated £10. All brick, stone, cob, timber and slated except the Hall.

£1,000

118/155873

BAWDEN, Richard, Plush and   20 Jan. 1757
Woollen Manufacturer.

Dwho. and offices adj. in the Friars without the South Gate of the City, brick, cob and slated £300; Hshld gds and stk in trd. therein £300.

£600

122/161841

BAWDEN, Richard, Plush and   29 March 1758
Woollen Manufacturer.

Hshld gds and stk in trd. in his dwho. in [?] Gandy Street [Candy Lane]. Brick and slated.

£600

172/242877

BRYANT, Samuel, Worsted Maker and Shopkeeper.   18 Feb. 1767

Hshld gds in his dwho. in Southgate Street £50; Utensils and stk therein £200; Utensils and stk in his workshops and warerooms adj. £50. Brick, timber and slated.

£300

88/121859

WITHERS, Benjamin, KENNAWAY, William, Jnr.   6 July 1750
Trustees to the last will of Nicholas Brinley,
for the benefit of Mrs. Hannah Kennaway.

Ho. and offices on the left and wash-ho., dyeho., warerooms and chamber over on the right hand behind, all adj., in tenure of Robert Kennaway, sergemaker, stone, brick, lath, plaster and slated £195; Brick, lath, plaster and slated ho. adj. in tenure of William Kennaway, sergemaker £170; Slated dyeho. in the court £5; One tenement and offices adj., part in William Kennaway's tenure and part in tenure of Susanna Soper, widow, £30.

£400

GREAT TORRINGTON

36/58049

MOORE, George, Clothier.   6 June 1732

Ho., stone and slated, known by the sign of the 'Black Horse,' in tenure of Peter Grater, innholder £200; A brewho., stable and linney adj. thatched £100.

£300

205/295740

GREENSLADE, Nathaniel Isaac, Sergemaker   26 March 1771

Dwho., stone and slated £140; Hshld gds therein £50; Bakeho. separate, stone and slated £10.

£200

85/115556

MOORE, George, Sergemaker.   7 March 1748

Stk in trd. in his wareroom in the dwho. of Thomas Harris, plumber, in the Sergemarket, St. Mary Major parish, Exeter.

£200

39/61357

MOORE, George, Jnr., Sergemaker.   12 July 1733

Dwho. only, stone, cob and thatched.

£300

67/96053

MOORE, George, Jnr., Shopkeeper and Sergemaker.   30 Aug. 1743

Hshld gds and stk in trd. in his new dwho., stone, cob and thatched.

£400

102/136564

JOY, William, Clothier.   10 July 1753

Hshld gds and stk in trd. in his new dwho. only, stone, cob and slated.

£200

33/54547

MOORE, George, MOORE, Richard,   24 June 1731

   SWEETE, Hugh, SWEETE, John,

   MOORE, George, Jnr., Clothiers.

Stk in trd. in their brick, stone, cob and slated wareho. in St. Mary's parish, Exeter.

£500

102/136563

SAUNDERS, Ester, Clothier.   10 July 1753

Dwho. and office, stone, cob and slated £100; Hshld gds and stks in trd. £200.

£300

63/92109
SAUNDERS, William, JOY, Richard and   27 July 1742
JOY, William, Sergemakers.
Stk in trd. in their warechamber in the dwho of Thomas Clutterbuck,
grocer, in the Sergemarket in Exeter, stone, timber and slated.

£300

85/115858
COLWILL, William, Fuller.   31 March 1749
Dwho., stone and slated £100; Hshld gds, utensils and stk in trd.
therein £100.

£200

121/159353
JOY, William, Pressman.   6 Oct. 1757
Press shop, storeroom and chamber over £50; Utensils, stk in trd. and
gds in trust therein £250; Dyeho., millho. and chamber adj. £100;
Utensils, stk in trd. and gds in trust £100. Stone, cob and thatched.

£500

HARTLAND

105/140654
ROBINS, John, Yarn Jobber.   23 April 1754
Stk in trd. in his wareroom in the dwho of Joseph Willsons, innkeeper,
known as the Angel Inn, Crediton, stone, brick and thatched.

£100

HATHERLEIGH

136/182548
COOMBE, John, Sergemaker.   16 May 1761
Hshld gds and stk in trd. in his dwho. and combshop adj. £160; Gds
and stk and linney adj. £10; Ho. in tenure £30. All stone, cob and
thatched in Hatherleigh.

£200

HEAVITREE

55/83174
COGGAN, Samuel, Sergemaker.   27 Feb. 1739
Hshld gds, utensils and stk in trd. in his dwho., stone, brick and slated.

£200

167/232075
COGGAN, Samuel, Sergemaker.   27 March 1766
Hshld gds in his dwho., brick and slated £50; Utensils and stk therein
£150.

£200

149/199906
COGGAN, Samuel, Jnr., Sergemaker. 22 June 1763
Hshld gds and stk in his dwho. and pleasure ho. adj., stone, plaster and slated.

£200

HEMYOCK

149/202660
FRY, Richard, Sergemaker. 24 Sept. 1763
Dwho., tending shop, sorting chamber, yarnho. and offices adj., stone and thatched £150; Hshld gds and stk therein £100; Stable, combshop, dyeho., linney adj. £50.

£300

153/209045
SCADDING, John, Sergemaker. 15 May 1764
Dwho., offices, cowhos and linneys adj. in the village [sic] of Shuttleton £130; Hshld gds and stk therein £60; Stable and barn adj., thatched £10.

£200

HILLMORE
[Culmstock]

179/250286
SHEARS, William, Sergemaker. 23 Oct. 1767
Dwho., stone, cob and thatched £50; Hshld gds therein £20; Utensils and stk therein £30.

£100

HOLCOMBE ROGUS

176/247801
DICKENSON, Henry, Sergemaker. 28 July 1767
Hshld gds in his dwho. £50; Utensils, stk, not hazardous, therein £340; Dwho. of the New Inn in the Sampford Peverell in tenure £60; Stable, strawho., barn, hogsty and linneys adj. each other £20; Ho. opposite called Patches in tenure £30; Dwho. in Uplowman in tenure £60; Double barn, poundho., and linneys adj. each other £40. All stone, cob and thatched.

£600

HONITON

28/47987
MAYNARD, Jerom, Woolstapler. 26 June 1729
Hshld gds and stk in trd. in his dwho., thatched £200; Stk in trd. in his ho., on the right hand of his dwho., containing seven rooms £300; Stk in his sundry wareho. in the yard behind his said ho., thatched £100.

£600

31/50106
MAYNARD, Jerom, Woolstapler.   25 March 1730
Stone, cob, timber and thatched:—Dwho. £80; Wareho. on the right
hand side of his dwho. £80; Wareho. in the yard on the right £15;
Wareho. in the yard on the left £25.

£200

114/152601
BLEW, Thomas, Sergemaker.   10 June 1756
Dwho. and workshop adj., stone, cob and slated £100; Hshld gds and
stk therein £100.

£200

164/225543
BLEW, Thomas, Sergemaker.   5 Oct. 1765
Dwho., parlour, cellars, linney and shops all adj., brick, slated and
thatched £150; Hshld gds and stk therein £50.

£200

56/86512
GREY, Abraham, Sergemaker.   8 Jan. 1740
Dwho., stone, brick and thatched £200; Hshld gds and stk in trd.
therein £150; Maltho. adj., stone, brick and thatched£100; Utensils
and stk therein £50; Range of offices only, adj., stone, brick and
thatched £50; Utensils and stk in trd. therein £50.

£600

97/130103
GREY, Abraham, Sergemaker and   N.S. 9 April 1752
    Maltmaker.
Dwho. and shop under one roof, stone, cob and thatched £200; Hshld
gds and stk in trd. therein £200; Maltho. and millho. under one roof,
stone, brick and thatched £100; Utensils and stk therein £100; A range
of offices and rooms to the right of the dwho., not finished, brick, cob,
slated £100; Stk in trd. therein £100.

£800

105/139894
GREY, Abraham, Sergemaker.   6 March 1754
Ho. in two tenements in tenure of William Isaacks and John Brocks,
weavers, stone, brick and slated, exclusive of all outhos adj. buildings.

£200

76/106023
MAYNARD, James, Sergemaker.   18 Sept. 1746
Hshld gds, utensils and stk in trd. in his dwho., warehos and chambers
over adj., stone, cob, slated and thatched.

£200

86/118784
MAYNARD, James, Sergemaker.   22 Nov. 1749

Gds and stk in trd. in his dwho., shop and chambers over, stone, cob and thatched £400; Stk in trd. in his new chambers, adj. each other in Honiton, brick, stone, lath, plaster and tiled £400.

£800

96/132072

MAYNARD, James, Sergemaker.   1 Sept. 1752
Dwho., workshops adj. and chambers over, stone, brick, tiled and slated £300; Hshld gds and stk in trd. therein £400; Weighing shops, combshops, drying hos. rooms over; stone, brick, slated and tiled £100; Gds and stk in trd. therein £100.

£900

101/136110

MAYNARD, James, Sergemaker.   15 June 1753
Three tenements under one roof, one adj. behind and offices in Wellington, brick, slated and thatched £160; Separate maltho. behind £30; Adj. stable and pigsties £10.

£200

44/69910

MAYNARD, Jerom, Sergemaker.   1 April 1736
Part brick, stone, cob, timber, all thatched: — Dwho., £125; A cellar and outhos adj. £5; One ho. in occupation of David Cockram, sergemaker, £40; A range of outhos behind, on the right, in Cockram's occupation £20; A range of outhos behind, on the left, in Maynard's occupation £40; Wareho. between the two hos in his own occupation £70.

£400

88/121154

MAYNARD, Jerom, Sergemaker and Shopkeeper.   2 May 1750
Hshld gds and stk in trd. in his dwho. and shop under one roof £150; Stk in trd. in his wareho. between the dwho. of late Maynard and Cockram £230; Stk in trd. in his comb shop and chamber over £20. All above stone, cob, timber and thatched. Ho. in four tenements in tenure of four persons and a wareroom over in his own occupation, stone, brick, timber and tiled £100; Stk in trd. in said wareroom £100.

£600

97/130104

MAYNARD, Jerom, Sergemaker.   N.S. 9 April 1752
Intended dwho. and shops, stone, brick and slated £100; Hshld gds and stk in trd. therein £200; Workshop, wareho., comb shop, cellar and offices with lofts over, stone, brick, tiled and slated £50; Gds and stk in trd. therein £150; Stone, brick and tiled ho. adj. west £100; Stk in trd. in his wareho. at the top of the above mentioned ho. £100; Brick, stone and tiled Baptist Meeting Ho., behind the above £100.

£800

180/254263
MAYNARD, John, Sergemaker.   9 Feb. 1768
Utensils and stk in his workshops behind dwho., stone, cob and
thatched £200; Ho., offices and stable in tenure, stone, cob and thatched
£100.
                                              £300

157/213187
NEWBERY, Samuel, Sergemaker.   18 Oct. 1764
Hshld gds and stk in his dwho., wareho., shops and offices under one
roof in New Street, brick and slated.
                                              £200

205/296854
SMALE, George, Jnr., Sergemaker.   23 April 1771
Hshld gds in his dwho. £40; Wearing apparel therein £10; Utensils, stk
and gds in trust or on commission in the said dwho. £120; In the
combshop and rooms near £10; In the drying loft £20. All stone, lath,
plaster and slated.
                                              £200

153/208208
SNOOK, John, Sergemaker.   4 April 1764
Two dwellings under one roof and outhos adj. in tenure of bakers,
stone, slated and thatched.
                                              £100

119/155948
EARLE, James, Clothier and Sergemaker.   26 Jan. 1757
Hshld gds and stk in trd. in his dwho. and offices adj., stone, cob and
thatched £50; Stk in his workshops and warehos behind £150.
                                              £200

114/152641
HAKE, Samuel, Clothier.   15 June 1756
Intended dwho. and shops adj., stone, brick and tiled £400; Hshld
gds and stk therein £500; Stable, dyeho. and linney adj. intended to
be built at a distance from the above. Stone, cob and thatched £30;
One ho. and five tenements in tenure £70. Stone, cob and thatched.
                                              £1,000

85/114740
HAKE, Samuel, Jnr., Clothier.   5 Jan. 1748
Hshld gds and stk in trd. in his dwho., stone, brick and slated £100;
Utensils and stk in trd. in his workshops, dyeho., cellars, linney and
stable adj., stone, brick, cob and thatched £200.
                                              £300

36/59283
HEWES, Thomas, Clothier.   13 Nov. 1732
Dwho., kitchen and brewho. belonging, brick and timber £150; Hshld

gds and gds in trd. in the above buildings £150; Three shops, a stable and woodho. belonging to the said dwho., thatched £100; Gds in trd. and utensils in above buildings £100.

£500

68/97526
HEWES, Thomas, Clothier.   5 Jan. 1743
Dwho., kitchen and brewho. under one roof, stone, cob, tiled and thatched £100; Hshld gds and stk in trd. therein £100; Three shops, a stable and woodho. adj., stone, cob, tiled and thatched £50; Utensils and stk in trd. therein £50.

£300

80/110430
HEWES, Thomas, Clothier.   17 Dec. 1747
Dwho. under one roof, stone, brick and slated £150; Hshld gds and stk in trd. therein £50.

£200

61/89584
HEWES, Thomas, Jnr., Clothier.   15 Dec. 1741
Dwho., workshop and offices adj., under one roof, stone, cob and thatched £90; Hshld gds and stk in trd. therein £100; Stable and linney adj., cob and thatched £5; Dyeho., stone, cob and thatched £5.

£200

123/161659
MAYNARD, James, Clothier.   16 March 1758
Ho. and tenements and offices adj. in tenure £50; A set of fulling mills, two tenements and office adj. in tenure of Sampson Long £150; Stk £50; One ho., two tenements and office in Weston in tenure £50. All stone, cob and thatched.

£300

151/203124
MAYNARD, James, Clothier.   7 Oct. 1763
Ho. and shop adj. in tenure of comber, weaver and tanner £100; Workshop, wareho., cellar and offices adj. in his own tenure £50; One ho adj. in tenure £100. The above are stone, brick, tiled and slated. One ho. in tenure of carrier, stone, cob and thatched £30.

£300

164/226558
MAYNARD, John, Clothier.   30 Oct. 1765
Hshld gds and stk in his dwho., brick and slated £70; Wearing apparel therein £30; One ho. and workshop adj. in tenure, stone, cob and thatched £50; One ho. on *Brimble Hill* in tenure, stone, cob and thatched £50.

£200

136/181757
SNOOKE, John, Clothier.   10 April 1761
Hshld gds and stk in trd. in his dwho. and offices adj., stone, cob and
thatched.

£100

174/244239
SNOOKE, John, Clothier.   2 April 1767
Hshld gds in his dwho., offices and workshops adj., stone, cob and
thatched £50; Utensils and stk therein £150.

£200

IDE

176/246361
KNOTT, Richard, Sergeweaver.   17 June 1767
Three dwellings in tenure under one roof called *Warns Cotts* £70, one
may be converted as poundho.; Tenements, stables and outhos adj. in
the court in his own tenure, stone, cob and thatched £30.

£100

63/92004
WHITE, John, Sergemaker and Maltster.   14 July 1742
Dwho. and maltho. adj. under one roof, stone, cob and thatched £80;
Hshld gds and stk in trd. therein £80; Linney, brewho. and comb shop
near the same, stone, cob and thatched £20; Two tenements near the
above £20.

£200

KENTISBEARE

94/128513
STONE, Anthony, Sergemaker.   18 Dec. 1751
Dwho., offices and comb shop adj. £100; Hshld gds and stk in trd.
therein £80; Breaking shop, yarn and weighing shop, woodho. and
comb shop with chambers over opposite the dwho. £40; Utensils and
stk therein £120; Dyeho., linney, double linney, barn, stable and linney
adj. at the head of the court £40; Utensils and stk in trd. therein £20.
All stone, cob and thatched.

£400

120/160286
STONE, Anthony, Sergemaker.   14 Dec. 1757
Dwho., milkho., wring ho., cellar and poultry ho. with chamber over,
stone, cob and thatched £60; Hshld gds and stk in trd. therein £40;
Breaking shop, yarn shop, woodho. and combshop with chamber over
on the opposite side of the court £30; Gds and stk therein £20; Dyeho.,
linney, double linney, barn, stable and linney adj. at the end of the
court £30; Gds and stk therein £20.

£200

134/178584
STONE, Anthony, Sergemaker. 22 Oct. 1760
Dwho. and offices adj. not yet finished £110; Hshld gds and stk therein £50; Wearing apparel therein £10; Ho. opposite his dwho. £30; Gds and stk therein £20; Dyeho., barn, stable and linney adj. £60; Gds and stk therein £20. Stone, cob and thatched.

£300

KINGSBRIDGE

131/173941
HINGSTON, John, Shopkeeper and Sergemaker. 26 Feb. 1760
Dwho. and workho. adj., stone, lath, plaster and slated £100; Hshld gds and stk therein £300.

£400

MODBURY

26/44103
COLLINS, Richard, Sergemaker. 24 Feb. 1727
Dwho., timber, plaster and tiled £300; Hshld gds and stk in trd. therein £300.

£600

101/135707
GEST, Jonathan, Sergemaker. 9 May 1753
Two tenements and adj. woodho., stone and slated.

£200

93/127549
PERRING, Phillip, Jnr., Sergemaker. 3 Oct. 1751
Dwho., workshop and stable adj., stone and slated.

£200

112/149878
WAKEHAM, Robert, Sergemaker. 9 Dec. 1755
Dwho., brick and slated £250; Hshld gds and stk in trd. therein £350; Dyeho. behind, stone and slated £100; Gds and stk therein £100; One ho., stone and slated, in tenure to a woolcomber £100; Ho., stone, timber and slated £100.

£1,000

MORETONHAMPSTEAD

91/124759
BRIDGMAN, John, Sergemaker. 14 Feb. 1750
Three stone and slated tenements in tenure of himself and two others £300; Ho., stone, lath, plaster and slated, in tenure of two persons £100.

£400

136/181755

BRIDGMAN, John, Sergemaker and   10 April 1761
    Shopkeeper.
Hshld gds and stk in trd. in his dwho., timber and slated.

£200

203/292055

BRIDGMAN, John, Jnr., Sergemaker.   3 Jan. 1771
Hshld gds in dwho., workshop and outhos adj., stone, cob and thatched
£30; Utensils and stk therein £70.

£100

86/117510

EDWARDS, Joseph, Sergemaker.   25 Aug. 1749
Dwho. and offices adj., stone, cob and thatched £40; Hshld gds and stk
in trd. therein £60.

£100

26/45367

JACKSON, Abraham, Sergemaker.   1 Aug. 1728
Dwho., timber and slated £150; Hshld gds and stk in trd. therein £150.

£300

26/45637

JACKSON, Abraham, Sergemaker and   11 Sept. 1728
    Woolcomber.
Nine hos, a barn, a stable, part thatched/slated, in occupation of nine
persons [named], £30 on each, £270; Barn and stable in his own tenure
£30.

£300

26/45366

JACKSON, Jabez, Sergemaker.   1 Aug. 1728
Dwho. only, timber and slated £150; Hshld gds and stk in trd. therein
£150.

£300

154/210909

JACKSON, James, Sergemaker.   18 July 1764
Dwho. and offices under one roof, stone, lath and plaster £200; Hshld
gds and stk therein £200.

£400

160/220434

JACKSON, James, Sergemaker.   15 June 1765
Ho. and offices and stable adj., thatched.

£100

65/94016

MARWOOD, William, Sergemaker.   2 Feb. 1742
Dwho., stone and thatched £180; Outhos adj. each other, stone and
thatched £20.

£200

100/134387

PARR, William, Sergemaker. 8 Feb. 1753
Ho. in Moretonhampstead in tenure of Edward Pethybridge, sergemaker, stone, slated or thatched.

£200

118/156173

PARR, William, Sergemaker. 10 Feb. 1757
Ho. and four tenements adj. in the tenure of James Biggs, farmer, and
his under tenants, stone, plaster, slated and thatched £200; One ho. and
offices adj. in tenure, thatched £100.

£300

82/112054

PETHYBRIDGE, Edward, Sergemaker. 3 May 1748
Hshld gds in his dwho., wareho., wool chambers and yarn chambers
under one roof, stone slated and thatched.

£200

117/153145

PETHYBRIDGE, Edward, Sergemaker. 8 July 1756
Dwho. and offices adj., stone and thatched £100; Hshld gds and stk in
trd. therein £200.

£300

202/292209

PUDDICOME, Thomas, Sergemaker. 19 Dec. 1770
Hshld gds in his dwho. and office adj., stone, cob, slated and thatched
£50; Utensils and stk therein £100; Utensils and stk in comb shop,
sorting shop and outho. adj. £50; Utensils and stk in his wareho.,
thatched £100.

£300

114/152211

SMALE, George, Sergemaker. 4 May 1756
Hshld gds and stk in trd. in his dwho., ware-rooms and working rooms
under one roof, stone, cob, weather boarded and slated.

£200

164/228119

SMALE, George, Sergemaker. 4 Dec. 1765
Three tenements under one roof in reversion in tenure, stone, cob and
thatched £50; Three tenements under one roof in reversion £50. Stone,
cob and thatched.

£100

203/291214

SMALE, Robert, Sergemaker. 15 Nov. 1770
Hshld gds in dwho., stone, slated and thatched £50; Utensils, stk and
gds in trust therein £140; Wearing apparel £10.

£200

95/129161
VARDER, Richard, Sergemaker.   N.S. 29 Jan. 1752
Hshld gds and stk in trd. in his dwho. and offices under the same roof,
stone, lath, plaster and slated.

£200

206/298504
WEBBER, Joseph, Sergemaker.   18 June 1771
Hshld gds in his dwho. and offices adj., stone, cob and thatched £50;
Utensils and stk therein £50; Four tenements under one roof in West
Crediton in tenure of weavers, stone, cob and thatched £100.

£200

31/51356
WHITEWAY, Alexander, Clothier.   26 Aug, 1730
Dwho. only £200; One ho. in tenure of William Quath, blacksmith,
and Ann Sowland, widow, £100; One ho. in tenure of Sarah Neckland
£25; One ho. in tenure of Stephen Berry, carpenter £25; Maltho. in
tenure of George Leslie £50.

£400

119/156382
WHITEWAY, William, Clothier.   1 March 1757
Ho. and offices adj. in the tenure of Samuel Vile, apothecary, stone,
plaster and slated £200; One tenement, stable and drying ho. adj.
behind but separate from above in tenure, stone, cob and thatched £50;
One ho. in tenure, stone, cob and thatched £100; One tenement, stable
and cellar and two other tenements under the same roof, all in tenure
£150.

£500

NEWTON ABBOT

51/79481
FLAMANK, Samuel, Sergemaker and Shopkeeper.   11 Jan. 1738
Hshld gds and stk in trd. in his dwho., stone, timber and slated £800;
Stk in trd. in his warechamber in the dwho. of Thomas Clutterbuck,
shopkeeper, Exeter, £200.

£1,000

53/81411
FLAMANK, Samuel, Sergemaker and Shopkeeper.   25 July 1739
Hshld gds and stk in trd. in his dwho., stone, timber and slated £800;
Stone, timber and slated ho. in tenure of victualler £100; Stk in trd. in
his wareho. in the dwho. of shopkeeper, Exeter, £100.

£1,000

87/117332
FLAMANK, Samuel, Sergemaker.   12 Aug. 1749
Ho. and maltho. adj., in tenure of Thomas Jore, maltmaker, stone, cob,
timber and thatched.

£200

143/190325
FLAMANK, William, Sergemaker. 25 June 1762
Dwho., stone, timber, tiled and slated £200; Hshld gds and stk therein
£100; Range of outhos and stables and offices £100; Stone, cob and
timber and slated and thatched.

£400

169/235380
FLAMANK, William, Sergemaker. 9 July 1766
Ho. and offices adj. in Stokeinteignhead in tenure £100; Pound ho.,
pound engine, press and utensils for making cider, barn, stable, outhos,
styes £50; Cellar, chamber opposite £30; Stable, cellar and shippen
£40; Barns and linneys at a distance £50; Tenement, barn and linney
in Stokeinteignhead £30; Stone, cob and thatched.

£300

88/120346
GOODRIDGE, John, Sergemaker. 14 March 1749
Hshld gds and stk in trd. in his dwho. and shop in the dwho. of John
Brooking in Newton Abbot, stone, cob, lath, plaster and slated £200;
His stk in trd. in his wareroom in the 'Bear Inn' in the Sergemarket, St.
Mary Major parish, Exeter, £100.

£300

95/128409
GOODRIDGE, John, Sergemaker. N.S. 11 Dec. 1751
Hshld gds and stk in trd. in his dwho., stone, brick, plaster and tiled
£300; Stk in his wareroom in the 'Bear Inn', Exeter, stone, timber and
slated £100.

£400

118/157847
MACEY, Peter, Shopkeeper and Sergemaker. 16 June 1757
Hshld gds, stk in trd. in his dwho., pantry and offices adj., timber,
stone, slated £360; Stk in his coalshop and room over behind the ho.,
stone, cob and slated £40.

£400

37/58308
MATTHEWS, Andrew, Sergemaker. 7 July 1732
Dwho. with a stable adj. under one roof, stone, cob and slated £100;
Hshld gds and stk in trd. therein £100.

£200

71/100171
MATTHEWS, Andrew, Sergemaker. 27 Sept. 1744
Dwho. and offices under one roof, stone £200; Hshld gds and stk in trd.
therein £150; Stone, cob and slated ho. in tenure of tailor and others
£50; Stk in trd. in his chamber in a vacant ho. in St. Mary's parish.
Exeter, stone, timber and slated £100.

£500

170/239047
PINSENT, Robert, Sergemaker and Shopkeeper.   31 Oct. 1766
Dwho., stone, timber and slated £100; Hshld gds £100; Utensils and
stk. £300.

£500

78/108208
RUNDLE, George, Sergemaker.   23 April 1747
Hshld gds and stk in trd. in his dwho., stone and slated £100; Stk in
trd. in his wareroom in a vacant ho. in St. Mary's parish, Exeter, stone,
brick, timber and slated, £100.

£200

48/75743
TOZER, Aaron, Sergemaker.   5 Jan. 1737
Dwho., woodho. and stockho., all under one roof, stone, cob, lath, plaster and slated £160; Hshld gds and stk therein £290; Linney at the end
of the garden £5; Stk in the linney £5; Cellar and stable adj. the ho.,
slated £30; Stk therein £10.

£500

52/81630
TOZER, Aaron, Sergemaker.   28 Aug. 1739
Dwho., woodho. and stockho., all under one roof, stone, cob and lath
£120; Hshld gds, utensils and stk in trd. therein £220; A stable and
cellar adj. his dwho. £10; Stk in trd. in his wareho. behind the dwho.
of Thomas Clutterbuck, shopkeeper in Exeter, stone, timber and slated
£150.

£500

63/92938
TOZER, Aaron, Sergemaker.   22 Oct. 1742
Ho. in tenure of George Rendal, comber, and others, stone, cob, lath,
plaster and slated £200.

70/99109
TOZER, Aaron, of Newton Bushell   8 June 1744
    Sergemaker.
Hshld gds and stk in trd. in his dwho., stone, brick, cob, some lath and
plaster £400; His stone and timber slated ho. in tenure of George Rendall, woolcomber and Mrs. Holliwell, widow £200; His stk in trd. in a
chamber in a vacant ho. in the Sergemarket, Exeter, stone, timber and
slated £400.

£1,000

76/105355
TOZER, Aaron, Sergemaker.   26 June 1746
Dwho., stone, brick, cob, lath, plaster and slated £100; Hshld gds and
stk in trd. therein £250; Stone, lath, plaster and slated ho. in the
tenures of George Rendall, woolcomber, and the Widow Hollwell

£100; Stk in trd. in a chamber in a vacant ho. in the Sergemarket in Exeter, stone, timber and slated £250.

£700

158/216242
TOZER, Solomon, Sergemaker. 15 Jan. 1765
Hshld gds and stk in his dwho., stone, brick, plaster and slated £200; Gds and stk in wareho., brewho. and chamber over, slated £30; Gds and stk in cellar and stable adj., thatched £10; Stk in workshop, lath and barn thatched £250; Stk in poundho. of Aaron Tozer, thatched £10.

£500

48/75373
VICARY, Robert, Sergemaker. 23 Nov. 1737
Hshld gds and stk in trd. in his dwho., stone, cob and slated.

£300

86/116619
RANDLE, George, Clothier. 15 June 1749
Ho. in tenure of four persons, stone, cob, lath, plaster and slated.

£200

89/119734
RANDLE, George, Clothier. 25 Jan. 1749
Dwho., stone, cob, lath and plaster £200; Hshld gds and stk in trd. therein £100.

£300

NORTH TAWTON

122/163095
BROCK, John, Sergemaker. 13 June 1758
Dwho., workshop and office adj. £60; One ho. and office adj. in tenure £40. Stone, cob and slated.

£100

163/224842
BROCK, John, Sergemaker. 21 Sept. 1765
Dwho., workshop and offices adj. £100; Hshld gds and stk therein £60; Ho. and offices adj. each other opposite aforesaid in tenure £40. Stone, cob and thatched.

£200

86/117511
DAY, Thomas, Sergemaker. 25 Aug. 1749
Dwho., workshop, combshop, sorting ho., wareho., dyeho., stable and shippen adj., forming a court, stone, cob, slated and thatched £100; His hshld gds and stk in trd. therein £100.

£200

92/127274

DAY, Thomas, Sergemaker.   18 Sept. 1751

Hshld gds and stk in trd. in the 'New Inn', cellars and stables in tenure of Samuel Day, innholder.

£100

109/145374

DAY, Thomas, Sergemaker.   11 March 1755

Dwho., workshop, comb shop, sorting ho., wareho., dyehos, stable, sheep pen and linney adj. forming a court £150; Hshld gds and stk in trd. therein £150. Stone, cob, slated and thatched.

£300

137/183482

DAY, Thomas, Sergemaker.   3 July 1761

Dwho., workshop, sorting ho. and wareho., dyeho., stable, linney adj. and forming a court £150; Hshld gds and stk in trd. therein £150; Four tenements under one roof with hanging linneys in tenure £100. Stone, cob and thatched.

£400

138/184168

DAY, Thomas, Sergemaker.   11 Aug. 1761

Hshld gds and stk in trd. in dwho. of the George Inn with cellar and offices and stables adj. in tenure of innholder, stone, cob and thatched.

£100

152/206056

SOMMERS, John, Sergemaker.   12 Jan. 1764

New built dwho., kitchen, cellars and brewho. adj., stone, cob and slated £240; Hshld gds therein £60.

£300

80/110022

SOMMERS, Richard, Sergemaker.   29 Oct. 1747

Dwho., milkho., kitchen, cellars, shops and chambers over and shippen adj., stone, cob and thatched £240; Hshld gds and stk in trd. therein £200; A tenement near the above, in tenure of William Innocent, and stable adj., stone cob and thatched £60.

£500

153/206741

SOMMERS, Richard and John, Sergemakers.   9 Feb. 1764

Dwho., milkho., kitchen, cellars, shops, chambers over and shippen adj. the sole property of Richard Sommers £240; Utensils and stk, their joint property therein £400; Barn and linney adj., sole property of Richard Sommers £40; Stable, his property £20. All stone, cob and thatched.

£700

OKEHAMPTON

194/279764
BURD, John, Sergemaker.   12 Jan. 1770
Utensils and stk in his shop, warerooms and workshops communicating,
stone, slated and thatched.
£200

132/175797
BURD, Rebecca, Shopkeeper and Sergemaker.   30 May 1760
Dwho., stone and slated £200; Hshld gds and stk therein £300; Hshld
gds and stk in her ho. and outhos adj. in Back Lane, stone, cob and
thatched £300.
£800

143/191297
BURD, Rebecca, Shopkeeper and Sergemaker.   23 July 1762
Dwho., stone and slated £150; Hshld gds and stk therein £550.
£700

103/136884
BURD William, Sergemaker.   3 Aug. 1753
Hshld gds and stks in trd. in his dwho. and range adjoining on the
left hand behind, stone, plaster and slated.
£300

161/221844
BURD, William, Sergemaker and Shopkeeper.   11 July 1765
Dwho., stone and slated £150; Hshld gds and stk therein £550.
£700

194/279765
BURD, William and STONE, Samuel, Sergemakers.   12 Jan. 1770
Utensils and stk in the dwho., brick and slated.
£500

106/141359
COLLING, Joel, Sergemaker.   20 June 1754
Ho. in the tenure of himself and others, stone and tiled £150; Small
tenement and stable adj., in tenure of John Lane, stone and thatched
£20; Three stables adj. aforesaid, stone and thatched £30.
£200

79/109144
DODGE, William, Sergemaker.   4 Aug. 1747
Ho. divided into tenements with offices and three stables adj., in
tenures of himself and others, stone, cob and thatched £100; Stk in trd.
in his wareho. £200; Ho. and offices adj. in tenure of Johanna Dodge,
widow, part in his own tenure, stone and thatched £40; Stk in trd. in
that part in his own occupation £250; Stable and shippen behind the
above, thatched £10.
£600

91/123565
DODGE, William, Sergemaker.   13 Nov. 1750
Ho., divided into tenements with offices and three stables adj. forming
a court in tenures of himself etc. £100; dwho. and offices adj. £40; Stk
in trd. therein £250; Stable and sheep pen behind the above £10.

£400

164/228122
DODGE, William, Sergemaker.   4 Dec. 1765
Stk in his dwho. and offices, stone, cob and thatched.

£700

106/142213
REEVES, Richard, Sergemaker.   8 Aug. 1754
Dwho., wareho., workshop and offices under one roof, stone and slated
and thatched £100; Hshld gds and stk in trd. therein £100.

£200

123/162918
SPRAGUE, Walter, Sergemaker,   31 May 1758
      Shopkeeper and Baker.
Dwho., brewho., bakeho. and chamber over stable and wool chamber
adj., stone and slated £60; Hshld gds and stk therein £40.

£100

OTTERY ST. MARY

201/288202
TAYLOR, Robert of Tipton St. Johns,   21 Aug. 1770
      Blacksmith and CHANNON, William
      of Ottery St. Mary, Sergemaker.
Five tenements adj. in Sandhill Street in Ottery St. Mary in tenure, cob
and thatched £95; Linney near £5.

£100

105/140517
COLES, John, Sergemaker.   11 April 1754
Hshld gds and stk in trd. in his dwho. and offices of stone, cob and
thatched adj. each other.

£100

159/217430
COLES, John, Sergemaker.   5 March 1765
Ho. in two tenements in tenure of two persons £60; Four tenements
behind above, workshop, woolchamber, brewho. and cellar in tenure
£40; Hshld gds and stk in his dwho., workshops and offices adj. £100.
All stone, cob and thatched.

£200

104/140353
COPLESTONE, Edmund Sergemaker.   3 April 1754
Dwho. and office adj., stone, cob and thatched £200; Hshld gds and stk
in trd. £400.

£600

140/188860
COPLESTONE, Edmund, Sergemaker.   8 April 1762
Dwho. and adj. offices, stone, cob and thatched £200; Hshld gds and
stk therein £200.

£400

161/220631
DARE, Robert, Sergemaker.   19 June 1765
Hshld gds and stk in his dwho., linney, brewho., pigloose, gateway,
stable, wareho. adj. in Back Street £300; Three tenements in Bass
Lane in tenure £100. Stone, cob and thatched.

£400

164/226362
DARE, Robert, Sergemaker.   25 Oct. 1765
Hshld gds and stk in his dwho., small linney, brewho., pigloose, gate-
way, stable and wareho. adj. £200; Three tenements under one roof in
Bass Lane £100; Ho., barn, linney, stable under one roof called
Norwell £95; Linney £5. Stone, cob and thatched.

£400

174/243234
DARE, Robert, Sergemaker.   3 Feb 1767
Hshld gds in his dwho. with linney, brewho., pigloose, etc. in Back
Street £60; Utensils and stk therein £200; Three tenements in Bass
Lane in tenure £100; Tenement in Bass Lane in tenure £40; Ho.,
barn, linney, stable called *Norwell* in tenure £95; Linney £5. All
stone, cob and thatched.

£500

170/238022
DOWNE, Richard, Jnr., Sergemaker.   9 Oct. 1766
Hshld gds in his dwho., office and linney, stone, cob and thatched £40;
Utensils and stk therein £60.

£100

92/125976
EVANS, William, Sergemaker and Shopkeeper.   10 June 1751
Dwho., two tenements adj., brewho., stable, woodho. and stable in his
own tenure, brick, cob, lath and plaster £300; Hshld gds and stk in trd.
therein £300.

£600

179/250497
EVANS, William, Sergemaker and Shopkeeper.   28 Oct. 1767

Dwho., brick and tiled £550; Hshld gds therein £50; Utensils and stk therein £450; Stable and woodho. adj. £40; Gds therein £10.

£1,100

174/244488
KEYS, John and Elizabeth, Sergemakers.   8 April 1767
Her ho. in three tenements in tenure, stone, cob and thatched £190; Stable and linney near, thatched £10.

£200

33/53328
LATHROP, Robert, Sergemaker.   18 Feb. 1730
His six thatched hos adj., one in his own occupation, one in occupation of William Laskew, shoemaker, one in occupation of Robert Shannon, husbandman, one in occupation of William Marshall, weaver, one in occupation of Joan Lipincord, widow, one empty. £16. 13s. 4d. on each.

£100

86/116243
LATHROP, Robert, Sergemaker.   29 April 1749
Dwho. and offices adj. £100; Six tenements under one roof, in the tenures of six persons £100.

£200

60/90670
LONG, Robert, Sergemaker, Vintner and Glazier.   30 March 1742
Ho. in tenure of Robert Clapp, attorney £80; A maltho. and stable behind the above, intended to be converted into comb shop and weaving shop, cob, shingle and thatched £20; Hshld gds, utensils and stk in trd. in his new dwho £100.

£200

119/155582
LONG, Robert, Glazier, Sergemaker and Shopkeeper.   15 Jan. 1757
Hshld gds and stk in trd. in his dwho., stone, cob and thatched.

£200

126/166759
LONG, Robert, Sergemaker, Glazier and Vintner.   12 Jan. 1759
Dwho., office, weaving shop, stable and linneys adj., brick, stone, cob and slated £100; Hshld gds and stk in trd. therein £200.

£300

153/207509
LONG, Robert, Sergemaker.   13 March 1764
Dwho., offices weaving shops, stable, linney adj., brick, stone, cob and slated and thatched £100; Hshld gds and stk therein £100.

£200

171/239286
LONG, Robert, Sergemaker. 5 Nov. 1766
Dwho., shop, outho., office adj. £150; Hshld gds £20; Utensils and stk
£50; Barn £30; Utensils and stk therein £20; Stable £10; Stk £20.
Stone, cob and thatched.

£300

78/107896
MARKER, Gideon, Sergemaker. 26 March 1747
Dwho. and offices under one roof, brick, cob and thatched £250; Drying
linney, stable and cellar adj. only, brick, cob and thatched £50.

£300

80/109642
MARKER, Gideon, Sergemaker. 30 Sept. 1747
Ho., maltho., stable and chamber over adj., in tenure of Richard
Upham, maltster, stone, cob and thatched £160; Ho., cellar and linney
adj., near the aforesaid tenements, stone, lath, plaster and thatched
£140.

£300

27/46345
MARTIN, John, Sergemaker. 7 Dec. 1728
Dwho. and five hos adj., thatched, in occupations of five persons
(named).

£100

34/56161
REWALLING, Ralph, Sergemaker. 2 Nov. 1731
Stone, cob and thatched: — One ho. in tenure of John Robinson, John
Wills, sergemaker, and Elizabeth Guines, spinster £80; One ho. in
tenure of John Evely £20.

£100

197/284047
SANDERS, Benjamin, Sergemaker. 24 April 1770
Hshld gds in dwho. and adj. offices, stone, cob and thatched £30; Uten-
sils and stk therein £160; Utensils and stk in combshop and linney £10.

£200

203/291988
SAUNDERS, Benjamin, Sergemaker and Shopkeeper. 11 Dec. 1770
Dwho., office and combshops adj., brick, cob and tiled £200; Hshld gds
therein £50; Utensils and stk therein £750.

£1,000

59/87849
WEEKES, James, Sergemaker. 10 June 1741
Dwho. and offices adj. to the same, cob and thatched £200; Hshld gds
and stk in trd. therein £300; Ho. divided into four tenements £100.

£600

98/133700
WEEKES, James, Shopkeeper and Sergemaker.   N.S. 29 Dec. 1752
Dwho., brewho., working shops on the right hand and working shops
and wool chambers over, stable on the left hand £300; Hshld gds and
stk in trd. therein £500; Four tenements in tenures of four weavers
£90; Large linney behind the above £10, all thatched.

£900

PLYMOUTH

77/106780
BROWNE, John, Merchant.   19 Nov. 1746
Gracechurch St., London, and
SHEPHERD, Thomas, Baymaker, Plymouth
Storehos in one building at Coxside, Plymouth, stone and slated
£400;; Stk £400; Tucking mills in one building, St. Charles Parish,
Plymouth £200; Stk £200.

£1200

PYWORTHY

85/113958
PHILIP, John, Yarn Jobber.   25 Oct. 1748
Stk in trd. in his shop and room over in Holsworthy, Devon £100; Stk
in trd. in his chamber in the dwho. of [   ] Dicker, hatter, Crediton
£100.

£200

ST. THOMAS THE APOSTLE
[Exeter]

77/106314
BIDWELL, William, Sergemaker.   8 Oct. 1746
Hshld gds and utensils and stk in trd. in his dwho., brewho., dyeho.
and warehos and lofts over all, brick, timber and slated.

£200

92/127199
BIDWELL, William, Sergemaker.   10 Sept. 1751
Hshld gds, utensils and stk in trd. in his dwho., brewho., dyeho. and
lofts adj.

£300

102/137814
BIDWELL, William, Sergemaker.   4 Oct. 1753
Hshld gds, utensils and stk in trd. in his dwho., brewho., wareho and
lofts over and adj., brick, timber and slated.

£500

130/174242
BIDWELL, William, Sergemaker.   17 March 1760
Intended dwho., cellar and workroom adj., stone, cob, plaster and

slated £260; Loft over dwho. to be enlarged for shops and dyeho., slated £40.

£300

174/243782
24 March 1767
BINNS, Thomas, Sergemaker.
Hshld gds in his dwho., stone, cob and slated £50; Utensils and stk therein £150; Ho., cellar, stables, linney in Bovey Tracey, called Rockwell Ho. now empty, stone, cob and thatched £100.

£300

203/292850
30 Jan. 1771
BOND, Samuel, Sergemaker.
Ho. and offices adj. in tenure, stone, cob, slated and thatched.

£100

47/72580
26 Jan. 1736
BURNETT, Thomas, Sergemaker.
Brick and tiled dwho. £200; Hshld gds and stk in trd. therein £300.

£500

93/127550
3 Oct. 1751
BURNETT, Thomas, Jnr., Sergemaker.
Dwho., cellar and chamber over, in the tenure of himself, stone, cob, lath, plaster and slated £190; Hshld gds and stk therein £280; Wash-ho. and lofts over behind, stone, cob, timber and slated £10; Gds and stk in trd. therein £20.

£500

94/129056
N.S. 21 Jan. 1752
CASELEY, John, Sergemaker.
Hshld gds and stk in trd. in his dwho., cellar and wash-ho. adj., brick and slated £200; Stk in trd. in his worsted wareho. and wool chambers over, stone, cob and thatched £200.

£400

170/239045
31 Oct. 1766
CASELEY, John, Sergemaker.
Hshld gds in his dwho., offices and shop adj., brick and slated £200; Utensils and stk therein £300; Utensils and stk in wareho., woolchamber and dyehos £300. Brick, timber and slated.

£800

111/146567
8 May 1755
CASELY, John, MANNING, Robert and
    WILLIAMS, Joshua, Sergemakers
Stk in trd. in wareroom over dwho., brick, cob and thatched.

£200

169/234257
COLES, Joseph, Sergemaker.   10 June 1766
Hshld gds in his dwho., kitchen, office, shop and rooms over, all adj.,
forming a court, stone, brick, timber and slated £50; Utensils and stk
therein £150; Ho. in tenure and range of offices adj., brick, brick
nogging and slated £150; Workshop at end of court behind, stone,
brick and slated £50.

£400

51/78050
COULDRIDGE, John, Sergemaker.   28 Aug. 1738
Dwho. and offices, brick, timber and slated £100; Hshld gds and stk in
trd. therein £200; A dyeho. behind the dwho. £10; Ho. and linney,
under the same roof, cob and thatched £30; Utensils and stk in trd. in
said ho. and linney £50; A stable and linney, thatched, at the end of
the garden £10.

£400

120/159820
COULDRIDGE, John, Sergemaker.   4 Nov. 1757
Dwho., outho., dyeho., working hos, linney and offices adj. forming a
court, brick, cob, timber, slated and thatched £140; Hshld gds, utensils,
stk in trd. therein £230; Stable, outho., linney adj. at end of garden,
thatched £15; Gds and stk therein £15.

£400

59/88281
EVANS, John, Sergemaker.   14 July 1741
Half part of his dwho., wash-ho and brewho. adj., brick and slated
£145; Hshld gds and stk in trd. therein £420; Half part of the dyeho.
behind the dwho., brick, timber and slated £5; His utensils and stk in
trd. therein £30.

£600

121/158878
EVANS, Richard, Sergemaker.   25 Aug. 1757
Moiety of his dwho., wash-ho. and brewho. adj., brick and slated £145;
Hshld gds and stk in trd. therein £420; Moiety of the dyeho. behind,
brick, timber and slated £5; Utensils and stk therein £30.

£600

62/91936
FORD, John, Sergemaker.   9 July 1742
Dwho. only, brick, cob, lath and plastered, thatched and slated £200;
Hshld gds and stk in trd. therein £100; Dyeho., wareho., rooms over
and a hanging linney behind, brick, lath, plaster and slated £50; Uten-
sils and stk in trd. therein £50.

£400

83/113391

FORD, John, Sergemaker. 19 Sept. 1748
Dwho., stone, lath, cob and plaster and slated £200; Hshld gds and stk in trd. therein £100; Kitchen, cellar, offices and dyeho. with warerooms over and hanging linney adj. behind his dwho., stone, brick, cob, lath, plaster and slated £100; His gds and stk in trd therein £200.

£600

90/123713

FORD, John, Sergemaker. 22 Nov. 1750
Ho., stone, brick, plaster and slated, in tenure of Samuel Stevens, gent. £160; Outho. with chambers over, stone, brick, plaster and tiled £40.

£200

108/143513

FORD, John, Sergemaker. 7 Nov. 1754
Hshld gds in his dwho. stone, slated and timber.

£300

129/171703

FORD, John, Sergemaker. 24 Nov. 1759
Ho. in Preston Street, Exeter, in tenure of Thomas Bickford, tinker £40; Outhos and wareroom above £5; One ho., offices and rooms over, west of above, in tenure of Widow Fox £45; Outho. and room behind the above £10.

£100

157/213188

FORD, John, Sergemaker. 18 Oct. 1764
Ho. in tenure £200; Kitchen, cellars, offices, dyeho. with warerooms over and linney behind and adj. £100. All stone, brick, cob, lath, plaster and slated.

£300

151/203558

FRY, Thomas, Sergemaker. 18 Oct. 1763
Hshld gds, utensils and stk in trd. in his dwho., shops and woolchambers over all adj. each other, brick, lath, plaster and slated £400; On his ho. only used as a wareho. distant from aforesaid, stone, cob and thatched £200.

£600

176/247802

HILL, Thomas, Sergemaker. 28 July 1767
Hshld gds in his dwho. £50, brick and slated; Utensils and stk therein £50; Utensils and stk in his shop, worsted wareho. and rooms at the right of the entrance adj. separate from the ho., stone, brick and thatched £200.

£300

64/94737
HOLWORTHY, Archilaus, Sergemaker and 20 April 1743
 Shopkeeper.
Hshld gds and stk in trd. in his dwho., workshops and warerooms
under one roof, stone, cob, lath, plaster and slated.

£400

95/129163
HOOPER, William, Sergemaker. N.S. 29 Jan. 1752
Dwho., brick and slated £140; Hshld gds and stk in trd. therein £200;
Drying linney behind, brick, timber and slated £15; Gds and stk
therein £30; His other brick and slated ho. £60; Gds and stk therein
£55.

£500

152/208411
HOOPER, William, Sergemaker. 11 April 1764
Dwho., brick, tiled and slated £84; Hshld gds and stks therein £120;
Drying linney behind adj., brick and slated £9; Gds and stk therein
£18; Ho., brick and slated £36; Gds and stk therein £33; Ho. in tenure
of woolcomber, brick and slated £85; Brewho. behind the above, brick
and slated £15.

£400

62/91937
JEFFERY, Mary, Sergemaker and Shopkeeper. 9 July 1742
Hshld gds and stk in trd. in her dwho., brick and slated £200; Utensils
and stk in trd. in her warping chambers, shops, dyeho. and wareho., all
adj. each other, brick, timber and slated £100.

£300

53/81783
LANGDON, John, Sergemaker. 29 Sept. 1739
Cob and thatched dwho. £95; Stable and woodho., thatched £5; Five
hos, four occupied by four persons at £40, £25, £20, £5 and £10—
£100.

£200

178/250074
LUSCOMBE, Kellande, Sergemaker. 11 Nov. 1767
Hshld gds in one building, stone and slated £150; Utensils and stk
therein £150.

£300

157/215004
LUSCOMBE, Thomas, Sergemaker. 12 Dec. 1764
Dwho. and offices behind and adj., brick and slated £150; Hshld gds
and stk therein £250; Dyeho., combshops, cellars and wareho. adj.,
brick, timber and slated £110; Gds, utensils and stk therein £190.

£700

56/85715

LUSCOMBE, Thomas, Jnr., Sergemaker.   17 Oct. 1740
Dwho., brick and slated £90; Hshld gds and stk in trd. therein £100;
A small office only behind, brick and slated £10.

£200

81/109555

LUSCOMBE, Thomas, Jnr., Sergemaker.   24 Sept. 1747
Dwho., brick and slated £100; Hshld gds and stk therein £100; Small
office adj., brick and slated £20; Stk in trd. therein £80; A little combshop adj., brick, lath, plaster and tiled £10; Dyeho. and chamber over
it, brick, timber and tiled £40; Utensils and stk in trd. therein £50.

£400

95/129826

LUSCOMBE, Thomas, Jnr., Sergemaker.   N.S. 27 March 1752
Dwho., brick and slated £100; Hshld gds and stk in trd. therein £110;
Small offices adj., behind, brick, lath, plaster and tiled £30; Stk therein
£100; Dyeho., combshop, cellar and wareho. over adj., further back,
brick, timber and slated £110; Utensils and stk therein £150.

£600

56/85714

LUSCOMBE, Thomas, Snr., Sergemaker and   17 Oct. 1740
    Maltmaker.
Brick and slated dwho. £150; Hshld gds and stk therein £50; Brick,
lath, plaster and slated maltho. £100.

£300

91/122328

MANNING, Robert, Sergemaker.   14 Aug. 1750
Hshld gds and stk in trd. in his dwho., workshops and warerooms
under one roof, stone, timber and slated £500; Utensils and stk in trd.
in his yarnshop, on the left hand, stone, timber and slated £75; Utensils and stk in trd. in his dyeho., on the right hand, stone, timber and
slated £25; Ho. and maltho. in Stockland, Dorset, cob and thatched, in
tenure of John Galpin, schoolmaster £80; Stable and linney adj., stone,
cob and thatched £20.

£700

204/296659

MANNING, Robert, Sergemaker.   16 April 1771
Hshld gds in his dwho., workshops and warerooms under one roof,
stone, timber and tiled £110; Utensils and stk therein £360; Utensils
and stk in his yarn shop on the left hand behind, stone, timber and
slated £100; Utensils and stk in his dyeho. on the right hand £20;
Utensils and stk in his new built warehos adj. at bottom of the court,
brick built nogging and tiled £200; Little stable in the court, slated
£10; Utensils, stk and gds in trust or on commission in ho. consisting

of two under rooms, cellar and three chambers, stone, cob, lath, slated and plaster £225; Ho. in two tenements and linneys adj. in tenure in Stockland (Dorset), stone, cob and thatched. £75.

£1,100

63/92402
ROWDEN, William, Fuller and Vintner.   9 Sept. 1742
Stk in his dwho. £20; Stk and utensils in his pressho. and offices near, brick, timber and slated £20, the above the lands of Mrs. Ann Seth; Utensils and stk in trd. in his dwho. and pressho., under one roof, fronting the street, the land of Mr. Brown, and hshld gds therein £60; Ho. in Exeter in tenure of Elizabeth Bung, widow, stone, timber and slated £100.

£200

67/96868
ROWDEN, William, Fuller.   2 Nov. 1743
Stk in trd. and gds on commission in his dwho., brick, timber and tiled, the lands of Ann Seth £300; Stk in trd. and gds on commission in his dwho., the lands of Tobias Brown, brick, timber and slated £200.

£500

109/143748
SHEPHARD, Frederick, Pressman and Tucker.   21 Nov. 1754
Utensils and stk in trd. and gds on trust in his mother's dwho. £200; Utensils, stk and gds in his press shop and offices £250; Utensils, stk and gds in his packing rooms £50.

£500

103/137988
SPARKS, Joseph, Sergemaker.   12 Oct. 1753
Buildings, two tenements under one roof in the tenure of Peter Stocker, grazier and [ ] Bond, woolcomber, stone, cob and slated £200; Range of offices on the right hand behind, thatched £5; Linney on the left hand, slated £5; Linney on the left hand of Bond's tene-ment, thatched £5; Linney further back, thatched £2. 10s. 0d.; Tenement in tenure of John Bayley and others, stone, cob and thatched £100; Hot shop and offices under one roof and adj. the tenure of Joshua Williams, sergemaker and Widow Splatt, stone, cob slated and thatched £167 10s. 0d. Range of offices on the left hand behind the above, thatched £10; Open dyehos and offices adj. on the right hand £5.

£500

48/75377
TROTT, John, Sergemaker.   23 Nov. 1737
Dwho., cob, nogging and thatched £170; The dyeho. behind, cob and thatched £30.

£200

68/97996
TROTT, John, Sergemaker.   8 Feb. 1743
Ho. divided into tenements, brick, timber and thatched £170; A range
of linneys and outhos under one roof, thatched £30.

£200

162/222728
WESTCOTT, Robert, Sergemaker.   26 July 1765
Hshld gds and stk in his dwho. and shops under one roof, brick and
thatched £180; Wearing apparel therein £20.

£200

103/137989
WILLIAMS, Joshua, Sergemaker.   14 Oct. 1753
Hshld gds and stk in trd. in his dwho., shops and offices under one roof
and adj., stone, cob, slated and thatched.

£200

SAMPFORD PEVERELL

135/179442
DICKINSON, Henry, Sergemaker.   19 Dec. 1760
Hshld gds, utensils and stk in his dwho. and offices adj., stone, cob and
thatched.

£300

168/233253
DICKINSON, Henry, Sergemaker.   29 April 1766
Hshld gds in his dwho. £50; Utensils and stk therein £150; Ho. known
as New Inn in tenure £60; Stable, strawho., hogsty, linney adj. £10;
Ho. opposite in tenure £30; Ho. in Uplowman known as Wood Farm
in tenure £60; Double barn, poundho. and linney adj. £40. Stone, cob
and thatched.

£400

SANDFORD

143/191119
BAKER, Mary, Sergemaker.   19 July 1762
Dwho. and offices adj. £70; Hshld gds and stk therein £30; Three tenements and adj. outhos in tenure of John Baring and others £85; Barn
£10; Two additional outhos £5.

£200

148/200842
BROWNE, Samuel, Sergemaker and Shopkeeper.   15 July 1763
Dwho., stable and offices adj. £95; Hshld gds and stk therein £100;
Chain linneys in the same land £5; Seven tenements under one roof,

linney and outhos behind and adj. in tenure £170; Tenements and linney adj. in tenure £30; All stone, cob and thatched.

£100

69/98401

ELLACOTT, Robert, Sergemaker and Shopkeeper.   22 March 1743
Hshld gds and stk in trd. in his dwho., stone, cob and thatched £150;
Stk in trd. in his wareho. and chambers over, stone, cob and thatched
£250; Two stone, cob and thatched tenements in tenures of two
weavers, one at £70, one at £30, £100.

£500

76/105248

ELLACOTT, Robert, Sergemaker.   13 June 1746
Ho. in the West town of Crediton, in tenure of Mary Bolt, ironmonger
and shopkeeper, brick and slated.

£200

89/120926

REEVE, John, Sergemaker.   14 April 1750
Ho. in the West town of Crediton in two tenements in tenures of
Samuel Dyer, sergemaker, and Robert Prickman, sergeweaver, stone,
cob and thatched.

£100

54/83883

SMALE, Augustin, Sergemaker.   29 April 1740
Ho. divided into tenements in tenures of himself and others, cob and
thatched £100; Hshld gds and stk in trd. in his part of the ho. £150;
One ho. in tenements, cob and thatched £50.

£300

115/151704

TUCKER, Robert, Sergemaker.   1 April 1756
Dwho. £30; Ho. in two tenements in the West town of Crediton in
tenure £70. Stone, cob and thatched.

£100

132/174821

VICARY, James, Sergemaker.   8 April 1760
Dwho., shops and offices adj. £150; Two tenements near adj. in tenure
of two persons £50. Stone, cob and thatched

£200

148/200128

VICARY, Richard, Sergemaker.   28 June 1763
Intended dwho., workshops under one roof and chain linney adj. not
finished £150; One ho. and weaving shop adj. near the above in tenure
£50. Stone, cob and thatched.

£200

SHEEPWASH

139/184740
ROBBINS, John, Yarn Jobber.   23 Sept. 1761
Intended dwho., stone and slated £200; Stk in warerooms in dwho. only
of the Angel Inn, Crediton £100.

£300

SILVERTON

78/107565
BROADMEAD, Philip, Sergemaker.   10 Feb. 1746
Dwho. and offices under one roof, stone, cob and thatched £160;
Dyeho., stable, linney and combshop under one roof, stone, cob and
thatched £40.

£200

132/176910
CHALLICE, Richard, Sergemaker.   18 July 1760
Hshld gds and stk in his dwho., combshop and offices adj., stone, cob
and thatched.

£100

60/89040
KINGDON, William, Sergemaker.   6 Oct. 1741
Dwho. £70; Combshop and chambers over £10; His stable and loft
over £10; A linney £10.

£100

105/139382
PETERS, William, Sergemaker.   16 Jan. 1754
Hshld gds, utensils and stk in trd. in his dwho., shop and offices adj.,
stone, cob and thatched.

£200

SOUTH MOLTON

135/179954
JONES, John, Woolstapler.   9 Jan. 1761
Hshld gds and stk in trd. in his dwho. adj. to the schoolho., stone,
slated and thatched £80; Stk in his wareroom in a ho. behind the
aforesaid, stone and thatched £20.

£100

167/230686
BISHOP, Thomas, Sergemaker.   4 Feb. 1766
Dwho., offices and stable, stone, cob, slated and thatched £200; Hshld
gds, utensils and stk therein £100.

£300

96/131220

DUNN, Michael, Sergemaker.　　　　　　　N.S. 2 July 1752
Dwho., brewho., shop, woodho., hayho., two stables and outhos, all adj.,
stone, cob and thatched £100; Hshld gds and stk in trd. therein £100.

£200

137/183429

TAPP, Philip, Sergemaker.　　　　　　　　3 July 1761
Dwho., offices and stable adj., stone, cob and slated, tiled and thatched
£100; Hshld gds therein £100.

£200

137/183577

TAPP, Philip Jnr., Sergemaker.　　　　　　8 July 1761
Dwho., trading shop, stable and linneys adj., stone, cob, slated and
thatched £80; Hshld gds and stk therein £100; Weaving shop in the
court, thatched £20.

£200

138/184008

WIDGERY, Philip, Sergemaker.　　　　　　28 July 1761
Dwho., offices, stable adj. £54; Hshld gds and stk therein £100; Tenement near the above in his own possession £15; Hshld gds and stk
therein £30; Woodho. £1.

£200

130/171936

JONES, John, Yarn Jobber.　　　　　　　7 Dec. 1759
Dwho., outho., stable and garret over, cob and thatched.

£200

TAVISTOCK

178/249638

WINDEATH, Thomas Jnr., Fellmonger and　　　7 Oct. 1767
　　Sergemaker.
Hshld gds in his dwho., lofts, stables and outhos adj., stone, brick, lath,
plaster and slated £60; Utensils and stk not hazardous therein £440.

£500

141/187511

BOND, John, Sergemaker.　　　　　　　28 Jan. 1762
Ho., offices, stables adj. in Launceston in tenure to innholder, stone,
thatched.

£100

125/165215

GARLAND, John, LANG, Roger and　　　　20 Oct. 1758
　　PRIDEAUX, John, Sergemakers.
Ho. in West Street, timber and slated £200; Stk therein £100.

£300

130/172603
LANG, Roger, Sergemaker. 4 Jan. 1759
Ho. in Plympton [St] Maurice Devon in tenure of widow, stone and
slated £100; Barn near ho., stone and slated £100; Pound ho. adj. ho.,
stone, timber and part thatched £100; Hazardous gds in ho. in tenure
of his son, stone and slated £200.

£500

137/180684
PARSONS, Thomas, Sergemaker. 11 Feb. 1761
Dwho., warerooms and working room under one roof, stone, timber and
slated.

£300

120/158346
PADDON, David, Clothier. 13 July 1757
Ho. in tenements in tenure, dyeho. in tenure of Thomas Parsons,
Clothier and offices adj., stone, timber and slated £350; Stable and room
over at the end of the yard, slated £50.

£400

THORVERTON

122/161859
KINGDON, Samuel, Sergemaker. 29 March 1758
Hshld gds and stk in his dwho. and office adj. £200; Ho., cellar and
office adj. called *Gillotts Hays* in tenure of John Pitts, farmer £100;
Pound engines, pound hos and mill therein £30; Pigs loose, stables,
linney, barn, hanging linney and strawho. and linney adj. in a court
fronting the dwho. £60; Barn, hanging linney and cellars adj. in Tan
yard £10. Stone, cob and thatched, all in Thorverton.

£400

39/61202
KINGDON, Zachariah, Sergemaker. 30 June 1733
Dwho., thatched £100; Hshld gds and stk in trd. therein £100; Stk in
trd. in one ho. adj. his dwho., thatched £100.

£300

72/102787
KINGDON, Zachariah, Sergemaker. 4 July 1745
Dwho., stone, cob, brick and thatched £100; Hshld gds and stk in trd.
therein £150; Ho. adj., part in his own occupation and part in occupation of Samuel Kingdon and John Head £100; His hshld gds and stk
in trd. therein £150.

£500

103/136891
KINGDON, Zachary, Sergemaker. 1 Aug. 1753
Ho. in tenements, stable, barns, poundhos and linneys under one roof.
Stone, cob and thatched.

£300

162/223940
MARSHALL, Thomas, Sergemaker.   27 Aug. 1765
Dwho., cellar and workshop, thatched £60; Hshld gds and stk therein
£20; One tenement, thatched £20.

£100

133/175021
MILFORD, John, Sergemaker.   17 April 1760
Ho. in tenure of husbandman, shops, cellars, wareroom, offices adj.
£200; Hshld gds and stks therein £100; Large linney near the above
£10; Stable, tallet over, barn, poundho., pound chamber, pound and
engine therein £40; Small ho. £5; Dyeho., vats and furnaces therein
£20; Small ho. near dyeho. £5; Ho. in tenure £20. Stone, cob and
thatched.

£400

67/96152
TURNER, Abraham, Sergemaker.   14 Sept. 1743
Dwho., stone, cob and thatched £145; Cellar, combshop and stable
with wool chambers and tallets over, thatched £10; Thatched barn
£15; Stone and thatched ho. nearby, in tenure of William Baker, woolcomber £30.

£200

TIVERTON

55/83645
OSMOND, George, Esquire.   11 April 1740
Stk in trd. in the dwho. and workshop of Thomas Davey £500; Stk in
trd. in the dwho. and workshop of Widow Cornish £600; Stk in trd.
in the dwho. and workshop of John Harris £1,000; Stk in trd. in the
dwho. and workshop of William Pitt £600; Stk in trd. in the dwho.
and workshop of John Davey £700; Stk in trd. in the dwho. and workshop of William Badcock £600; Stk in trd. in the dwho. and workshop
of William Sanders £600; Stk in trd. in dwho. and workshop of John
Grovier £600; Stk in trd. in dwho. and workshop and linney of Samuel
Var £800; Stk in trd. in dwho. and workshop and two linneys behind
John Daveys £100.

£6,100

71/100568
PEARD, Oliver, Merchant and Clothier.   29 Oct. 1744
Foreho., part stone, brick, timber and slated £300; Stk therein £1,900;
Dwho. part timber and slated £200; Hshld gds therein £100; West
workho., brick, stone, cob, mud and slated £200; Utensils and stk
therein £600; East workho., brick, stone, cob, mud and slated £200;
Utensils and stk in trd. therein £1,900.

£5,400

171/238684

PEARD and DICKENSON, Merchants.   23 Oct. 1766

Utensils and stk not hazardous in wareho., stone, brick and timber £1,500; In East wareho., brick, stone cob and slated £3,000; In finishing shop, separate, timber and slated £500.

£5,000

176/248277

SMALE, William, Tiverton.   18 Aug. 1767

BARING, John, Esquire, and Charles, Exeter.

Six hos and offices in Fore Street, Tiverton in tenure of William Smale, brick and slated £500; Hshld gds therein £100; Utensils and stk therein £900; Open linney standing on timber posts, back parts cob, walls covered with pantiles, wash-hos, rooms over, offices and stables adj. on the left hand behind above, stone, brick, cob, lath, plaster and slated £100; Utensils and stk therein £100; The Folly in the middle of Fore Street, lath, plaster and slated £300; Three tenements under one roof in Bampton Street now or late in tenure of a perukemaker, husbandman, and a gent, brick and slated £300; Ho. in St. Andrews Street in tenure of comber and others, stone, cob and thatched £50; Hos, offices, outhos, poundhos, pound engine and press therein called Lythycourt, two miles from town, in tenure of farmer, stone, cob and thatched £100; Double barns thatched £50; Linneys, outhos and stables adj. thatched £50; Ho., malthos, offices, stables and linney adj. called Middlemarsh, quarter mile from above, in tenure, stone, cob and thatched, £50; Ho., offices and stable adj. Bolham Inn in tenure of victualler, stone, cob and thatched £50; Stk in barn called Kings or Castle Barn on Collipriest Barton, stone, cob and thatched £25; Stk in the mowplot near £25; All in Tiverton. Hos formerly in tenements in Witheridge; Stayhos and offices adj. in tenure of innholder, stone cob and thatched £50; Stk in barn and linney adj. called Week House in parish of Winkleigh £50; stone, cob and thatched: Brick and stacks in the mowplot on the premises being the tythes of the parish £100. Sole property of William Smale. Joint property of utensils and stks in Folly above £3,000.

£5,900

227/331744

SMALE, William, Snr. and Jnr., Tiverton.   20 Oct. 1774

BARING, John and Charles, Exeter. Merchants.

Ho. in Fore Street, Tiverton £350; Hshld gds £150; Utensils and stk therein £750; Open linney, wash-ho., rooms over, offices and stables on the left hand behind above £100; Utensils and stk therein £75; Utensils and stk in yard £25; Folly in middle of Fore Street £250; Three tenements in Bampton Street in tenure £200; Ho. in St. Andrews Street in tenure £50; Ho. and new linney £100; Millho. with running tackle and materials in West Exe £50; Range of tenements in Hammetts Lane £50; Grist Mill ho., and mill ho., running tackle and materials at bottom of Hammetts Lane £125; Dyeho. for shelling oats

£25; Tenements adj. near Bolham £80; Hos in Bolham formerly Bolham Inn £50; Hayho. and offices in Witheridge £50; Utensils and stk
in barn at Weekhouse £35; Stack of corn and hay £25; Utensils and
stk in Folly, joint property £1,500; Utensils and stk in tenement in
Bolham £275; Utensils and stk in Mill Ho. in West Exe £25.

£4,300

177/246848

ACKLAND, William, Sergemaker.   1 July 1767
Hshld gds in dwho., woodho., warping shop, dyeho. and wool chamber
adj. £50; Utensils and stk therein £250. Stone, cob and thatched.

£300

53/79706

ALLISTONE, Robert, Sergemaker.   1 Feb. 1738
Hshld gds and stk in trd. in his dwho.* £180; Stk in trd. in his comb
shop behind the above, lath, plaster and thatched £10; Utensils and
stk in trd. in his dyeho. and linney under one roof £10.

£200

* On the Leat.

43/67975

ASHLEY, Henry, Sergemaker.   2 Sept. 1735
Hshld gds and stk in trd. in his dwho. and wareho. adj. together, brick,
plaster, tiled, slated and thatched. In Newport St.

£200

50/78951

ASHLEY, Lewis, Sergemaker.   23 Nov. 1738
Hshld gds and stk in trd. in his thatched dwho. £100; Utensils and
stk in trd. in a range of thatched buildings behind the dwho. £100.
In West Exe on the Leat.

£200

204/295251

BESLEY, Bernard, Sergemaker.   12 March 1771
Hshld gds in his dwho. and offices, warerooms, combshop and dyeho.
adj., brick, lath and plaster £100; Utensils and stk therein £200.

£300

35/55112

BESLEY, John, Sergemaker.   24 July 1731
Dwho., part thatched/tiled £300; Backho. and outhos adj. £200.

£500

37/58350

BESLEY, John, Sergemaker.   13 July 1732
Dwho., part thatched £250; The outhos thereto belonging £100; Three
small tenements adj., £50 on each, £150.

£500

152/207217
BESLY, Bernard, Sergemaker.   28 Feb. 1764
Hshld gds and stk in his dwho., workho. and rooms under one roof on
the left hand behind Bampton Street, stone, cob, slated and thatched.
£300

158/215768
BESLY, Francis, Sergemaker.   4 Jan. 1765
Intended dwho. in Bampton Street, stone, lath, plaster and slated £200;
Hshld gds and stk therein £100; Office, open dyeho. slated, wareho.,
shops, room over and linney adj. behind the above, stone, cob and
thatched £100; Gds, utensils and stk therein £100.
£500

98/133946
BESLY, John, Sergemaker and Dyer.   11 Jan. 1753
Dwho. and two tenements adj. in his own tenure and of Samuel Whit-
ney, comber £250; His hshld gds and stk in trd. therein £200; Dyeho.
and offices adj., brick, timber and slated £50.
£500

140/186933
BESLY, John, Sergemaker and Dyer.   7 Jan. 1762
Dwho. and two adj. tenements in own occupation, brick and slated
£300; Hshld gds, stk in trd. and gds in trust therein £350; Dyeho. and
adj. offices behind, brick, timber and slated £50.
£700

68/97518
BESLY, William, Sergemaker.   5 Jan. 1743
Dwho., offices, dyeho., stable and linney under one roof, stone, cob,
thatched and slated £250; Hshld gds and stk in trd. therein £150;
Three tenements under one roof, in tenures of Andrew Heard, comber,
Nicholas Chappell, woolcomber and Mrs. Besley, brick, cob and
thatched £100.
£500

46/73804
BIDGOOD, John, Sergemaker.   24 June 1737
Brick, cob, lath, plaster and thatched:—Dwho.* £100; A dyeho.,
comb shop and chamber over, adj. his dwho. £20; Two tenements in
tenures of Samuel Rice and John Richards, combers, £40 on each £80.

  * In West Exe.   £200

198/287065
BIDGOOD, John, Sergemaker.   11 July 1770
Ho. and stable adj. in High Street in tenure, brick, cob, timber and
slated £200; Hshld gds in dwho. adj., stone, cob and thatched £100;
Utensils and stk therein £100.
£400

88/119546
BIDGOOD, Thomas, Sergemaker.   12 Jan. 1749
Hshld gds, utensils and stk in trd. in his dwho., wareho., wool chambers and dyeho. adj. in West Exe, stone, cob and thatched.

£200

120/158276
BIDGOOD, Thomas, Sergemaker.   7 July 1757
Dwho. and woodho. under one roof in West Exe £150; Hshld gds and stk in trd. therein £150; Warping shop, dyeho. and wool chamber adj. £20; Hshld gds, utensils and stk therein £80; Five tenements under one roof in tenure £100. Stone, cob and thatched.

£500

176/246628
BIDGOOD, Thomas, Sergemaker.   23 June 1767
Dwho. in [St] Peter Street, Tiverton £250; Hshld gds therein £100; Utensils and stk therein £100; Wearing apparel therein £30; Dyeho. £20. All brick and slated.

£500

198/287595
BIDGOOD, Thomas, Sergemaker.   31 July 1770
In trust for Thomasin Down, shopkeeper. Hshld gds in dwho. of Down in West Exe, stone, cob and thatched £40; Utensils and stk therein £260.

£300

41/63823
BLAGDON, Leonard, Sergemaker.   28 May 1734
Dwho. with his warehos under the same roof £190; Hshld gds and stk in trd. therein £250; Dyeho. adj. £10; Two tenements in tenures of John Beere and Samuel Dunn, wool-combers, £25 on each £50. Part slated, part thatched.

£500

45/70456
BLAGDON, Leonard, Sergemaker.   1 June 1736
Dwho., stone, cob and thatched, in occupation of Edward Samon, husbandman, in Bolham £120; Barn £40; Poundho. £20; Shop adj. £10; Cowho. adj. £10.

£200

34/57041
BOWERMAN, John, Sergemaker.   10 Feb. 1731
Dwho. and maltho. under one roof, cob and thatched £150; Hshld gds and stk in trd. therein £50.

£200

37/60234
BOWERMAN, John, Sergemaker.   20 March 1732
Dwho. £50; Hshld gds and stk in trd. therein £25; Maltho. £20; Utensils and stk therein £25; One ho. in occupation of Thomas Hatsell, baker, £40; One ho. in occupation of Widow Gover £40. All thatched.

£200

53/81483
BOWERMAN, John, Sergemaker.   7 Aug. 1739
Dwho.* £60; Hshld gds and stk in trd. therein £50; Dyeho., workshop and chambers over £30; Cellar and woodho. only £10; Four hos, £40, £40, £20, £50=£150.

£300

* In West Exe.

44/70335
BRUSHFORD, Robert, Sergemaker.   18 May 1736
Plaster and thatched ho. in tenure of John Blacknall only, a clothier.

£100

54/82266
BRUSHFORD, Robert, Sergemaker.   8 Nov. 1739
Ho. in tenure of John Blacknall, clothier, £60; Ho. in tenure of Henry Lake, sergemaker £40.

£100

55/83650
BRUSHFORD, Robert, Sergemaker.   11 April 1740
Two hos in tenures of John Blacknall, clothier and Henry Lake, sergemaker, £30 on each, thatched £60; His ho. in tenure of tailor £40.

£100

85/115961
BRUSHFORD, Robert, Sergemaker.   6 April 1749
Two hos in tenures, £30 on each £60; Dwho. and maltho. adj. £60; Hshld gds, utensils and stk in trd. therein £80.

£200

153/209046
BURGES, George, Sergemaker.   15 May 1764
Dwho. and outhos adj. on the left hand behind in West Exe, stone, cob and thatched £150; Hshld gds and stk therein £50; Dyeho., combshop, maltho. and gateway on the left hand behind the above, slated and thatched and stable on the right hand, thatched, all adj. £50; Gds, utensils and stk therein £50.

£300

65/94596
BURGESS, George, Sergemaker.   7 April 1743

Hshld gds and stk in trd. in his dwho. and offices adj.,* stone, part timber, slated £150; Stk in his maltho. adj., stone and slated £50.

£200

* In Peter St.

148/202489
CARTER, Samuel, Sergemaker.   13 Sept. 1763
Five tenements under one roof or adj. in Barrington Street in tenure. Stone, cob and thatched.

£100

158/216831
CARTER, Samuel Sergemaker.   6 Feb. 1765
Court lodge consisting of nine tenements called Luggs Court in tenure. Stone, cob, thatched and tiled.

£100

169/236000
CARTER, Samuel, Sergemaker.   30 July 1766
Three tenements under one roof in tenure of himself and others stone, cob and thatched £100; Hshld gds £20; Utensils and stk therein £80. In West Exe.

£200

152/207216
CHILCOT, William, Sergemaker.   28 Feb. 1764
Four tenements under one roof in Newport Street in tenure of woolcomber and others, brick, cob, slated and thatched £80; Four tenements under one roof and offices adj. in tenure of himself and others, brick, slated and tiled £100; Hshld gds and stk therein £100; Seven tenements under one roof in Frog Street in tenure of labourer and others, stone, cob and thatched £120.

£400

194/279304
CHILCOTT, William and BONDON, Roger,   3 Jan. 1770
    Sergemaker and Miller.
Two hos and stable adj. in Bampton Street in tenure, stone, brick, cob, slated and thatched.

£100

87/116985
COLE, Thomas, Sergemaker.   7 July 1749
Hshld gds and stk in trd in his dwho., dyeho., combshop and offices adj., stone, cob and thatched £150; Stk in trd. in a ground room, two chambers forward and one chamber backward in a vacant ho. adj. his dwho., stone, cob and thatched £50. In Peter St.

£200

78/108331
CORNISH, John, Sergemaker.   7 May 1747
Hshld gds, utensils and stk in trd. in his dwho., combshop and warp-
ing shop adj. called Coldharbour, stone, cob and thatched.
                                                       £200

114/151888
CRUWYS, George, Sergemaker.   8 April 1756
Hshld gds and stk in trd. in his dwho., warerooms, combshops and
offices adj. in Newport Street £100; Ho., stable, poundho., pound and
engine therein in tenure, barn and linney adj. called Cowley Moor in
tenure of farmer £90; Milkho., two cellars and chambers £10. All stone,
cob and thatched.
                                                       £200

134/178153
DUNSCOMBE, Manby, Sergemaker.   8 Oct. 1760
Dwho., maltho., backho., cellar and offices adj. late Bowerman at pre
sent empty £110; Two tenements under one roof or adj. vacant £40;
Hshld gds and stk in trd. in his dwho. and warerooms under one roof
late Mr. Govetts £150. Stone, cob and thatched.   £300

52/79659
DUNSFORD, Martin, Sergemaker.   26 Jan. 1738
Ho. and offices adj. under one roof, in his tenure and under two
tenants, cob and thatched £80; Hshld gds, utensils and stk in trd.
therein £100; Offices and workshops behind said ho., cob and thatched
£40; His utensils and stk in trd. therein £50; Thatched warehos behind
the same £20; His stk therein £10.   £300

59/87355
DUNSFORD, Martin, Sergemaker and Maltster.   10 April 1741
Dwho. and offices under one roof, stone, cob and thatched £140;
Apparel, hshld gds, utensils and stk in trd. therein £60; The maltho.
and offices under one roof, stone, plaster and thatched £40; Utensils
and stk therein £30; Tiled linney near £5; Utensils and stk in trd.
therein £10; Tiled wareho. behind the maltho. £10. In Bampton St.
                                                       £300

38/61678
DUNSFORD, Robert, Jnr., Sergemaker.   28 Aug. 1733
Hshld gds, utensils and stk in trd. in his dwho. and workhos adj.,
stone, part timber and plaster.   £600

39/61345
DUNSFORD, Robert, Jnr., Sergemaker.   11 July 1733
Hshld gds, utensils and stk in trd. in his dwho. and workhos, adj., part
brick, stone, timber and plaster, all slated and leaded. £600

93/127659
FINIMORE, Thomas, Sergemaker.   N.S. 10 Oct. 1751
Ho., maltho., cellars and offices adj.* in tenure of Robert Evans, stone,
cob and thatched £200; Barn, poundho. and reed ho. adj., thatched
£50; Barn, stable, hanging linney adj., thatched £50.

£300

* Called Fire Beacon.

85/115960
GILL, John, Sergemaker.   6 April 1749
Pound ho. and chamber over, stone cob and thatched £40; Pound mill
and stk therein £30; Cellar and chamber over, stone, cob and thatched
£10; Stk therein £20.

£100

88/120773
GILL, John, Sergemaker.   5 April 1750
Poundho., pound therein and chamber over £30; Gds and stk in trd.
therein £30; Cellar and chambers over £20; Gds and stk therein £20;
Utensils and stk in trd. in his dwho.* £80; Gds and stk in trd. in yarn
shop, comb shop and dyeho. under one roof £20. Stone, cob and
thatched.

£200

* In Newport St.

137/183568
GILL, John, Jnr., Sergemaker.   8 July 1761
Dwho., workhos, offices adj. and one tenement under the same roof in
St. Andrews Street in tenure £60; Hshld gds and stk in trd. therein
£60; Dyeho., maltho. and woodho. adj. £20; Gds and stk therein £20;
Four tenements adj. in West Exe in tenure £40. All stone, cob and
thatched.

£200

44/69036
GOVETT, Clement, Sergemaker as Mortgagee.   17 Dec. 1735
Four tenements, three in tenures of Richard Lidder, carpenter, Richard
Gibb, victualler and George Clark, tailor, fourth empty £170; Work-
shops and outhos behind the said tenements, tiled £30.

£200

52/80651
GOVETT, Clement, Sergemaker.   3 May 1739
Ho., barn and linney adj. under one roof* in his own tenure, thatched
£50; Stk in said barn and linney and hay and corn unthrashed £10;
Thatched ho. in tenure of shop-keeper £40; Thatched ho. in tenure of
three persons £100.

£200

* Called Middle Hill in Ashley Park.

76/106083
GOVETT, Clement, Sergemaker.   25 Sept. 1746
Two tenements, maltho., barns and stables under one roof and linneys adj. in Hockworthy, Devon, part in the tenure of David Tozer, yeoman, and part in his own tenure, stone, cob and thatched.
£200

35/55286
GOVETT, Clement, Sergemaker.   16 Aug. 1731
Dwho., cob and thatched £200; Hshld gds and stk in trd. therein £100; Four hos under one roof, £25 on each £100.
£400

52/79652
HODGE, Henry, Sergemaker.   25 Jan. 1738
Hshld gds and stk in trd. in his dwho. and offices under one roof, cob and thatched, forming a small court, in West Exe.
£200

173/241421
HODGE, Thomas, Sergemaker.   8 Jan. 1764
Dwho., workho. and dyeho. adj. £100; Hshld gds therein £50; Utensils and stk therein £200; Four tenements under one roof in tenure £50. Stone, cob and thatched, in West Exe.
£400

54/82267
HOW, Thomas, Sergemaker.   8 Nov. 1739
Dwho., burling shop and other offices under one roof, brick, cob and thatched. In Broad Lane and West Exe.
£200

55/83651
HOW, Thomas, Sergemaker.   11 April 1740
Dwho., burling shop and other offices under one roof, cob and thatched. In Broad Lane in West Exe.
£200

73/101936
HURFORD, John, Sergemaker.   2 April 1745
Hshld gds and stk in trd. in his dwho. only, stone, cob and thatched £100; Utensils and stk in trd. in his dyeho., combshop and warerooms over adj. each other, stone, brick and slated £100. In Newport St.
£200

100/136094
HURFORD, William, Sergemaker.   14 June 1753
Hshld gds and stk in trd. in his dwho. and offices adj.,* brick, stone, lath and plaster £200; Two tenements in tenures of two persons, £30
* In Bampton St.

on each £60; One tenement in tenure of Robert Currain, weaver, £20;
One tenement in tenure of a person £20. Stone, cob and thatched.

£300

163/223332
JENKINS, William, Sergemaker.   7 Aug. 1765
Hshld gds and stks in his dwho., workshops, woolchambers and dyeho.
adj. in [St] Peter Street, stone, brick, cob, slated and thatched.

£100

172/241845
JENKINS, William, Sergemaker.   16 Jan. 1767
Dwho., workshop and office adj., brick, slated and leaded £200; Hshld
gds £100; Utensils and stk £100. In Peter St.

£400

72/101442
LANE, Henry, Sergemaker.   6 Feb. 1744
Dwho.* £80; Hshld gds and stk in trd. therein £20; Linney and wool
chamber adj. £30; Utensils and stk in trd. therein £40; Outhos adj.
£10; Ho. in two tenements £20. All stone, cob and thatched.
   * In Castle [Frog] St.   £200

204/296082
LANE, John, Sergemaker.   2 April 1771
Dwho.* £80; Hshld gds therein £40; Utensils and stk therein £30;
Dryho., slated and wareho. adj. behind £20; Utensils and stk therein
£30; Linney at the bottom of the garden £10; Four tenements under
one roof, two of them fronting the street adj. his dwho. and two
behind in tenure £70; Two tenements under one roof behind the last
mentioned £20. Stone, cob and thatched.
   * In Castle [Frog] St.   £300

88/120274
LANE, Samuel, Sergemaker.   7 March 1749
Hshld gds and stk in trd. in his dwho., stone, cob and thatched £20;
Gds and stk in trd. in his wash-ho., wool chambers and yarn chambers
over and dyeho. adj., near the above, stone, cob and thatched £80.

£100

110/146710
LANE, Samuel, Sergemaker.   16 May 1755
Hshld gds and stk in trd. in dwho., stone, brick and slated, in a court
in Fore St.

£300

160/221658
LIDDON, William, Sergemaker.   8 July 1765
Two tenements in tenure of himself and a weaver £60; Hshld gds and

stk therein £20; Tenement in tenure £20. All stone, brick, cob and thatched.

£100

117/155144
8 Dec. 1756

LOCKE, John, Sergemaker and Victualler.
Ho. in the tenure of James Quick and Grace Crudge £100; Hshld gds and stk in trd. in his dwho. and brewho. adj. *known by the Lower Boat,* £100. Stone, brick, cob and thatched.

£200

41/63819
28 May 1734

MORGAN, Peter, Sergemaker.
Thatched dwho.* £200; Another ho. in occupation of William Morgan, sergemaker, part slated £100; Three thatched tenements in occupation of Roger Wheatton, John Stanway and John Wood, woolcombers £100; Another ho. in occupation of Mary Osmond, widow, £200.

£600

* In Peter St.

52/80144
25 March 1739

MORGAN, Peter, Sergemaker.
Tiled or thatched dwho. in a court in Peter St., in occupation of two persons £200; Cob, timber and slated ho. in his own tenure at the entrance of the court fronting the street, £200; Three thatched tenements on the other side of the way, one empty £100; *Rock Mills,* a stable adj. £70. *Rock Mill* tenement, thatched £30.

£600

50/78949
23 Nov. 1738

MORGAN, Thomas, Sergemaker.
Hshld gds and stk in trd. in his brick, lath and plaster dwho. £100; Stk in trd. in his workshop and wool chamber in his yard behind the dwho., thatched £100.

£200

170/238016
9 Oct. 1766

NANSTONE, Francis, Sergemaker.
Dwho. and office under one roof, stone, cob and thatched £50; Hshld gds £25; Utensils and stk £25. In St. Andrew's St.

£100

152/208412
11 April 1764

OWENS, John, Sergemaker.
Hshld gds and stk in his dwho. and dyeho. adj.,* stone, brick and slated £100; Utensils and stk in his workshop and warerooms a little distant from the above, stone, cob and slated £200.

£300

* In a court in Fore St.

204/296658
OWENS, John, Sergemaker.   16 April 1771
Hshld gds in his dwho. and dyeho. adj., stone, brick and slated £100;
Utensils and stk therein £50; Utensils and stk in his workshop and
warerooms over, stone, cob and slated £450.

£600

114/150622
PEARCE, Samuel, Sergemaker.   20 Jan. 1756
Buildings in Tiverton, stone, cob and thatched viz: The front tenement in tenure £30; The second tenement in tenure £20; The third
tenement in tenure £25; The back dwho. only in tenure £25; Five tenements adj. in tenure £100; Hshld gds and stk in trd. in his dwho. and
offices adj. £100. All in St. Andrew's St.

£300

119/155587
PEARSE, John, Sergemaker and Clothier.   15 Jan. 1757
Hshld gds and stk in dwho. and offices adj. St. Andrew Street, part
slated £150; Three tenements under one roof in tenure £50.

£200

104/139134
PEARSE, Samuel, Sergemaker.   3 Jan. 1750
Hshld gds and stk in trd. in his dwho. and offices adj. £150; Front tene-
ment in St. Andrews Street in tenure of William Shorland, scribler,
£30; Second tenement in tenure of Richard Davis, woolcomber £20;
Third tenement in tenure of John Burrington and Thomas Rendalls
£50; Ho. and office adj. in Dulverton, Somerset, in tenure of William
Poole £50.

£300

130/173363
PEARSE, Samuel, Sergemaker.   24 Jan. 1760
Buildings in St. Andrews Street, stone, cob and thatched. One tenement
in tenure of weaver £30; One tenement in tenure of woolcomber £20;
Two tenements in tenure of two persons, weavers, £50; Five tenements
in tenure of five persons £100.

£200

176/247280
PULLING, James, Sergemaker.   10 July 1767
A college of tenements adj. St. Andrew Street in tenure, stone, cob and
thatched.

£100

160/221656
RADDON, Francis, Sergemaker.   8 July 1765
Hshld gds and stk in his dwho. and warerooms in Bampton Street

£150; Hshld gds and stk in his combshops, wareho. and offices adj. behind the above £50. All brick, cob, tiled and thatched.

£200

117/154351
SALTER, William, Sergemaker.   29 Sept. 1756
A college of tenements forming a court in tenure on the Leet in West Exe £150; Two other tenements under one roof in tenure £50; Dwho. on the Leet £80; Combshop, chamber over, brewho. and dyeho. adj. £20; Dwho., cellar, brewho. and stable adj. in tenure £100. Stone, cob and thatched.

£400

44/70664
SAUNDERS, Samuel, Sergemaker.   26 June 1736
Ho., part in his own occupation and part in the occupation of Frances Ruddington, widow, stone, cob and thatched £80; Shop and chambers adj. £20. In St. Andrew's St.

£100

73/102513
SAUNDERS, Samuel, Sergemaker.   12 June 1745
Stone, cob and thatched ho. in tenure of himself and under tenants £80; shop and chambers over adj. £20. In St. Andrew's St.

£100

47/72282
SELDON, Anna, Widow and Sergemaker.   28 Dec. 1736
Dwho. and workhos adj., stone, brick, part slated/thatched £200; Her other dwho. nearby in trust for Elizabeth Wood, fuller £100. On the Leat.

£300

37/58643
SELDON, John, Sergemaker.   31 Aug. 1732
Dwho., stone, cob, brick, timber and part thatched £300; Hshld gds, stk in trd. therein £100. In West Exe on the Leat.

£400

117/154350
SHORLAND, Peter, Sergemaker.   15 Oct. 1756
A college of tenements under one roof forming a court in tenure on the Leet in West Exe £100; Dwho., maltho., combshop and chamber over the Leet £50; Hshld gds and stk in trd. therein £50.

£200

39/63429
THORNE, George, Sergemaker.   3 April 1734
Dwho., stone, timber and slated £80; Hshld gds and stk in trd. therein £50; Stable, brick, timber and tiled £20; Two hos adj., thatched, in

occupation of John Tucker and Nathaniel Stephens, woolcombers, £25 on each, £50. In Peter St. and Back Lane.

£200

97/130105
THORNE, George, Sergemaker and Vintner.   N.S. 9 April 1752
Dwho.,* stone, timber and slated £100; Hshld gds and stk in trd. therein £100; Two stone, cob and thatched hos adj. on the back, in tenures of two persons, £25 on each, £50; Three stone, cob and thatched tenements in the tenures of three persons £50.
    * In Peter St.

£300

49/75208
VOYSEY, John, Sergemaker.   3 Nov. 1737
Hshld gds, utensils, stk in trd. in his dwho., workshops and other offices, including his furnace at the end of the said building, part slated/thatched.

£200

117/154354
VOYSEY, John, Sergemaker.   15 Oct. 1756
Hshld gds and stk in trd. in his dwho., wareho., combshop and offices, dyeho., linney, all adj., stone, slated and thatched.

£200

35/55544
WARREN, John, Sergemaker.   14 Sept. 1731
Hshld gds, utensils and stk in trd. in his dwho.

£200

171/238414
WARREN, John, Sergemaker.   16 Oct. 1766
Dwho. adj., stone, cob and thatched £50; Two dwellings under one roof in tenure £50; Ho. and office adj. in tenure £100.

£200

134/178439
WARREN, Thomas, Sergemaker.   16 Oct. 1760
Dwho. and offices under one roof in St. Andrew's Street £60; Hshld gds and stk therein £38; Outho. in the garden £2; Five tenements under one roof adj. in the tenure of Laurance Richards weaver and others £85; One tenement opposite the above in the tenure of Samuel Laryon, weaver £15.

£200

46/71652
WEBBER, John, Sergemaker.   12 Oct. 1736
Stone, brick, cob and slated dwho. in his and his son's occupation £200; Cob and thatched workho. and cellars, behind the dwho., in occupation of his son John £50; One thatched dwho. in occupation of

several persons £100; Three tenements under one roof in occupation of several persons £100; Another thatched ho. in occupation of one person £20; Another thatched ho. in occupation of several persons £30.

£500

49/75203
WEBBER, John, Sergemaker. 3 Nov. 1737
Stone, brick, nogging and slated dwho.* £150; One thatched ho. and offices above in his own and his daughter's tenure £100; One thatched ho. in tenure of three persons £100; Three tenements under one roof, in tenure of three persons £100; Thatched dwho. in tenure of one person £20; Thatched dwho. in tenure of three persons £30.

£500

* In Bampton St.

35/55215
WEBBER, John, Snr., Sergemaker. 6 Aug. 1731
Dwho. part in his son John's tenure, cob and slated £60;Workhos. in John's tenure, cob and thatched £50; Cob and thatched ho. in tenure of John Stevens, weaver, £20; One ho. in tenure of three persons, brick, cob, slated and thatched, £70.

£200

39/61949
WEBBER, John, Snr., Sergemaker. 4 Oct. 1733
Thatched dwho. in occupation of Abel Drew, weaver, £70; One other thatched tenement in occupation of John Farmer, blacksmith £30.

£100

168/234577
WILLIAMS, John, Sergemaker. 18 June 1766
Dwho. in Elmore, Tiverton £40; Hshld gds therein £10; Utensils and stk therein £20; Ho. in Elmore in the tenure of a weaver £30. Stone, cob and thatched.

£100

49/75202
WOODWARD, Daniel, Sergemaker. 3 Nov. 1737
Hshld gds, stk in trd. in his dwho., workshop and wareho. all adj. behind ho. in Castle [Frog] St.

£200

50/78950
WOODWARD, Daniel, Sergemaker. 23 Nov. 1738
Hshld gds and stk in trd. in his dwho., wareho. and workshop adj., brick, timber and slated. In Peter St.

£300

52/80650
WOODWARD, Daniel, Sergemaker. 3 May 1739
Ho. in Bampton, Devon, in tenure of William Brand, apothecary,

stone and thatched £130; Stable and linney behind the same, thatched £20; Two hos in tenures of two persons £50.

£200

99/113729

ZELLY, Robert, Sergemaker.   12 Oct. 1748
Hshld gds and stk in trd. in his dwho. and offices* £100; Stk in his warerooms adj. £50; Four tenements in tenures of four persons in Cocks Court, stone, cob and thatched £40.

* In Castle [Frog] St.   £200

99/132537

ZELLY, Robert, Sergemaker.   N.S. 12 Oct. 1752
Hshld gds and stk in trd. in his dwho., stone, cob and thatched and tiled £50; Gds and stk in trd. in his back kitchen and rooms over dyeho. opposite, combshop and warerooms over adj., brick, lath, plaster and slated £200; Four tenements adj. in tenures of four persons £50. In West Exe.

£300

143/192301

ZELLY, Robert, Sergemaker.   7 Sept. 1762
Hshld gds and stk in dwho., stone, cob and thatched £100; Gds and stk in back kitchen and rooms over dyeho. opposite, combshop and warerooms over, brick, lath, plaster and slated £400; Four adj. tenements, stone, cob and thatched £50; Four adj. tenements, stone slated and thatched £50. In West Exe.

£600

38/62183

PEARD, Oliver, Clothier.   23 Oct. 1733
Foreho. occupied by several persons £300; Stable and pumpho. adj. £20; Dwho., part timber and slated £200; Hshld gds therein £50; Stone; cob, mud, brick and slated woolho. on the west side of the court £200; Utensils and stk in trd. therein £600; Brick, stone, mud and tiled sergeho. on the east side of the court £180; Utensils and stk in trd. therein £350.

£1,900

34/56212

PEARSE, John, Clothier.   3 Nov. 1731
Dwho., cob and thatched £50; Ho., workshops and stable all adj. behind his dwho. £50.

£100

56/84670

PEARSE, Peter, Clothier.   4 July 1740
Dwho., stone, cob and thatched £80; Tenement £20. In St. Andrew's St.

£100

117/154352
PEARSE, Peter, Clothier.   15 Oct. 1756
Dwho. near Little Silver Bridge £80; Tenement in tenure of William
Bowden £20; One ho. in the parish of Talaton in tenure £50; Barn
and outhos adj. £20; Stable, shop, large linney adj. £30. All stone, cob
and thatched.

£200

97/130246
CORNISH, Thomas, Fuller.   N.S. 14 April 1752
Hshld gds, stk in trd. and gds on trust in his dwho. and workshop
under one roof, stone, cob and thatched. In West Exe.

£200

115/150813
CORNISH, Thomas, Fuller.   3 Feb. 1756
Hshld gds and utensils and stk in trd. and gds in trust and on commission in his dwho., shops and chambers and offices under one roof,
stone, cob and thatched, on the Leat in West Exe.

£600

36/58178
CORSWAY, Thomas, Fuller.   26 June 1732
Gds in trust in his new dwho. and workhos adj., thatched £200; Gds
in trust in a millho. 40 yards from the ho. £50; Hshld gds and utensils
in his above dwho. and workhos £50.

£300

43/68322
CORSWAY, Thomas, Fuller.   6 Oct. 1735
Dwho. and fulling mills at Bolham, thatched £150; Gds in trust therein
£200; Hshld gds therein £50.

£400

68/97439
COSSWAY, Thomas, Fuller.   29 Dec. 1743
Hshld gds in his dwho., thatched £50; Gds in trust in his dwho. and
shop, under one roof £300; Gds in trust in his fulling mill, thatched
£50.

£400

83/111921
COSWAY, Thomas, Fuller.   22 April 1748
Ho. and shippen adj. in Broadhembury, Devon, in tenure of Nicholas
Ellis, stone, cob and thatched £130; A barn and stable adj. £50;
Bakeho. £20.

£200

115/150802
COSWAY, Thomas, Fuller.   3 Feb. 1756
Hshld gds, utensils, stk in trd. and gds in trust and on commission in

his dwho., working rooms and offices adj., stone, cob and thatched, at Bolham.

£500

128/170850

COSWAY, Thomas, Fuller.　　　13 Oct. 1758

Hshld gds, stk and gds in trust or on commission in his dwho., brick and slated £225; Gds and stk and goods in trust or on commission in his workshop and rooms £75; Gds and stk and gds in trust or on commission in millho., thatched £100. All at Bolham.

£400

115/150806

DAVEY, Elizabeth, Fuller.　　　3 Feb. 1756

Dwho. and working rooms and offices adj. £150; Hshld gds, utensils and stk in trd. and gds in trust and on commission therein £400; Two linneys and outhos adj. behind the above £15; Stk and gds in trust and on commission therein £35. All stone, cob and thatched, in West Exe.

£600

49/75204

DAVEY, John, Fuller.　　　3 Nov. 1737

Thatched dwho. £100; Hshld gds and stk in trd. therein £200. In West Exe.

£300

52/79656

DAVEY, John, Fuller.　　　25 Jan. 1738

Dwho., stone, cob and thatched £150; Hshld gds therein £50.

£200

121/159635

DAVEY, John, Fuller.　　　20 Oct. 1757

Dwho., working rooms, offices, outhos and linneys, stone, cob and thatched £200; Hshld gds utensils and stk in trd. and gds in trust therein £400. In West Exe.

£600

74/103650

DAVEY, Thomas, Fuller.　　　16 Oct. 1745

Dwho.* and offices under one roof, stone, cob and thatched £100; Hshld gds and stk in trd. therein £50; Two stone, cob and thatched tenements in tenure of Thomas Pitt, fuller, and another £100; Three stone, cob and thatched tenements £50.

£300

* In Broad Lane in West Exe.

115/150807

DAVEY, Thomas, Fuller.　　　3 Feb. 1756

Dwho. and working rooms, offices, outhos and linneys adj. £100; Hshld gds, utensils and stk in trd. and gds in trust and on commission therein £400; Four tenements under one roof in tenure and two vacant £100. All stone, cob and thatched, in West Exe.

£600

42/66861
GALE, Simon, Fuller.   23 April 1735
Dwho.,* thatched £80; Hshld gds and stk in trd. therein £100; Two thatched stables, one behind the other £20; Three thatched hos divided into seven tenements £200.

£400

* In West Exe.

174/244255
GILBERT, George, Fuller.   2 April 1767
Hshld gds in two tenements and workshops and drying linneys in West Lane, stone, cob and thatched £100; Stk and gds on trust therein £300.

£400

83/111807
GILBERT, Richard, Fuller.   15 April 1748
Hshld gds, utensils, stk in trd. and gds on trust in his dwho. and workshops adj., under one roof in West Exe, stone, cob and thatched, in West Exe.

£300

115/150805
GORTON, David, Fuller.   3 Feb. 1756
Hshld gds in trust and on commission in his dwho., workshops and rooms over, part slated £500; Millho. and mills therein £50; Stk and gds in trust and on commission therein. All stone, cob and thatched.

£600

63/92937
GORTON, William, Fuller.   22 Oct. 1742
Dwho.* and workshops under one roof, stone, brick, slated and thatched £100; Hshld gds, utensils and stk in trd. therein £100; Ho., maltho. and adj. offices in tenure of George Burges, maltster and serge-maker, brick, stone and slated £200.
* In West Exe.

£400

101/135788
GORTON, William, Fuller.   18 May 1753
Dwho.,* stone, lath, plaster and slated £100; Malthos and offices to right, left and behind dwho., small part lath and plastered and stone and slated and a linney and stable adj., thatched, office £100; Gds and stk in trd. £100; Ho. and workshops under one roof in tenure of David Gorton, fuller, £100.

* In Peter St.   £400

38/61770
HARRIS, John, Fuller.   8 Sept. 1733
Hshld gds, utensils and stk in trd. in his dwho. and wareho. adj., part
thatched £100; Gds in trust for George Osmond therein £400.

£500

50/78946
HARRIS, John, Fuller.   23 Nov. 1738
Stone, timber, slated and thatched dwho. and workshop under one roof
£140; Thatched maltho. under the same roof £60. In West Exe.

£200

158/218431
HOW, James, Fuller.   4 April 1765
Dwho., burling shops, tenement and offices adj. in tenure, stone, cob,
slated and thatched £150; Hshld gds, utensils, stk and gds in trust
therein £50. In West Exe.

£200

97/130107
HOW, Samuel, Tucker.   N.S. 9 April 1752
Dwho. and small linney adj., stone, cob and thatched £100; Hshld gds
and stk in trd. therein £100. In West Exe.

£200

115/150808
HOW, Thomas, Fuller.   3 Feb. 1756
Dwho., burling shops, office, gateways, stable and linneys under one
roof and adj. in West Exe, stone, cob and thatched £200; Hshld gds
and utensils, stk in trd. and gds in trust therein £600.

£800

155/210626
HOW, Thomas, Tucker.   11 July 1764
Hshld gds, stk and stks in trust or on commission in his new dwho.,
shops, chambers adj. in the Leat in West Exe, stone, cob and thatched.

£100

158/218430
HOW, Thomas, Fuller.   4 April 1765
Dwho., burling shops, offices, gateway, stable and linney, stone, cob and
thatched £200; Hshld gds, utensils, stk and gds in trust therein £200.
Under one roof in West Exe.

£400

36/58520
PEPPIN, James, Jnr., Fuller.   2 Aug. 1732
Thatched dwho. in West Exe.

£100

102/136571
PITT, Roger, Fuller.   11 July 1753
Hshld gds, stk in trd. and gds in trust, stone, cob and thatched.
£100

83/111805
PITT, Thomas, Fuller.   15 April 1743
Utensils and stk in trd. and gds on trust in his dwho. and workshops
under one roof in West Exe, stone, cob and thatched.
£100

115/150804
REED, Peter, Fuller.   3 Feb. 1756
Hshld gds, utensils, stk in trd. and gds in trust and on commission in
his dwho., workshops under one roof £550; Stk and gds in trust and
on commission in his millho. £50. All stone, cob and thatched, in West
Exe.
£600

83/111806
RENDLE, Henry, Fuller.   15 April 1748
Utensils, stk in trd. and gds on trust in his dwho., workshops and cellar
adj. in West Exe, stone, cob and thatched.
£200

83/111804
SANDERS, William, Fuller.   15 April 1748
Utensils and stk in trd. and gds on trust in his dwho. and workshops
adj. in West Exe, Tiverton, stone, cob and thatched.
£200

115/150801
WEBBER, John, Fuller and Dyestuff Grinder.   3 Feb. 1756
Dwho., cellar, offices, millho., grist millhos under one roof and adj.
£200; Hshld gds, utensils, stk in trd. and gds in trust and on commission therein £500; Stable, loft over and linney adj. £20; Stk and gds
in trust and on commission £80; Ho. in tenure, brick and thatched
£80; Dyestuff millho. near the above, stone, cob and thatched £130;
Stk and gds in trust therein £20. All at Bolham.
£1,000

178/252826
WEBBER, John, Fuller.   6 Jan. 1768
Dwho., brick and slated £200; Hshld gds therein £200; Millho., mills
and running tackle therein separate from the ho., thatched £100; Utensils, stk and gds in trust and on commission therein £400; Stable and
linney adj. distant, thatched £40; Ho. and offices adj. in tenure, stone,
cob and thatched £100; Millho., mills and running tackle therein,
thatched £60. All at Bolham.
£1,100

170/238024
WILLY, Henry, Fuller.   9 Oct. 1766
Utensils, stk and gds in trust or on commission in dwho. and burling
shops, stone, cob, timber and thatched £400; Utensils, stk and gds in
trust or on commission in his millho., stone, cob, thatched and timber
£200.

£600

50/78952
WOOD, Robert, Fuller.   23 Nov. 1738
Ho. divided into two tenements with a shop and chambers in tenure
of William Pit, cob and thatched £95; A thatched stable opposite £5.

£100

54/83315
WOOD, William, Fuller.   25 March 1740
Dwho., stone, cob and thatched £70; Hshld gds, utensils and stk in trd.
therein £40; Burling shops, chambers over and cellar adj. the dwho.,
cob and thatched £30; Utensils and stk in trd. therein £60. In West
Exe.

£200

73/101936
WOOD, William, Fuller.   2 April 1745
Two tenements, £25 on each, £50; Five other tenements, £10 on each,
£50; Ho., stable, shippen and brewho. adj. in his own tenure £100.
Stone, cob and thatched.

£200

100/135258
WOOD, William, Fuller.   9 April 1753
Ho. and offices in tenure of William Rew, farmer, in [West] Marley,
Devon £100; Two barns, £25 on each, £50; Stable and linney adj. £25;
Maltho. £25. All stone, cob and thatched.

£200

173/241423
BESLY, John, Dyer.   8 Jan. 1767
Barn, stone, cob and thatched £20; Utensils and stk therein £180;
Utensils and stk and gds in trust in dyeho. on the Leat in West Exe,
brick and slated £100.

£300

53/81484
PATEY, Spurway, Dyer.   7 Aug. 1739
Dyeho., wareho. and linney adj.,* brick, timber and slated £100; Two
brick and slated hos adj. each other, in tenures of John Glover, blacksmith, and William Bryan, weaver, £50 on each, £100.

£200

* Near Loman Bridge

67/96600
FINNIMORE, Thomas, Hotpresser.   13 Oct. 1743
Dwho., brewho. and chamber over £200; Hshld gds, stk in trd. and gds
on trust therein £100; Pressho. and packing chambers under one roof
behind the above, brick, some timber and slated £100; Utensils, stk in
trd. and gds on trust therein £200. In Peter St.

£600

122/162221
HORABIN, William, Presser and Packer.   13 April 1758
Utensils and stk in trd. and gds in trust or on commission in his press
hos and rooms over, brick, stone, timber and slate £400; Hshld gds in
trust or on commission in his dwho. and wareho. adj. separate from
above, stone, cob and thatched £600.

£1,000

136/181752
HORABIN, William, Presser and Packer.   9 April 1761
Utensils and stk in trd. and gds in trust or on commission in his
pressho. and rooms, stone, brick, timber and slated £300; Hshld gds
and utensils of stk in trd. on gds in trust or on commission in his dwho.
or wareho. only adj., separate and distant from the above in West Exe
in Tiverton, stone, cob and thatched £200.

£500

153/207502
HORABIN, William, Hotpresser.   13 March 1764
Dwho., offices, press-shops, packing rooms and outhos adj. on the right
and left hand and at the bottom forming a court in West Exe, brick,
cob, lath, plaster and slated £500; Hshld gds and utensils and gds and
stk in trust or on commission therein £500.

£1,000

TOPSHAM

180/253547
DEWEY, Thomas, Maltster and Woolstapler.   21 Jan. 1768
Utensils and stk in his maltho., wareho. and stable, stone, cob, timber
and slated and thatched.

£200

TORRINGTON *see* GREAT TORRINGTON

TOTNES

149/202667
CUMING, William, Sergemaker.   24 Sept. 1763
Dwho., brewho., wareho. and shops adj., stone, timber and slated £300;
Hshld gds, utensils and stk therein £200.

£500

95/127907
HURRELL, Richard and PAYNE, William,   N.S. 24 Oct. 1751
Sergemakers.
Stk in trd. in the warehos in Barge Yard, Bucklesbury, brick and
timber.
£500

163/223648
PAYNE, William, Sergemaker.   13 Aug. 1765
Stk in his two warehos No. 10 and No. 14 in one pile of building
situated Haynes' Wharf near the Bridge Yard, Southwark, brick built.
£2,000

161/220656
TRIMLETT, Lawrence, Maltster and   20 June 1765
Sergemaker.
Hshld gds and stk in his dwho., warerooms, cellar etc. £200; Stk in
maltho. £100. Stone, lath, plaster and slated.
£300

178/249641
WINDEATH, Samuel, Jnr., Fellmonger and   7 Oct. 1767
Sergemaker.
Utensils and stk in two hos adj. east of dwho. of Samuel Windeath Snr.
in Bridge Town £250; Utensils and stk in ho. and wareho. adj. opposite
the above £200; The dwho. of Samuel Windeath Snr. £50. Stone, lath,
plaster and slated.
£500

29/47030
PAYNE, William, Clothier.   1 March 1728
Dwho., brick, timber and tiled £300; Hshld gds and stk therein, £150
on each, £300.
£600

71/100600
PAYNE, William, Clothier.   1 Nov. 1744
Dwho., stone, plaster covered, with shingle stones.
£300

120/160393
PAYNE, William, Clothier.   23 Dec. 1757
Stk in a pile of warehos called Youngs Buildings at Hays Wharf at the
Bridge Yard, Southwark now in the occupation of Messrs. Stargrave and
Charlton, brick.
£1,000

UFFCULME
99/133003
BURROW, Jonathan, Sergemaker.   N.S. 3 Nov. 1752
Hshld gds and stk in trd. in his dwho. and offices adj., stone, cob and

thatched £100; Dwho. and wash-ho. adj. each other in Topsham, Devon, in tenure of a tallow chandler whose workshop is distant, stone, brick, timber and slated £200.

£300

60/90746
BYRD, Barnard and Thomas, Sergemakers.　　5 April 1742
Dwho. and pantry adj. £160; Weighing shop, comb shops and wool chambers over all, under one roof, cob, thatched and tiled £200; Dyeho., wash-ho., brewho. and bakeho. under one roof with four coppers therein, cob tiled and thatched £100; Pound ho. with a pound therein with a stable under the same roof, thatched £30; Comb shop by itself, thatched £10.

£500

94/128981
BYRD, Thomas, Sergemaker.　　N.S. 16 Jan. 1752
Dwho., pantry and compting ho. adj. £90; Hshld gds and stk in trd. therein £70; Weighing shop, comb shop and wool chambers over £50; Utensils and stk in trd. therein £170; Dyeho. and wash-ho., brewho. and bake ho. under one roof £40; Utensils and stk in trd. therein £40; Cellar, pantry, wool chamber over, with a stable £40; Stk therein and cider for sale £45; Comb shop, chambers over and cellars adj. £20; Stk and cider for sale therein £35.

£600

122/163098
BYRD, Thomas, Sergemaker.　　13 June 1758
Dwho., maltho., comb shops, sorting shops, dyeho., pound ho., pound engine, linney and stable adj. £450; Hshld gds and stk in trd. £350. Brick, cob, tiled and thatched.

£800

73/102338
BYRD, Thomas and William, Sergemakers.　　16 May 1745
Dwho., pantry and compting ho. adj. £90; Hshld gds and stk in trd. therein £70; Weighing shop, comb shop and wool chambers over £70; Utensils and stk in trd. therein £170; Dyeho., wash-ho., brewho. and bakeho. under one roof £40; Their utensils and stk in trd. therein £40; Cellar, Pantry and wool chamber over and stable adj. £40; Stk in trd. therein £10.

£600

128/169434
BYRD, William, Sergemaker.　　30 Jan. 1759
Buildings and gds, dwho., dyeho., combshops and cellars adj., brick, tiled and thatched £250; Hshld gds, utensils and stk in trd. £150; Tending shop, linney and barn adj., cob and thatched £100; Stk in trd. therein £80; Ho., cob and thatched £20; Stk therein £10; Set of grist mills and millho. adj., cob and thatched in tenure £150; Maltho.

in tenure £20; Dyeho. and bakeho. in tenure £20; Ho. in tenure and stable adj. £40, cob and thatched; Ho. in tenure £20, cob and thatched; Ho. in tenure £20; Ho. in tenure, cob and thatched £30; Ho. in tenure, cob and thatched £30; Ho., barn, stable and other ho. adj. cob and thatched in tenure £80; Ho. and hos adj. in tenure £20; Bakeho. and hos adj. in tenure £40; Stall and linage adj. in tenure £30; Barn in tenure £20; Ho., cob and thatched in tenure £20; Above in Coombe Raleigh. Following in Tiverton. Ho. in tenure, brick and thatched £100; Ho. in tenure £50; Ho. in tenure £50; Ho. in tenure £10; Ho. in tenure £40; Hos in tenure, cob and thatched £100; Ho. in tenure, cob and thatched £40; Gds, utensils and stk in trd. in ho. in Tiverton, brick, lead and slate £300.

£1,900

146/197205
BYRD, William, Sergemaker.   25 Feb. 1763
Ho., dyeho., comb shop and cellar adj., brick, stone and slated £350; Hshld gds, utensils and stk therein £250; Tending shop, stable, poundho., wool chamber and ho. adj. in tenure £150; Utensils and stk therein £300; set of grist mills and mill ho. adj. in tenure £200; Maltho. separate £20; Brewho., dryho. adj. £20; Hos adj. in tenure £40; Ho. in tenure £20; Ho. in tenure £20; Ho. in tenure £30; Ho. in tenure £30; Ho., barn and stable and outho. adj. in tenure, £80; Ho. in tenure £20; All the above in parish of Uffculme. Ho. and outho. adj. in tenure £80; Bakeho. and outhos adj. £50; Salt stable and linney adj. £30; Barn only £20; Cottage only £20; Above in Coombe Raleigh. Following in Tiverton. Ho. in tenure £100; Ho. in tenure, cob and slate £50; Ho. in tenure £25; Ho. in tenure £25; Ho. in tenure £10; Ho. in tenure £100; Ho. in tenure £40; Ho. in tenure £200; Hshld gds, utensils and stk therein £280; Ho. and outhos adj. in tenure £40. All thatched except as mentioned.

£2,600

180/255479
DUNSFORD, Stephenson, Sergemaker.   29 March 1768
Dwho. and offices £250; Hshld gds therein £100; Utensils and stk therein £360; Corn shop, woodho. and chambers £100; Utensils and stk therein £350. All brick, stone and tiled. Dyeho., comb shop and wool chambers, stone, brick, timber and tiled £40; Utensils and stk therein £100; Two tenements, workshop, woodho. in tenure of wool-combers, with linney and stables adj. £60; Stk therein £40.

£1,400

137/118004
DYMOND, George, Sergemaker.   4 March 1761
Hshld gds and stk in his dwho., offices and stable and barn and outhos adj., stone, cob and thatched.

£300

86/118247
FARR, Nicholas, Sergemaker.   13 Oct. 1749

Five tenements under one roof in Sampford Peverell, Devon £100; Hshld gds and stk in trd. in his new dwho., barn, stable, comb shop, yarn ho. and linney under one roof in Uffculme, stone, cob and thatched £100.

£200

119/157977

HOW, John, Sergemaker and Maltster.　　23 July 1757

Hshld gds, utensils and stk in trd. in his dwho. and maltho. adj. £180; Utensils and stk in his comb shops and dyeho., barn and stable adj. £20; Ho., comb shop and offices adj. called Coldharbour, in tenure of Sarah How, Sergemaker £100. Stone, cob and thatched.

£300

145/195225

HOW, Sarah, Sergemaker.　　8 Jan. 1763

Hshld gds and stk therein in her dwho., stone, cob and thatched.

£100

116/153661

MARSH, Thomas, Sergemaker and Shopkeeper.　　27 Aug. 1756

Dwho., wareho. shop and country ho. adj., brick, stone and thatched £150; Hshld gds therein £50; Utensils and stk in trd. therein £300; Comb shop, dyeho., sorting chamber and stable adj. each separate from the aforesaid, brick, stone and thatched £50; Utensils and stk in trd. therein £50.

£600

116/153750

MARSH, Thomas, Sergemaker.　　7 Sept. 1756

Ho. occupied £20; Three hos adj. occupied £150; Three hos only on the other side of the bridge occupied £30. All stone, cob and thatched.

£200

114/151171

STARK, William, Sergemaker.　　3 March 1756

Hshld gds and stk in trd. in his dwho. and wareho., rooms over and small offices adj., stone, cob and thatched.

£200

126/168233

STARK, William, Sergemaker.　　28 April 1759

Ho. and offices adj. in tenure of Eleanor Birdnor in the village [sic] of Ashill £80; Barn £10; Stable and linney adj. £10; Stone, cob and thatched.

£100

137/181851

STARK, William, Sergemaker.　　24 April 1761

Dwho. and office adj. £170; Hshld gds and stk therein £100; Barn £10;

Stk therein £5; Poundho., pound and engine therein, stable and linney adj. £10; Stk therein £5. All stone, cob and thatched.

£300

168/233252

STARKE, William, Sergemaker.   29 April 1766
Ho., comb shop, dyeho. and tending shop under one roof in Ashill in his tenure £110; Hshld gds therein £20; Utensils and stk therein £35; Barn only £10; Poundho., stable, hogsty adj. £10; Cider engine, press in above £5; Linney separate £10; All stone, cob and thatched.

£200

83/111483

SWEATLAND, Hugh, Sergemaker.   31 March 1748
Dwho. and cellar, milkho., stable, warping shop, wareho., yarnho., comb shop, dyeho. and coalho. with a linney and barn adj., forming court, stone, cob and thatched £100; Hshld gds and stk in trd. therein £200.

£300

141/189406

SWEATLAND, Hugh, Sergemaker.   5 May 1762
Dwho., cellar, milk ho., stable, warping shop, wareho., yarn ho., comb shop, dyeho., coalho., linney, barn adj. forming a court, stone, cob and thatched £100; Hshld gds and stk therein £100.

£200

68/97126

SWEATLAND, William, Sergemaker.   30 Nov. 1743
Dwho., comb shop, stable, linney cellar, woodho., dyeho. forming a court, stone, cob and thatched £150; Hshld gds, utensils and stk in trd. therein £150.

£300

UPTON HELLIONS

168/233276

VICARY, John, Sergemaker.   29 April 1766
Three tenements and cellars under one roof in tenure, stone, cob and thatched.

£100

UPTON PYNE

178/251007

REYNOLDS, Roberts, Ironmonger, Exeter and   17 Nov. 1767
   WOODMAN, John, Miller (Fuller),
   Upton Pyne.
Dwho., mill, dryho. with three pairs of stones; two waterwheels and all the running tackle, stone, brick and tiled £300; Hshld gds therein £25;

Stk and gds in trust and on commission therein £75; Stable and cellar adj., separate from the above, thatched £20; Utensils, stk and cider therein £30; Ho., shammy millho. with four stocks, two water wheels and cellar adj., separate from the above in Upton Pyne in tenure of Samuel Stephens, shammyman, brick, stone and thatched £250.

£700

[N.B. This policy has been included because the second mill may have been used for fulling cloth as well as leather work.]

WILLAND

97/130116

SWEATLAND, Hugh, Sergemaker. N.S. 9 April 1752

Hshld gds and stk in trd. in his dwho. and offices, cob and thatched £100; Stone and thatched tenements in Sampford Peverell £200.

£300

WOODBURY

102/137807

DAGWORTHY, Samuel, Sergemaker. 4 Oct. 1753

Dwho. and dyeho., comb shop, tending shops and rooms over all adj. in the village of Woodbury Salterton and Woodbury, stone, cob and thatched £150; Hshld gds and stk in trd. therein £150.

£300

132/176906

DAGWORTHY, Samuel, Sergemaker. 12 July 1760

Dwho., cellar, tending shop, comb shop, linney and chambers over the whole length £150; Hshld gds and stk therein £145; Stable and open linney £5; Stone, cob and thatched.

£300

APPENDIX

Name	Occup'n		Vol.	Date	Prop.	Val.
Thos Reeve	S	Crediton	14	8 Mar. 1722	H &c.	280
Saml. Hele	C	Kingsbridge	14	8 Mar. 1722	H &c.	300
John Chaple	S	Wolborough	14	8 Mar. 1722	H	500
Jacob Splatt	S	Exeter	14	8 Mar. 1722	H & G	300
Geo. Moore	C	Gt. Torrington	14	8 Mar. 1722	G	500
Jacob Rowe	F	Exeter	14	8 Mar. 1722	H	500
Wm.Potter	S	Plymtree	15	4 July 1723	H & G	300
Jerome Menard	WS	Honiton	15	4 July 1723	G	300
Robt.Saunders	S	Exeter	15	31 May 1723	H & G	300
Thos.Tillmann	S	Colliton	15	4 June 1723	G	500
Joseph Ellis	S*	Bradninch	15	25 June 1723	G	500
John Farringdon	S	Ottery	15	2 July 1723	H & G	1000
John Marks	S	Exeter	15	3 July 1723	G	500
Wm.Dewdney	S	Chudleigh	15	5 July 1723	H & G	300
John Northcott	C	Honiton	15	19 Oct. 1723	G	500
Thos. Speed	S	Colliton	16	20 Feb. 1723	H & G	300
Saml. Rawson	C	Axminster	16	23 Aug. 1723	H & G	500
Wm.Warren	C	Axminster	16	8 Apr. 1724	H & G	500
Edw. Bilke	C	Axminster	16	8 Apr. 1724	H & G	500
Nick Churley	S	Culmstock	16	9 June 1724	H	500
Ab. Jackson	S	Moretonhampstead	17	25 July 1724	H	500
Jabez Jackson	S	Moretonhampstead	17	25 July 1724	H	500
Anthony Bale	S	Uffculme	17	7 Aug. 1724	H & G	300
Edw. Skinner	S	Uffculme	17	19 Aug. 1724	H & G	300
Hugh Ellis	S	Uffculme	17	19 Aug. 1724	H & G	300
Thos.Finnymore	S	Cullompton	17	14 Sept. 1724	H &c.	500
Henry Wilmott	D	Exeter	17	23 Oct. 1724	G	500
Joseph Howe	S	Uffculme	17	6 Nov. 1724	H & G	300
Jas. Harris	S	Crediton	17	26 Feb. 1724/5	G	500
Sam Tremlett	S	Exeter	17	31 Mar. 1725	H & G	300
Chas. Reeve	S	Crediton	19	31 Dec. 1724	H	500
Sam Liddon	C	Axminster	19	27 Feb. 1724	H & G	1000
Rich'd Gill	S	Uffculme	20	30 Aug. 1725	H & G	500
Rich'd Collins	C	Modbury	22	29 July 1726	H & G	1000
Henry Willcocks	S	Exeter	22	5 Dec. 1726	G	300
John Keagle	S	Crediton	23	24 June 1726	11 H	300
Edw. Mann	F	Exeter	23	6 July 1726	H & G	1,000
Ab. Badcock	S	Bampton	23	10 Apr. 1727	H	200

Key:	C	=	Clothier	*	=	and Shopkeeper
	D	=	Dyer	H	=	Dwelling house
	F	=	Fuller	2H	=	Two houses
	S	=	Sergemaker	G	=	Goods
	WS	=	Woolstapler	&c.	=	outbuildings (with house)

INDEX OF PERSONS INSURED

153

156

INDEX OF PERSONS INSURED

Searle, Samuel, 49
Seldon, Anna, 135; John, 135
Shears, William, 91
Shellabear, Walter, 2
Shephard (Shepherd), Frederick, 116; John, 30, 31(3); Samuel; 31(2); Thomas, 110
Sherive, Samuel, 6
Shorland, Peter, 135
Short, Arthur, 76(3)
Shute, Stephen, 39(3), 40(2); Thomas, 31, 32, 33(15)
Skinner, Edward, 152; Thomas, 33
Slade, John, 14(2); Nathaniel, 13(2)
Smale, Augustine, 33, 34, 118; George, 99(2); George, Jnr., 94; Robert, 99; William, 123; William, Jnr., 123; William, Snr., 123
Snook (Snooke), John, 94, 96(2)
Sommers, John, 104(2); Richard, 76, 104(2)
Soper John, 1
Sparks, Joseph, 116
Speare (Spear), Arthur, 76(2); William, 76(2)
Speed, Thomas, 152
Splatt, Jacob, 61, 152
Sprague, Richard, 34; Walter, 106
Sprey (Spry), Benjamin, 77(2); Benjamin, Jnr., 77; Benjamin, Snr., 77
Spurway, John, 14
Spying, Thomas, 77
Stark (Starke), William, 149(3), 150
Stephens, William, 8
Stokes, John, 83(3)
Stone, Anthony, 96(2), 97; Samuel, 105
Stoodly, Charles, 61
Sunter, William, 1
Sweatland, Hugh, 150(2), 151; William, 150
Sweete, Hugh, 89; John, 89

Tapp, Philip, 120; Philip, Jnr., 120; Robert, 34
Taylor, Robert, 106
Thomas, William, 5(2)
Thorne, George, 135, 136
Tillmann, Thomas, 152
Tothill, Robert, 77
Tozer, Aaron, 102(5); John, 1(2); Richard, 1; Solomon, 102
Treddle, George, Jnr., 34
Tremlet (Trimlett, Tremlett), Anthony, 61; Lawrence, 146; Robert, 34; Samuel, 61(2), 152
Trewman, John, 84
Trott, John, 116, 117
Trump, Charles, 49

Tucker, John, 61; Peter, 35(2); Richard, 62; Robert, 118
Turner, Abraham, 122; Isaac, 11; Zachary, 84(5)

Upcott, Nehemiah, 49(2)

Varder, Richard, 100
Vesey, Hugh, 49
Vicary, Elizabeth, 13; James, 118; John, 150; Richard, 118; Robert, 103; Samuel, 35(2)
Vosper, Elizabeth, 87
Voysey, John, 136(2)

Wakeham, Robert, 97
Wardall, Matthew, 77
Warren, John, 6, 136(2); Thomas, 136; William, 152
Webber, John, 136, 137, 143(2); John, Snr., 137(2); Joseph, 100; Thomas, Jnr., 51
Weekes, James, 109, 110; Nathaniel, 35
Welsford, Giles, 35; Giles, Jnr., 36; Giles, Snr., 36; John, 36(2); Richard, 36(3); Roger, 33(4), 37(5)
West, James, 14
Westcott, Elizabeth, 12; John, 12; Robert 62, 117
Whitby, Richard; 50; Robert, 40, 41, 50; Robert, Jnr., 41; Thomas, 50(2)
White, John, 96
Whiteway, Alexander, 100; William, 100
Widgery, Philip, 120
Wilcocks (Willcocks), Henry, 62(2), 152
Williams, John, 137; Joshua, 111, 117; William, 62
Willmott (Wilmot, Wilmott), Henry, 84(2), 85(4), 86(3), 152
Willy, Henry, 144
Windeath, Samuel, Jnr., 146; Thomas, Jnr., 120
Winsor (Windsor), John, 2, 10(3)
Withers, Benjamin, 88
Wood, John, 7; Robert, 144; William, 144(3)
Woodman, John, 150
Woodward, Daniel, 137(3)
Wooley (Woolley), John, 6; Joseph, 6
Worth, Joseph, 37
Worthy, Jonathan, 78
Wyne, Thomas, 51

Yeatherd, Joshua, 37, 38(6); Mary, 38; Samuel, 38, 39

Zelly, Robert, 138(3)

INDEX OF PERSONS OTHER THAN
THE INSURED